HAUNTS
OF THE
WHITE CITY

HAUNTS
OF THE
WHITE CITY

GHOST STORIES FROM THE WORLD'S FAIR, THE GREAT FIRE AND VICTORIAN CHICAGO

URSULA BIELSKI

FOREWORD BY JEFF MUDGETT

Published by Haunted America
A Division of The History Press
Charleston, SC
www.historypress.com

Copyright © 2019 by Ursula Bielski
All rights reserved

First published 2019

Manufactured in the United States

ISBN 9781467139656

Library of Congress Control Number: 2019943352

For Dan Carroll
Who appreciates my ghosts—and my demons

CONTENTS

CONTENTS

Love, thieves and fear make ghosts.

—German proverb

FOREWORD

My introduction to Ursula Bielski's work was a signed copy of her 1997 historical *Chicago Haunts*, a masterful review of everything Chicago pertaining to the city's tall tales, the supernatural, the paranormal, interspersed with Ursula's own harrowing adventures exploring "plain old" haunted houses. That first went on to become the immensely successful series known for all things ghosts in Chicago.

What always struck me about those books, even more so than Ursula's fine ability putting pen to paper, was her fertile imagination and utter lack of fear actually going down into the dark, damp, scary places most of us would have refused visiting. Her get-to-the-bottom-of-things and let-it-all-hang-out honesty made her writing about those same visits completely relatable for the normal folk, which is where so many of the other authors attempting these identical harrowing subjects fail. Ursula writes about recognizable human characters with realistic emotions instead of the more common, and quite often silly, horror movie creations.

Reading *Haunts of the White City*, I immediately recognized the same being true of this, her newest work. Once again, Ursula has given us the opportunity to relate to some of the strange, harrowing historical figures who time and time again picked Chicago as their playground for committing strange acts, supernatural episodes and, often, evil deeds.

Many of these characters were true monsters. And while, thankfully, very few of us live these experiences, sadly the stuff of life, I'm quite certain Ursula gives her readers the ability to recognize each and every one of them—particularly my horrible ancestor, serial killer H.H. Holmes.

Ursula first sought me out almost eight years ago after learning that I was in Chicago exploring H.H. Holmes's haunts while writing a new exposé of my great-great-grandfather, who many believed to be the most evil man in American history. In fact, she was paramount in helping me gain entrance to the United States Post Office basement at Sixty-Third and Wallace, the same location of the "Murder Castle," Holmes's house of horror and terror. When I finished *Bloodstains*, Ursula again tracked me down, allowing me the opportunity of presenting my admittedly controversial theories about Chicago's serial killer and Jack the Ripper to a live crowd of her adoring fans. Always willing to go where others are afraid to tread, no matter who benefits: that's the type of historian and author Ursula Bielski is.

As with everything Ursula writes, you will quickly realize there is something more going on beneath the surface. How there's nothing trivial here. For me, without giving away too many secrets, *Haunts of the White City*'s chapter about Holmes and, in particular, Ursula's incredible description of the Holmes Curse had me on edge from start to finish. Presenting startling new facts that even I was unaware of. Incredible. In fact, I read the chapter twice. I wouldn't be surprised if the Hollywood producers in charge of creating the new television series based on *The Devil in the White City* do so as well.

It's all here. Verified facts, true history, legend, lore, interspersed with a tall tale or two that make the reading fun. All honestly expressed with that serious purpose Ursula is famous for, but never forgetting the fearlessness I've always admired in her. Boldly going where no other Chicago historian dares enter and explore.

There is no doubt that for Ursula Bielski, writing *Haunts of the White City* was a labor of love.

For you, I know reading her book will be as well.

—Jeff Mudgett
Author, *Bloodstains*
Co-Host, *American Ripper*

ACKNOWLEDGEMENTS

I would like to thank my dear friend Dan Melone for all of his assistance with Cook County history, especially the history of the Alexander Robinson family. I would also like to thank the Chicago History Museum, the Newberry Library, the University of Illinois at Chicago, the Library of Congress, Pat Camalliere and the Lemont Historical Society, Dan Terras of the Grosse Point Lighthouse National Landmark, Nancy Webster of the Highland Park Historical Society, the Tinley Park Historical Society, Dave Cowan for his notes on the introduction, Jeff Mudgett for his all too generous foreword, Carlos Alvarado for his help on Chicago Spiritualism, Eva Cowan for her supreme cheerleading and Ilse Cowan for being there every day to smile at me and encourage my work. A very special thanks also to our wonderful tour guides—Tony, Larry, Mark, Nick and the whole Joliet gang—for sharing my research with others through our tours. You are more appreciated than you can ever know. Lastly, thanks to Ben Gibson, my editor, for letting me publish a book that is three times as long as it was supposed to be and for having so much patience with me during these difficult last years of family struggle and loss. I hope that you will find the wait was worth it.

The Columbian Exposition of 1893 captured the imagination of the world and inspired both the best and worst of humanity, as chronicled in Erik Larson's *The Devil in the White City*. It was the perfect endcap to Chicago's century of darkness and light. *Library of Congress.*

INTRODUCTION

In January 1901, Captain O'Neill of Chicago's Woodlawn Police Department received an unusual letter from a citizen. It was from Mrs. S.A. Stuart, of 10 North State Street, who asked O'Neill to help her find a haunted house to live in. Stuart, however, didn't want any old haunted house, with "second rate spirits who get out of the cemetery once or twice a month." It had to be occupied by a family of ghosts insidious in their attentions to the lessees. They must be on hand every night to clank through the corridors in their chains, open and shut doors mysteriously and shriek murder until sleep is out of the question.

O'Neill found Stuart a house to live in, near Forty-Eighth and Lake, but apparently the ghosts were "second rate," because she refused it.[1]

Not long after Stuart made her public announcement, another woman, a Mrs. F.P. Lanigan, threw her hat in the ring and said she wanted a haunted house, too. However, Lanigan said she shouldn't have to pay to live in it—that the owners should be happy to lease such a house to her for free, since she would prove by her tenancy that there were no ghosts and raise its value exponentially. After all, she reasoned, "Anyone who is willing to dwell with ghosts should at least have the privilege of doing so without paying for it."[2]

In fact, a kind of haunted house frenzy had gripped the last decades of nineteenth-century Chicago. The legends of these fearful sites were rampant on the streets of the Windy City, and it wasn't uncommon for mobs of people numbering in the thousands to gather at the sites of reported hauntings, leading to Mrs. Stuart's disgusted offer of tenancy in one of them in order to stop the propagation of what she felt was stuff and nonsense.

There had been the "extremely modern and up to date ghost" said to walk the house of the late Mary Ford, who had been an art critic of some renown when she died while living in a house on Lake Avenue near Forty-Eighth Street, in swanky Hyde Park. "The Lane Ghost," as the former tenant's phantom was known around the neighborhood, soon forced out any tenant who dared to take up residence, as his spirit was known to walk "by day as well as night," and the property fell into decay. According to the story, Mary Ford found the ghost to be actually helpful, claiming that it told her what kind of coal to buy for the tricky furnace. When she ordered it from the coal dealer, he reportedly said, "That's strange, nobody else has ever ordered that particular combination before."

The late Charles Smith was said to wander the empty grounds of his former house at Fifty-Third and Greenwood. After heirs no longer lived in the house, the ghost stories began, and it seems the wraith successfully chased the outsiders away. The house was eventually razed.

A place at Grand and Forty-Third was known to be "infested with ghosts," drawing nightly crowds to witness the various manifestations such as rattling windows and doors, while the ghost of a murder victim haunted the empty house on Cottage Grove near Forty-Ninth Street.

A little farther up Cottage Grove, near Thirty-Fifth Street, a woman remained behind after she died and the house decayed. Left behind was a profusion of lilac bushes heavy with flowers in the spring. The local children, however, were too terrified to pick them because of the ghost, believed to be a bitter woman who was abandoned by her children late in life. A streetcar driver claimed to see a "frail old woman" picking the lilacs on many of his late-night runs past the home. Even when a skating pond was built after the house's demolition, the local children refused to use it.[3]

At Robey Street and Washington Boulevard, the first Mrs. Robey was said to walk the rooms of the family home after her death, dressed in a black robe and wringing her hands, and a "Grey Man" was seen wandering the neighborhood of Grand Crossing, as even police were quick to testify. Police also swore to the existence of the ghost of a 350-pound woman named Annie Kline of Fourth Street. "Big Annie" went on the rampage after the woman's death in 1899, warning old neighbors to pay her relatives the money they owed them or she would haunt the offenders until their dying days. When one victim of Annie's threats brought a police officer to investigate, the ghost threw a brick at him.[4]

ON THE NEAR WEST Side, in Holy Family Parish near Taylor and Blue Island, a well-known ghost was that of Charles Fanning, a stonecutter and old scrooge who built his own house, including a crypt in the basement where he wanted to be buried. That wish was denied for unknown reasons. Similar legends told that he also buried his treasure in the backyard, causing the ghost to wander from house to cellar to yard, as was its habit, according to the testimony of the locals. Whenever someone moved in, the neighborhood kids predicted a swift moving out. As they told one reporter: "The ghost don't let nobody stay."[5]

There had been a contagion of haunted houses in the suburb of Englewood—reports of which had been totally overshadowed by the story of the "Murder Castle" of H.H. Holmes, whose own demons put all other area ghosts to shame.

MANY OF CHICAGO'S GHOST stories, however, were and are not as personal. They are, instead, stories that reflect the deeply shared experiences of Chicagoans in times and places of great joy or sorrow. For more than three decades, I have told Chicago's story through this supernatural folklore. I can tell you from many years of learning about little else that there is no time in Chicago's history—not the Gangland days of Al Capone and Bugs Moran; not the days of massive twentieth-century tragedies like the *Eastland* Disaster, the Our Lady of the Angels Fire and the Crash of Flight 191; not in the legacy of John Wayne Gacy; and not the modern era of mass shootings, rampant lawlessness and corruption—where ghosts take over the storyline more than in the city's first pages: during that century when Chicago struggled to grow from the virgin native prairie, and then again from the ashes of 1871, and when waves of disease, destruction and uncertainty led to not only constant upheaval but also epidemics of crime, killing and, most tragically of all, suicide.

Indeed, historian Paulette D. Kilmer, in her essay, "Haunted Times? Ghosts in Crime Stories Printed by the *New York Times* 1851–1901," writes that, while researching this topic, she found—after sorting through thousands of search results and eliminating the misses—179 *New York Times* articles from the latter half of the nineteenth century that specifically covered the appearance of ghosts in true crime reports.[6] I can tell you that I have utilized in my own research at least that many from our own local papers—most notably the *Chicago Tribune* and the *Inter Ocean*. Both papers seized every opportunity to run features that included the appearance of ghosts.

Some of the ghost stories that grew in this world were deliberately planted: newspaper coverage of the often unhinged world of nineteenth-century Chicago largely comprised bizarre incidents chronicled by reporters who were often given free rein in the form of unchecked literary license to mingle reality and imagination, embellishing facts with rumors and hearsay, creating thrilling serial-like dramas out of the news. Ghosts often appeared in courtrooms or to victims or perpetrators of crimes in their bedrooms at night during trials. Phantasmal sightings were regularly entered as evidence by judges, and convictions based on the testimony of ghosts were not uncommon.

Much of this occurred during the heyday of Spiritualism, when thousands of desperately sincere mediums and sitters strove to make contract with departed loved ones. It was an earnest pursuit, but "flimflammers" staged elaborate scams to transform the sorrow into sawbucks, and more than one medium was hauled into the hoosegow on charges of fraud, deception and theft.

Two of the "good ones" were George and Sylvia Stickney. The home the couple built in remote Bull Valley, northwest of the city, was deemed by critics "as out of place as a medieval castle in a junkyard." But unlike their hyper-competitive, upscale peers, for whom every goal was a contest, the Stickneys didn't care. They had no desire, as their fellows did, to lure the rich and famous to their home. The only guests they really desired were dead ones. The Stickneys were Spiritualists, and they designed their house—which still stands today—to have no ninety-degree angles so as not to trap evil spirits in the house after their legendary séances.

IT SHOULD NOT SURPRISE us that Spiritualism was such a life raft for those living in nineteenth-century Chicago. For Spiritualism offered—contrary to popular impression—not a curious and adventuresome lifestyle, but order and stagnancy in an ever-changing world. Séances held to rigid routines, the messages of spirits held only comfort and kindness and the séance parlor was a haven of that familiar and cozy world of sitting rooms and tea services that seemed to be ever slipping away. At the same time, the modern world could be let in a little at a time: the use of graphite pencils, the typewriter and other modern tools by mediums was daring but containable—a small but important "proof" that Spiritualism was not backward but forward-thinking and in sync with modern life.

Nowhere was the uncertainty of that life more obvious than in Chicago. Indeed, perhaps no city in modern times has been more equally elegant and chaotic than nineteenth-century Chicago. What began as a remote trading outpost on the Great Lakes rose in the span of a few decades to become a world center of commerce, art and ideas, only to see its core razed by a conflagration of biblical proportion.

Yet as the city still smoldered, it began to rebuild, and following the destruction of 1871, in little more than twenty years Chicago doubled its population to 1.2 million and in 1893 beat out New York City to host the Columbian Exposition—the World's Fair—whose illuminated "White City" of buildings and brilliant ideas would influence every corner and discipline of the modern age.

The juxtaposing images presented by the 1871 City of Ashes and the 1893 White City was so stark a picture and so polar a comparison that its marvel created a sense of magic that even now inspires. The ideas, art and innovation introduced at the fair continue to affect thinkers, artists and designers everywhere. Meanwhile, Jackson Park (the former fairgrounds site on Chicago's South Shore), its Museum of Science and Industry (the fair's former Palace of Fine Arts) and myriad other physical locations connected to the fair remain key points of pilgrimage for both Chicagoans and tourists alike.

But while the elegance and beneficence of the White City continue to inform, equally compelling is a legacy of chaos and malice that also befell nineteenth-century Chicago. Rightly called the "City of the Century" by historian Donald Miller, Chicago saw among the very best—and worst—of modern life, from the carnage of the Fort Dearborn Massacre played out on the bloodied sand dunes of 1812 to wholesale death brought by cholera, tuberculosis and smallpox. The Civil War did not spare Chicago the anguish of witnessing the black-draped funeral train of the assassinated President Abraham Lincoln pass through the city's mournful gates on the final leg of its somber journey home to Springfield, Illinois—this after five thousand imprisoned Confederate soldiers died miserably in notoriously inhumane conditions at Camp Douglas, their bodies buried in mass graves along the lakefront.

Thus as the Gilded Age emerged with its competing realities, it's no surprise that one of the most notorious figures in Chicago's multicolored history would be a person of deeply evil motive, a serial killer. The exploits of "America's Serial Killer," Herman Webster Mudgett (a.k.a. H.H. Holmes), stunned a world that, like us still today, could not manage to reconcile the diabolical Holmes with the inspiring fair—a place that inspired Holmes to only evil. Holmes's nefarious exploits were chronicled brilliantly by author Erik Larson in his epic volume *The Devil in the White City*. In the book, alongside Holmes's sordid tale is told that of another man, Daniel Burnham, who possessed one of the era's most enlightened minds and was the gifted architect of the World's Fair. These two figures represent perfectly the dueling nature of Victorian Chicago: one, a shining beacon in the world of architecture, engineering, commerce and art, the other a soulless pit of greed, chaos and death. Like the city in which they thrived, they were a study in light and darkness, good and evil.

Erik Larson's story of Holmes and Burnham has touched so many because it rings so true. It is, indeed, a story hauntingly representative of Chicago in its century. As is the story of George and Sylvia Stickney.

A flaw in the Stickney house plans led to one room having a perfectly squared-off corner. And it was here, in this corner, that George Stickney was allegedly found one day, dead from no traceable cause. The story of it fit perfectly in the newspapers of the time, leaving readers to ask: Had George been killed by ghosts because of his flawed architectural plan, or did he simply perish after the dream of Spiritualism had, pardon the pun, failed to materialize?

The stories in this book tell the tale of a city balancing—like the rest of the modern world of the "progressive" nineteenth century—between a millennium of custom and tradition, rural life, certain faith traditions and attendant folklore and an untold new one of innovation, communication, industrialism and iconoclasts. The stories in this book tell of plans for paradise that, despite many beauties, almost never quite worked out. There are stories of demons who plagued both farmers and slum dwellers, of men and women hypnotized by mesmerists, of ship captains who spoke to the dead, of birds of ill omen and of phantoms of avarice, hopelessness and payback. There are stories of undertakers trying to preserve corpses forever and of corpses that didn't need their help to do that. There are stories of love and of loss. So many stories of death.

They all tell the same tale: the posh mansions built on massacre grounds...the White City with a killer in its streets...the manicured parkland as a haven for suicides.

This was Chicago in its grand century. And it is Chicago today. A beautiful plan with a fatal flaw: an insidious, shadowy corner where the ghosts get caught.

THE MASSACRE TREE

In Chicago's South Loop neighborhood, a little park rests between the new, expensive condominium complexes along Calumet Avenue, where Eighteenth Street cuts from Indiana Avenue East to the lake, skirting the stately Prairie Avenue historic district. It is a strangely small patch of grass, but there is a historic marker designating it as one of the most important sites in the city's history. But before the bronze marker was forged, a much different, much older monument stood: an ancient cottonwood known for generations as the "Massacre Tree." The tree was believed by many to have marked ground zero of the gruesome Fort Dearborn Massacre of 1812, a defining moment in Chicago's memory and one of the most truly haunting in American history.

In the summer of 1812, the settlement at Fort Dearborn was young, diverse and fatally unstable, composed, in the words of Nelson Algren, of "Yankee and voyageur, the Irish and the Dutch, Indian traders and Indian agents, half breed and quarter breed and no breed at all." By 1800, the competition for hunting areas and trade routes had ruined much of the independence natural to the Great Lakes tribes. The native element of the emergent pan-Indian culture could not avoid engaging in trade-based subsistence and became largely dependent on trade goods. Their pottery making had become extremely rare by 1780, and the cultivation of maize, once a unifying tribal activity, had devolved into a means of supporting white populations. Soon, the inevitable depletion of wild game forced the Potawatomi to repurchase their own harvests from white traders.

A section of the so-called Massacre Tree is said to still exist in the collections of the Chicago History Museum. *Chicago Public Library.*

The toppling of the Chicago area's native equilibrium happened in the blink of an eye. Jean Baptiste Point DuSable, a mixed-race fur trader from Santo Domingo, had been the area's first settler, living at the river for twenty years before the turn of the nineteenth century. During his residence there, the wilderness had remained literally unbroken. After living peaceably in a modest home for nearly two decades, DuSable sold his land to a man named John Lalime, who aimed to take up indefinite residence in DuSable's quiet cabin at the mouth of the river. That intention was abruptly halted when John Kinzie arrived in Chicago and seized the property in 1803. Although the Kinzie title has still not been found, most historians agreed that the house, on the bank of the Chicago River opposite the fort, was the same lot that DuSable sold to Lalime in 1800. Records in Detroit, however, show the sale of that same land to Kinzie by Pierre Menard, who passed the parcel to Kinzie for fifty dollars, claiming to have purchased it from an Indian named Bonhomme. When Kinzie arrived in Chicago, he assumed the right to the disputed title, at the same time beginning a rivalry with Lalime that would end in the murder of the latter at the hands of his foe.

Yet, only with Kinzie's whirlwind arrival, less than a decade before the fort's destruction, did the settlement at the river begin to come alive. Preceded by his reputation as a quick-witted Indian trader, Kinzie, a British subject born in Detroit's Grosse Point area, immediately settled his family in the safe shadow of Fort Dearborn.

For nearly ten years, he ruled the realm of settlers and "savages" that together began to suggest civilization, at least when Kinzie himself wasn't sparring with his fellows. For Kinzie was a melding of opportunism and temerity, and when he came to Chicago, aiming to position himself between the portage fur trappers and the Detroit market, he brought along his whole collection of brash personality traits to help him, using what one critic called "guile, intimidation, and the soporific effects of British rum" to "persuade" Detroit-bound trappers to undersell him their pelts.

Kinzie's attitude set the standard for the business relationships that affected every aspect of life at Fort Dearborn. That attitude took its life largely from the shared distaste of men like Kinzie for all others, something that overshadowed any feelings of community.

Still, Kinzie's self-assuredness served to comfort and encourage those who sensed in him a certain quality of leadership. And it was this self-styled security enjoyed by Kinzie and his comrades that left them ill-prepared for the events to come. Eventually, the resentment of the native population became too strong for even a charmer like Kinzie to dismiss.

The inevitable slap of reality came in 1812 when fighting erupted along the northwestern frontier. The fate of more than the fort was sealed when a pair of decisions was delivered. General Hull's order of the evacuation of the fort was quickly followed by Captain Nathan Heald's own demand that the settlers and soldiers destroy all whiskey and gunpowder—a decision that enraged the Native Americans.

On August 15, 1812, Captain Billy Wells arrived at Fort Dearborn, escorted by friendly Miami Indians from his home of Fort Wayne, Indiana. His plan was to give the hostile natives at Fort Dearborn everything his band could carry, in hopes that the Indians would allow the Fort Dearborn settlers safe passage across the dunes to Fort Wayne. But while Wells had a plan, he didn't have a hope: he arrived at the fort that morning with black paint smeared over his face, a sign he believed his death would come before day's end.

Predictably, as the grim procession of soldiers and settlers crossed into the open landscape headed toward Indiana, Indian allies of the British beheld them with bitter eyes. When the line reached a smattering of cottonwood saplings near what is today Eighteenth Street and Indiana Avenue, a group of Potawatomi pounced.

Of the 148 members of the exodus, 86 men and women and 12 children were brutally scalped and murdered, a wagon of children axed in their skulls (claimed by the Indians to have been an act of mercy because their parents had been killed). Billy Wells fell with the dead, and the Indians promptly cut out his heart and ate it to absorb his immense courage.

Those who survived were taken as prisoners. Some of these died soon after, while others were enslaved and later sold to the British and into freedom. Appealing to the Potawatomi on the strength of the business relationships that he had forged, Kinzie and his family were spared.

The fort was burned down.

The scalped corpses of victims remained unburied where they fell, splayed across the Lake Michigan dunes or half buried in the loamy soil. When troops began arriving four years later, they were met by a ghastly host of images: the pitiful skeleton of the erstwhile fort, the abandoned Kinzie cabin, the decaying bodies of settlers and soldiers, all returned to the prairie, all victims of the wilderness and of a desperate, undeclared war.

By the time John Kinzie returned to his property soon after, troops erecting the new Fort Dearborn had re-buried many of Kinzie's neighbors in the new fort's cemetery. Never looking back, Kinzie sought in vain to climb again to his old seat at the peak of the portage fur trade. When his bitter efforts went unsatisfied, he stooped to employment with the new king, the American Fur Company.

The gruesome events that occurred on the Chicago dunes that summer day in 1812 seem to demand commemoration via haunting legends. Indeed, the site of the fort itself is reported to be well protected by marching troops of massacred soldiers who stand guard over the phantom fort site, now the south end of the Michigan Avenue bridge. Yet the site of the actual massacre remained placid until many decades later, after the physical formation of the city of Chicago. Only then, during routine roadwork near the site, did workers uncover the likely remains of massacre victims dating to the early 1800s. Whatever the identity of the remains, after the accidental excavation, apparitions described as "settlers" began to present themselves to passersby near Eighteenth and Calumet.

For many years, Kinzie himself was left to the quiet of his grave. Lauded by the histories penned by his own kin and taught for years as part of the Chicago public schools' curriculum, Kinzie became the city's first hero. This entitlement went largely undisputed until historian Joseph Kirkland began to focus a more critical eye on the figure of Kinzie. As the truth unfolded, Chicagoans began to learn more about the city's mythical founding father. Summing up the new research was the sentiment expressed in Nelson Algren's commentary of early settlement in his classic, *Chicago, City on the Make*. There, he described the city's early settlers as simply the first in a long line of hustlers, as those who would "do anything under the sun except work for a living, and we remember them reverently under such subtitles as 'Founding Fathers' or 'Far-Visioned Conquerors,' meaning merely they were out to make a fast buck off whoever was standing nearest."[7]

ON VISITING JOHN KINZIE'S grave today, one may be stricken by its placement at the outer edges of prestigious Graceland Cemetery, far from the plots of the Pullmans, the Fields, the Palmers and the architects, artists, writers and inventors who came after him to build Chicago into a world presence. Symbolic of his own ultimate place in Chicago's history, Kinzie has found himself on the outside, looking in on all he imagined himself to have been: courageous, enterprising, visionary and faithful. An outsider he wanted to be, and an outsider he most certainly is.

As for the massacre victims, exactly where they were buried—or "half buried"—along the sandy lakefront is hard to discern. Some accounts placed the mass grave at the house of Fernando Jones, 1834 South Prairie. Others thought the burials were done near the Pullman mansion, which stood until its 1922 demolition at 1729 South Prairie. Most, however, believe that the burials occurred at Eighteenth and Calumet, the site of today's "Battle of Fort Dearborn Park," and early maps show a "Massacre Cemetery" at that site.

It is also not entirely certain that all or any of the massacre victims were reinterred at the Fort Dearborn Cemetery along the river when the complex was rebuilt in 1916. In fact, it is more certain that at least some remain at the ambush site, turned into the soil and built on by the Chicagoans who came after.

Those who survived the Fort Dearborn Massacre, however, always marked the spot in their memories by the cluster of cottonwood saplings that had sprung up shortly before the fateful day. The tender shoots that witnessed the horror on the dunes that summer mostly died away as the years went on, except for one: a towering specimen that became known as the Massacre Tree. When locals called it an eyesore and petitioned for its removal, old-

The now-demolished Pullman mansion at Prairie Avenue and Eighteenth Street, circa 1900. The controversial sculpture titled *Black Partridge Saving Mrs. Helm*, also now gone, can be seen to the right of the house. Legend holds that Pullman had the statue commissioned to quiet the ghosts of the Fort Dearborn Massacre, which had occurred on this very spot. *Detroit Publishing Company, Library of Congress.*

timers asked the Chicago Historical Society to protect it, which it did. When a storm finally killed the tree, a portion of its felled trunk was reportedly sawn out and given to the society, where it is said to remain today, stored among its countless curiosities.

After the loss of the tree, George Pullman commissioned a monument for erection on the site. Carl Roehl-Smith forged the mammoth bronze, titled *Black Partridge Saving Mrs. Helm*, depicting a scene from the gruesome clash of 1812. Legend has it that the commission stemmed at least partly from Pullman's wish to placate the massacre victims he believed haunted his Prairie Avenue home. The monument did not remain long at the site, as it was removed not long after the demolition of Pullman's mansion and the deterioration of the elegant Prairie Avenue district. In 1931, it was installed in the lobby of the Chicago Historical Society before disappearing into storage in recent years, the victim of lobbying by the American Indian Center, which called the monument racist. According to accounts, the piece is now in storage in a garage near Roosevelt and Wells. The park replaced it, marked by the bronze plaque remembering the "Battle" of Fort Dearborn.

Today, condominium complexes shadow the park below, where Calumet Avenue skirts a row of new, million-dollar townhomes. The Illinois Central tracks run behind it to the city center, where the body of President Lincoln passed through Chicago after his assassination, and beyond that lie Soldier Field and the dark waters of Lake Michigan.

But the wind still whistles off the waves, the sand still blows up from the shore. And ghosts still wander here, both in and out of these new posh digs. Long-skirted wraiths of settlers are seen fading around dark corners. Phantom horses are heard galloping down the hall of a Prairie Avenue complex built in 2002. Footfalls follow behind strollers down these streets. If you listen closely on a summer night as you walk, you can sometimes still hear above the breeze what sounds like the screams of the massacre victims and the war cries of Indians.

Farther up the lakeshore, at the mouth of the river, phantom soldiers still keep watch where the fort once stood, in the shadow of a bridge relief showing Billy Wells locked in battle with an Indian opponent, his final moments captured in stone.

Meanwhile, at Graceland Cemetery, far from the wild shores where his fellow settlers found an earlier, though more honest rest, John Kinzie may now wish for the violent but valiant death he once fled, a death to which some massacre victims may still be calling him from a little patch of grass at Eighteenth and Calumet, where the Massacre Tree once stood.

THE DOORS OF PRAIRIE AVENUE

Today, the site of the Fort Dearborn Massacre is barely distinguishable as the place where, over two centuries ago, an iconic scene played out on the bloodied sands of the fledgling Checagou. A handful of the old mansions still stand along cobblestoned Prairie Avenue, most of them demolished and rebuilt, ironically, "in the fashion of" the destroyed houses.

And what houses they were.

For years after Great Fire, Prairie Avenue was Chicago's "easy street," where the wealthiest of the city's movers and shakers made their homes. But while the digs were unrivaled as the century turned, in short order the avenue fell into darkness and decline, affected by the busy Illinois Central railroad tracks immediately east and, much worse, the nearby Levee vice district in present-day Chinatown.

After the exodus, only a half dozen of almost one hundred of the mansions here were left standing.

Behind the door of 1800 South Prairie Avenue, the John Glessner House retains all of the vitality envisioned for it by its architect, Henry Hobson Richardson. The house, with its Arts and Crafts feel a harbinger of the great architects to come, was popularly believed to have been Richardson's last commission. In July 1885, however, more than a year after the plans were drawn up for Glessner House, Frank Mac Veagh, who would later become secretary of the treasury of the United States, requested that Richardson design a home at 1220 North Lake Shore Drive. The architect agreed and went on to witness the completion of his design for a lakefront Romanesque brownstone after that of Glessner House.

According to Glessner's accounts, Richardson toured the lots at South Prairie Avenue and Eighteenth Street and drew up the sketches for the house the very next day. Glessner, loving the house as much as the architect did, wrote a book for his children about his time there. Through its doors, the elite of Chicago came and went, as they did through many thresholds on this fabled street. Glessner was not Henry Richardson's last creative gesture, but to him and the majority of his peer architects, it was the pinnacle of his genius.

It should not be surprising, then, that this is where Richardson's spirit is rumored to linger. For years, inhabitants have identified their unseen boarder as the house's designer and not its owner. The giveaway is the manner in which he manifests: to visitors touring the house, who are delighted by their docent's intense understanding of and love for the house's architectural nuances. Often, when these same guests have commented on their charming guide to the house staff, they are informed that no guides were on duty that day—their tour was given by a ghost.

While Richardson walks the rooms of Glessner House, his ghost is not alone on this storied street. Phantoms are said to still hover around the old Clarke House, situated in a small park in the center of the block. Tales of phantom horses are told by strollers, their clip-clopping echoing on the cobblestones, and now and then a woman in settler's dress flits from bush to flower in the moonlight before vanishing in the mist. The Clarke House is a much older house than the Prairie Avenue mansions, as it was moved from its original location on the Chicago prairie. It was thought to be the oldest house in Chicago until Norwood Park's Seymour Noble-Crippen House was found to have an earlier pedigree.

The Kimball mansion still stands on the southeast corner of Eighteenth and Prairie, across from Glessner House. Built for the founder of Chicago's famed organ manufacturing company, the house is both stately and supernatural. Behind its doors walks the ghost of Evaline Kimball, the music magnate's wife, who has been known to rattle the windows at all hours of the day and night for nearly a century.

The mammoth doors of the Elbridge Keith mansion are often visited by guests to magnificent weddings and other events still held here. In between sips and dances, they sometimes encounter an invisible attendee or two. In fact, during one paranormal-themed event, three separate mediums claimed to sense strong spirits in many corners of the rooms.

All other houses on Prairie Avenue—enduring or demolished—pale, however, in comparison to the thirty-thousand-square-foot fortress of

The Marshall Field Jr. mansion on Prairie Avenue in the late 1990s, before its renovation into condominiums. *Author's photograph.*

Marshall Field Jr., which has been converted in recent years into six luxury condominiums. The building was used as a hospital and as a nursing home, among other things, since its abandonment during the street's decay. But at least one resident stayed behind: the house's namesake.

Field Jr.—son of Chicago's department store king—was reportedly given the house as a wedding gift by his father. The house, however, proved to be much bigger than the groom's vows. When he was found shot to death in a bedroom of the house in the fall of 1905, rumor had it that he had been involved with a woman from the notorious Everleigh Club brothel in the Levee district nearby. Though the shooting was explained by the family as an accident that occurred while Field Jr. was cleaning a hunting rifle, it was whispered that he had been shot at the club and then carried home under cover of darkness and silence. Left behind were a widow and three young children, who deserted the house, never to return.

Modern owners of the main front unit today talk about a filmy figure of a man seen and heard pacing the halls and treading the stairs regularly—an entity believed by most to be that of the tragic figure of Field.

AN OCCURRENCE AT SAG BRIDGE

Just southwest of Chicago, past the bend at Harlem Avenue, a street leaves the city to run through the outlying industrial towns of Bedford Park and Summit to villages farther south and the heavily forested Palos division of the Forest Preserve District of Cook County. It is an old road, originally an Indian trail with its origins on the shore of Lake Michigan, in Chicago's present-day Chinatown. The road takes its name from one of the most important events in American history and runs, too, through the imaginations of many, both skeptics and believers, for there is a magic along its path generations have longed to hold—or tried to dispel. It's a highway populated with ghost lights and vanishing hitchhikers—and a road flooded with the tears of laborers, murder victims and the countless mourners who have carried their dead to the seven cemeteries that flank it. That old road, built up by Irish workers on the Illinois and Michigan Canal in the 1830s and '40s, has established itself as no less than the magnetic center of Chicago's supernatural forces and is known today as one of the most haunted roads on earth.

That road is Archer Avenue.

The anchor of Archer Avenue's preternatural notoriety is a wildly sloping churchyard in south suburban Lemont. It is the oldest established cemetery in the county, and its point seems to mark the southern end of the "haunted" portion of Archer Avenue, just north of the old Sag Quarries, where the Cal-Sag Channel and the Des Plaines River rendezvous.

Like Archer Avenue itself, the parish and its cemetery date to the early 1800s, when Irish canallers, most of them from the town of Bridgeport

St. James Church at Sag Bridge, one of the oldest sacred sites in the Chicago area, hosts some of Chicago's oldest ghost stories as well. *Author's photograph.*

(now part of Chicago), put down this road along the route of the Illinois and Michigan Canal under the direction of Colonel William B. Archer. Construction of the canal, financially cursed from the outset, resulted in frequent periods of unemployment for the would-be workers, who often labored under slave-like conditions of thirst and hunger, disease, infighting and death. Nonetheless, they built the road and completed the canal. Many of them moved southwest of the city, to live and die along their Archer Avenue and ultimately to be buried in the bluff-side burial ground that grew up there: a churchyard called St. James of Sag Bridge, or simply "St. James Sag."

Legends abound regarding the sacred nature of this site, which was reportedly a French signal fort in the days of French exploration of the American interior, a site where Marquette and Joliet stopped on their travels and Pere Marquette celebrated Mass. An earlier Catholic church stood here in those days, replaced later by the current limestone structure, the cornerstone of which was laid in 1853 and took local men six years to complete. Workers hauled limestone from the Sag Quarries south of the site to build the structure. Legend says that during the building of the Illinois and Michigan (I&M) Canal, poor canallers who died without funds for a proper burial were cremated, with their ashes scattered over these quarries. Tradition has long told that an Indian burial ground preceded the European lots here—another possibility often brought to explain the site's impressive host of hauntings.

Supernatural events have been reported at St. James Sag since at least 1847, when phantom monks were first seen gliding up this bluff along Archer near its intersection with the Sanitary and Ship Canal, the I&M Canal, the Des Plaines River and the Cal-Sag Channel. In November 1977, 130 years later, a Cook County sheriff was passing the grounds late one night and reportedly saw eight hooded figures floating from the adjacent woods toward the rectory. As he pursued what he assumed to be pranksters, the figures moved toward the top of the hill and vanished. The sighting of these phantom friars long ago earned the church's social hall—with its earlier, castellated roof—the name of "Monk's Castle" in local lore, though no record exists of brothers ever living here.

The priests who made their home at this sacred site, however, have had their own stories to tell. A former pastor claimed to regularly witness the cemetery ground rising and falling as if the entire landscape was one great body of water. Additionally, the unmistakable sound of Gregorian chant has been heard in the vicinity, and a ghost light has been reported, bobbing among the tombstones.

While buried in microfilm at the Chicago Public Library one day in 1996, I came upon the bizarre experience of two young Chicago musicians detailed in both the *Chicago Tribune* and the local *Lemont Observer* of September 30, 1897.

St. James's pastor had decided to hold a fundraising fair at the church. In order to attract the younger parishioners, Father Bollman hired two Chicago musicians, William Looney and John Kelly, to provide harp and flute music. After the affair, exhausted from the long night of playing to a good crowd, the two musicians decided to bed down in the upper floor of the church's parish hall, Saginaw Hall—which was at the time a frame building located at the west end of the parking lot on the parish grounds—rather than risk the late drive back to the city. Settling in on bedrolls sometime after one o'clock in the morning, the two looked forward to a sound sleep. For Looney, however, sleep wouldn't come.

The chilly night and the bright moonlight kept the musician tossing and turning until he was alerted to a commotion outside: the unmistakable galloping and rumbling of a horse and carriage. Curious about the frantic nature of the sound, Looney ran to the window to observe the scene. But although the sound from the road continued with increasing strength, no horse or carriage could be seen. Perplexed and quite shaken, Looney awakened his friend and told him of the incident. As he told his tale, the sound began again, growing in strength as before. This time, both men stood at the window, searching the landscape for a sign of the carriage. What they finally saw was something quite unexpected. In the middle of the road stood a tall young woman in white. Her hands were raised and moving above her head of tangled, dark hair. The two men would later comment that she seemed filled with despair.

Sensing something amiss, the men were on the verge of calling out to her when, to their shock, she floated through the cemetery fence and began wandering around the tombstones. Soon, the sound of the carriage began again. At last the sound produced a visual counterpart, as the musicians witnessed the approach of galloping horses, which were, in their words, "snow white and covered with fine netting. A light of electric brilliance shone from the forehead of each." The animals preceded a "carriage…a dark vehicle of solemn outline. No driver could be seen." As the transport approached the dance hall, the woman returned to the road. Then, as the carriage whipped past her, a shadow enveloped her and "she began sinking into the center…until she was swallowed up."

Silenced by the spectacle, Looney and Kelly froze as the sound of the horses returned yet again and the woman reappeared. Finally, when the horses and carriage materialized for the second time, the woman called, "Come on," waved her hand once more and "disappeared into the ground." Badly shaken, the two men left their window post for their cots, where they waited in fear through the night. In the morning, they took their story to the local police.

In response to their testimonies, Marshall Coen of the Sanitary Police admitted that both of the witnesses obviously saw something that

> *impressed them greatly. I do not believe there is anything of a practical joke in the affair. That would be dangerous in this locality. Everyone out here carries weapons since the rough characters have been brought in for the building of the canal [and] would be tempting death to try such a thing, for any person so foolish would be likely to receive a bullet. Both men are sober fellows. There was no liquor at the dance. I believe these boys are telling the truth.*[8]

SOME LEGENDS MAINTAIN THAT the haunting scene witnessed by Looney and Kelly in 1897 was the result of an elopement attempt gone awry. According to lore, a young man came to St. James in the 1880s to serve as assistant to the pastor and shortly won the affections of one of the pastor's housekeepers. Unable to fight their feelings for each other, the couple decided to run away and be married. Late one night, the young man hitched up the team of horses and advised his fiancée to await him halfway down the hill. As the young man stepped down to help her board the carriage, however, the animals suddenly bolted. Tragically, the carriage overturned on top of the couple. They were both crushed by the weight and buried together in an unmarked plot at St. James Sag. Those who believe in this tale and the ensuing haunting assume that the couple was forever doomed to reenact their elopement as punishment for disregarding social convention.

The late great Chicago historian Kenan Heise documented the supernaturality of a phantom hearse carriage here in his book *Resurrection Mary: A Ghost Story* and wrote about the ongoing sightings of a phantom hearse carriage along Archer near St. James, even in the 1970s. He writes, "The terror of the hearse rips a hole in the frightened soul of anyone who has ever encountered it," and recounts that residents of the region still claim to see it, along Archer Avenue between Resurrection and St. James Sag Cemeteries, a stretch where one may leave the road and wander through the trees to the old Archer Woods burial ground on Kean Avenue. According to descriptions given to Heise by locals, the vehicle is built of black oak and glass through which the unsuspecting viewer might glimpse its ghastly cargo: the luminous casket of a child. Driverless, its horses hurl the carriage through the darkness "with the panting of creatures trying to escape hell itself."[9]

The thrilling stories of St. James Sag have made it a natural attraction for local teenagers, who have flocked to the site for generations under cover of darkness, hoping for a glimpse of the phantom monks and other wraiths said to be seen here. Locals tell that these late-night expeditions became so bothersome at one point that priests serving at the parish took to dressing up in robes to chase the encroachers away. Apprehended trespassers were forced to kneel on broom handles or stones for hours in penance for their offense.

Another Mr. Kelly was at the center of supernatural shenanigans at the Sag in 1897, when the skeletons of Indians were unearthed on the land of the Kelly brothers, just north of St. James Church, on the bluff inside present-day Red Gate Woods. A total of four skeletons were found, with

The story of the Sag Bridge Ghosts dates to the late nineteenth century and appeared in the newspapers the day after two musicians had their harrowing encounter. *Chicago Tribune illustration.*

only the skulls in a state of decent preservation, along with flint spearheads, mortars and stones for grinding corn and shells, which were believed to have been used for money. When the discovery went public, Kelly made an extraordinary announcement to the press. He said that nine years earlier, he had discovered a similar skeleton on his property and took it to his house, wanting to preserve it. In the days that followed, strange things happened on his farm, including sounds of "such a weird, uncanny character as to arouse the...fears of the family, who...connected them with the grim skeleton." Kelly decided to put the skeleton back where he had found it, and after doing so, no more activity was experienced.

After Kelly's second excavation, however, anthropologists from Chicago's Field Columbian Museum (today's Field Museum of Natural History)[10] swept in to take over, and the skeletons ended up in the permanent collections of the museum, presumably raising a ruckus there—which may still be part of the many hauntings of the place today.

THE QUARRIES AND THE CANAL

The limestone quarries of the Sag Bridge area are so closely connected to Chicago's history that it is hard to tell the city's tale without telling this story, too—and impossible to tell its ghost stories without delving into these now water-filled depths.

Chicago's progressiveness has always been coupled with an awe of the spiritual, likely born of the fact that the city has always been caught between two great natural forces: Lake Michigan to the east and the seemingly endless midwestern prairie to the west. These awesome presences have certainly inspired Chicagoans to make a mark here, to create a city as natural and as grand as the water and the grass. Chicago architects have been the most influential of the modern age, but their sensible designs have some strange stories to tell. In fact, some of the city's most haunted places are the striking structures concocted by its most controversial designers, from those who built early on, in stone, to the contemporary members of Chicago's most prestigious firms.

In the nineteenth century, when Chicago was burgeoning, no stone was more appealing than our local limestone. Hailing from the region just southwest of the city, beginning near Sag Bridge, "Lemont limestone" (Joliet limestone from the area a bit farther south) became some of the most desirable building material in Illinois, its buttery yellow hue and softness of appearance joined with a stability that made the stone irresistible to many builders in Chicago, including architects who designed some of Chicago's most recognizable—and haunted—nineteenth-century structures.

The presence of limestone at any ostensibly haunted site sends up the antennae of most modern paranormal researchers, who seem to be constantly looking for limestone as a culprit in reports of the paranormal, believing that its presence can "explain" everything from apparitions to footsteps and cold spots. Limestone is believed to influence the EM field, "holding onto" energy from the past. This theory is known as the Stone Tape Theory (from the 1970s-era British miniseries called *The Stone Tape*), and according to believers in it, the Stone Tape phenomenon can include ghost lights and cold spots; visual, audio and even olfactory apparitions; and more. True, visitors to quarries and to buildings made of limestone often report euphoric feelings, physical illness such as disorientation, malaise, gastrointestinal issues, hallucinations and other symptoms, which can be the result of high EM levels.

In Chicago, many of our limestone buildings are haunted, with good ghost stories to go with them—some of which you will read about in this book—including Holy Name Cathedral, the gate of Rosehill Cemetery and that mysterious church on the bluff at Sag Bridge. Doubtless, the most iconic of Chicago's Lemont limestone structures is the Chicago Water Tower, enduring (and haunted) emblem of the city and, indeed, one of the only structures to survive the Great Chicago Fire of 1871.

However, Chicago's limestone has an additional ingredient beyond any natural ability to encourage the ghostly activity. And that story starts, like many of Chicago's stories, along the building route of the Illinois and Michigan Canal.

The I&M Canal remains one of the most significant engineering projects in American history, as it effectively opened up the portage that had existed between the Great Lakes (Lake Michigan) and the Mississippi River (via the Illinois River), thereby clearing a water trade route between the Atlantic Ocean and the Gulf of Mexico.

Such a project had been envisioned as early as the seventeenth century, when Pere Marquette and Louis Joliet traveled through the Chicago Portage, with the latter remarking that the French could create a North American empire if the passage could be opened to allow for trading. It was Stephen Long, however, who in 1816 surveyed the portage to propose the actual endeavor. Two others, Nathanial Pope and Ninian Edwards, supported the initiative, suggesting that the border of Illinois be moved north from the tip of Lake Michigan to allow the canal to be built entirely in one state: the future state of Illinois. Despite having an insufficient number of residents to apply for statehood, their proposal won Illinois just that.

The water-filled Sag Quarries are now part of the Forest Preserve District of Cook County and are known to be haunted by workers on the Illinois and Michigan Canal as well as locals said to have drowned here. *Author's photograph.*

Construction on the canal began in 1836, but the Panic of 1837 soon threw a wrench in the works and forced the canal commission to borrow money from East Coast banks and even British investors.

As for the hard labor, it was performed primarily by Irish immigrants, most of whom had worked to build the famed Erie Canal. The work conditions have gone down in Chicago legend. Canal workers, being first Irish and then manual laborers, were considered subhuman by many Chicagoans as well, adding insult to the physical injury of the deplorable conditions. Hunger, thirst, infighting and disease—much of it from the ill funding of the project—led to countless deaths along the canal building route, which trudged along the ancient Indian trail that later became known as Archer Avenue, after Colonel William B. Archer.

According to southwest side legend, dead canallers without families to care for the remains of the early immigrants were cremated rather than buried. Those stories tell that their cremains were scattered over the stone quarries of Sag Bridge and Lemont, near the canal route that had taken their lives. A history of St. James at Sag Bridge also includes stories of ghosts said to haunt the Sag Quarries area—today a forest preserve featuring the now water-filled quarries—tying the tales to the drowning of a parishioner there.

Whether the haunting of Chicago's limestone structures can be connected to the quarries, the canallers or both is anyone's guess today. There can be little doubt, however, that a foundation stone of Chicago was hulled from the mysterious quarries of the Sag—and the toil of the canallers who literally opened the way for a Chicago only dreamed of by those who traveled an earlier portage.

THE INDIAN CEMETERY

I f you travel west on Lawrence Avenue beyond the Harlem Avenue outskirts of the city, the houses and strip malls soon give way to sprawling forest preserves on the south side of the road. These preserves stretch far to the south and are some of the most beautiful among the 700,000 acres of the Forest Preserve District holdings, as the stately Des Plaines River runs through them, and the preserves here draw tens of thousands of visitors each year.

Though most come to enjoy hiking, canoeing and sports on the wide fields and picnics with families and organizations, others have come to these woods, sometimes famously, on grim errands. These are the woods, after all, where John Wayne Gacy dumped at least four of his thirty-three victims, having lived just a few blocks away on Summerdale Avenue before his arrest in December 1978. These woods, too, are where the naked bodies of young teens John and Anton Schuessler and Robert Peterson were found in 1955. Their murderer, a stable hand named Kenneth Hansen, was not convicted until forty years after the deed.

Chicago newspapers through the years have been dotted, too, with stories of suicides in these woods—businessmen and family men who left the neighboring houses on evening walks, never to return.

Despite the lingering pall from these tragedies, there is an ethereal shine to these woods, too. Anyone driving west on nearby Irving Park Road will see—in every season—a line of people with plastic jugs at a nondescript well pump just past Cumberland Avenue, for many believe this pump taps a magical spring of healing water. Some also believe these preserves are home to wild men or bigfoot-like creatures, the reports of them sporadic but reaching well back into the nineteenth century. Others believe the flowing waters of the Des Plaines River create a conduit for spiritual and paranormal activity, much of which has been reported throughout the preserves.

No part of these woods, however, is more magical than the lands—and burial ground—once claimed by the family of Chicago's most influential Native American leader, Chief Alexander Robinson.

The burial ground of the Robinson family is today part of the Forest Preserve District's northwest side holdings and is easily accessed by pulling into the site's own wayside at Lawrence Avenue and East River Road. At one time, travelers on a nearby highway were drawn here by a sign inviting sightseers to "a real Indian cemetery," but today only a Forest Preserve District sign at the wayside and a battered showcase full of worn and faded documents hint at the wealth of history at this storied site.

Alexander Robinson is also known as Chief Che-Che-Pin-Qua ("Blinking Eye") and was one of the most active and important players in pre-founding Chicago. A leader of the Potawatomi, Ottawa and Chippewa tribes, Robinson profoundly enhanced relations between the native and early white residents of the city in a time when stresses between them threatened new wars at every turn. Best known for ferrying Anglos to Michigan—and safety—during the time of the 1812 Fort Dearborn Massacre, Robinson was awarded by the Treaty of Prairie du Chien a large segment of land and an annuity for his role in the negotiations and the support given to settlers during the early years of Chicago. According to Chicago-area archaeologist and Robinson family historian Dan Melone, however, Robinson was also given this land because he helped the government secure the lead mines in Galena, Illinois, thus giving the government control over the mines and the procurement of lead for the production of ammunition.

But the land awarded by the treaty, a bountiful expanse of prairie and woodlands along the Des Plaines River, became the family farmsteads and burial ground. The farmsteads remained into the mid-twentieth century, when the last of the family homes burned in a 1955 fire that led, eventually, to the bulldozing and torching of the remaining farm structures. And while the burials of Robinson, his second wife, Catherine Chevalier, his son, David, and a number of descendants remain, the original Victorian marble and concrete markers have disappeared, replaced by a single stone boulder bearing the story of Alexander Robinson and his ties to this land and to Chicago and American history.

But very little of Robinson's real story is recorded here. And neither is the legend of the family's troubled tenure on this land. Robinson was mixed-blood or Métis. His mother was Ottawa, and his father was Scottish. Hailing from the Perth area of Scotland, Robinson's ancestors were Highlanders who traced their genealogy back to a Viking called Ivan the Black, who at one time aspired to invade England. The king caught wind of it and sent his people with money and gifts to try to hold Ivan off. Ivan greeted the king's men, confiscated the booty and cut off the heads of messengers, sending back a message to their king that read, "Do not ever send a second in command to do the job of a King. The next head rolling will be yours." The king packed up and fled the country, leaving Ivan to walk in without a fight.[11]

Unlike his ancestor, Chicago's Robinson became known for his peacemaking. According to Melone, Robinson created and fostered alliances between the native peoples of the prairie and the encroaching white settlers throughout the turbulent nineteenth century. In addition to his work in Chicago, Robinson was called on occasion to Springfield, Illinois, by up-and-coming attorney Abraham Lincoln to consult on various land trials, as Robinson was highly informed about Chicago property and knew all the key players of the day.

Robinson moved among local, state and national circles with ease. At one point, he was hired by the federal government to take thirty-five men in pursuit of Sauk leader Black Hawk. The team left on the trail of the legendary leader, trailing him into Wisconsin, where he was brought to his demise along the Mississippi River bluffs.

Though Robinson lived in town (in a home near present-day Schiller Park), his descendants lived a robust life on the land now popularly known as "Robinson Woods." But as they farmed and canned and raised their children, as the rest of their neighbors did, unsavory legends of the Robinson family abounded throughout the first half of the twentieth century. Locals often talked of rowdy parties, drunken brawls and carousing on the enigmatic "Indian land." Stories even circulated that "debaucherous" Indians had burned down the last house during a particularly devilish escapade, or that the City of Chicago had staged a fire to force the ne'er-do-well Robinsons off the site. All of this, it turns out, is untrue.

Ironically, according to Verlyn "Buzz" Spreeman, authorized historian of the Robinson family (and himself a Robinson descendant), most of the family followed Alexander's lead and did not drink. Robinson himself was a teetotaler and never touched liquor, though he ran the quite prosperous first tavern in Chicago, the inn at Wolf's Point at the mouth of the Chicago River. The only one of the descendants who did drink was one of Robinson's great-grandsons, a colorful character who was often found sleeping in the basements of local homes and businesses, including Schiller Park's Great Escape Restaurant, still in operation today. As for the mysterious conflagration, it was a kitchen fire, started accidentally by an aging Catherine Boettcher, one of Robinson's granddaughters and the last descendant to live on the land.

Along with his abstinence, another surprising fact about Alexander Robinson was that he was a Roman Catholic. During the drafting of the Treaty of Prairie du Chien in 1829, Robinson tried, without success, to have six sections of north side Chicago land deeded to the Church.

Today, the Robinsons have mysteriously vanished from the land deeded "forever" to the descendants of one of the most influential personalities in Chicago's history. All that remains are a few farm furrows, visible after controlled burns, a rusted section of farm fence here and there and a boulder to mark the remains of the old family cemetery. Where the tombstones went no one knows. Where the property title went was anyone's guess—until recently, when archaeologist Dan Melone, descendant Verlyn Spreeman and historian Scott Markus recovered the stone fragments from a warehouse at the Illinois State Archives in Springfield, bringing them back to the chief's hometown of Schiller Park and returning them to his descendants.

Today, after more than a century as the centerpiece of tribal ceremony, impromptu celebration and everyday life, the remains of the Robinson family farms lie mixed with the soil of what is today Robinson, or Che-Che-Pin-Qua Woods. There, a dozen yards from Lawrence Avenue and its manicured homes, the Robinson family marker stands, though the actual burial site is unknown by the public. Two benches invite visitors to rest here and reflect on the chief's influence, told in the stone's inscription:

> *Alexander Robinson—(Chee-Chee-Pin-Quay)* [sic]
> *Chief of the Potawatomi, Chippewa, and Ottawa Indians who died April 22, 1872—Catherine (Chevalier) his wife who died August 7, 1860—And other members of their family are buried on this spot—Part of the reservation granted him by the Treaty of Prairie Du Chien—July 29, 1829, in gratitude for his aid to the family—of John Kinzie and to Capt. and Mrs. Heald at the time of the Fort Dearborn Massacre.*

In 1973, one of Robinson's great-grandsons died, and sanitation officials worked to block his burial at the Robinson gravesite. Thereafter, peculiar events began to be reported by visitors to Robinson Woods, and rumors of paranormal phenomena spread quickly.

These firsthand accounts ranged from the sighting of "Indian" faces and strange lights among the trees to the unmistakable sound of tom-tom drums and the chopping of wood, to a sudden and pungent scent of lilacs at the Robinson gravesite, even in winter.

Among various investigations conducted at the site over the years, one of the most compelling was conducted by students from Northeastern Illinois University, which at the time offered a course of study in parapsychology. That investigation yielded some interesting evidence in favor of witnesses' allegations, including audio tape recordings of the beating of drums. In addition, numerous investigations have produced some especially compelling photographic images of the site, a site which is known for producing visual evidence. In further testimony, Uri Geller's *Unexplained* magazine in recent years printed several photographs of Robinson Woods taken by Clarendon Hills resident James Hunter that seem to include human-like forms nestled among the trees.

Psychics claim to experience vivid visions at Che-che-pin-qua Woods. Lucy Solis, a southwest suburban student of Native American descent, reported having at least two "vision dreams" of the site. One happened while visiting the physical location, and a second occurred during sleep. During the first, Solis beheld a medicine man about five feet, eight inches tall wearing a round brimstone hat with a gray feather on the side and a worn jacket over dark trousers. He spoke silent and foreign words to her. She wrote them down and took them to the professor of her Native American Studies course at Moraine Valley Community College. She said, "My words weren't gibberish but had meaning. The words were similar to 'Washnita Taka Hielo.' The medicine man pointed to me and his chest repeating these words to me. My instructor said he was speaking Lakota."

Working from her instructor's translation, Solis interpreted the words, "Go on thy sacred path," as having a personal meaning for her—which made perfect sense to a student who at the time was engrossed in tracing her Native American ancestry. A later dream brought a supporting, similar message: "Kashniwa Taka Hey Washnita," "Go sacred younger one. Go sacred on thy path." Why there should be a Lakota presence at this Potawatomi memorial ground is an unanswerable question, one that—at least for Solis—in no way undermines the vitality of the message.

What lies in store for the "Indian lands" of Robinson Woods in anyone's guess. As the chief's descendants work to recover the land from the Forest

Preserve District, one only hopes that Robinson and his departed loved ones are guiding them to success.

Despite the glaring absence of Robinsons here, the preserve and the burial ground are considered extremely sacred ground by the Robinson family descendants and Native Americans as a whole. Both groups ask your profound respect if you visit. They ask that you do not litter, remove historic artifacts or feed the deer, whose digestive systems cannot handle human food.

THE WATCHMAN

One of the prettiest places in Illinois is certainly Ogle County, a place of refuge for many Chicagoans who take the long drive northwest there on Sundays to enjoy the rolling farmlands and quaint, historic towns near the Mississippi River—the state's western edge. A highlight is the region surrounding the Rock River, abutted by steep bluffs where hikers may climb for a grand view over the surrounding country. The peerless landmark here is a massive, forty-eight-foot-high sculpture of a Native American in seeming contemplation that overlooks the river. Reportedly, it is the second-largest monolithic concrete sculpture in the world (second only to *Christ the Redeemer* in Rio de Janeiro). Named *The Eternal Indian*, the figure memorializes the impact of one of the most legendary figures in American history: the enigmatic warrior who fought to remain just that, despite the demands of another culture's manifest destiny. Few know, however, that Black Hawk, in death, went on to become a key figure in many Spiritualist churches, a fact owing largely to a charismatic Chicago medium.

Black Hawk was not a hereditary chief but an influential Sauk leader. He sparked the Black Hawk War when, in 1832, he led members of his own tribe, along with Meskwakis and Kickapoos—all British allies—along the Mississippi River and into the state of Illinois, in defiance of the 1804 Treaty of St. Louis, in which the Sauk's tribal lands had been ceded to the United States.

Believing Black Hawk's action to be hostile—a point that is still one of dispute—the U.S. government sent in a militia, and on May 14, 1832,

Two young women pose at the construction site of Lorado Taft's mammoth sculpture known as Chief Black Hawk, which Taft titled *The Eternal Indian*. Black Hawk emerged as a "spirit guide" in Chicago Spiritualist séances and, later, a saint-like guardian in black Spiritual churches of New Orleans. *City of Oregon, Illinois.*

Black Hawk responded to the threat by attacking the Americans in the Battle of Stillman's Run. Black Hawk then led his followers into Wisconsin, where they were pursued by the militia. At the same time, other conflicts erupted, old hostilities flaring and fanned by Black Hawk's leadership. Among those who led the forces against Black Hawk was Chicago's Chief Alexander Robinson—the Potawatomi and Menomenee Métis chief who had worked to establish peace between the natives and whites.

In July, commanded by General Henry Atkinson, U.S. troops tracked the British-allied Indian forces to their stand. When Colonel Henry Dodge joined the troops soon after, the U.S. forces battled the British band at the Battle of Wisconsin Heights, defeating them. The final battle of the war raged on August 2, when U.S. soldiers attacked Black Hawk's followers, weakened by fighting, hunger and illness, in the Battle of Bad Axe. What many believe had begun with Black Hawk's attempt to quietly move back to his tribal lands ended in the American government's banishment of all Indians to land west of the Mississippi River.

Chief Black Hawk, circa 1836. *Library of Congress; Lehman & Duval, and James Otto Lewis. Mac-cut-i-mish-e-ca-cu-cac or Black Hawk, a celebrated Sac chief, painted from life by J.O. Lewis at Detroit, Lehman & Duval liths.*

In 1833, the year after the war, Black Hawk dictated his life story to a government worker and a Galena newspaper editor, telling a story of violence, frustration, anger and a lifelong search for justice. The rest of Black Hawk's days were lived in a poverty that he was quick to blame on Americans, always calling the British kinder, nobler and more honest than their American descendants. Forever in search of funds, the chief was even seen appearing as entertainment on a riverboat shortly before his death, collecting donations in exchange for his colleagues performing war dances for the benefit of spectators.

Even death brought no end to what the chief had seen as a lifetime of exploitation by the American people. Soon after burial, his grave was robbed. In *Bury My Heart at Wounded Knee*, Dee Brown writes that the governor of Iowa obtained the chief's skeleton and displayed it in his office. Eventually, the skeleton went to an Iowa museum. Sauk Indians burned down the museum in 1855.

IN NEW ORLEANS, MEMBERS of local black churches have for a century been calling on the spirit of Black Hawk for aid, for advice, for money in troubled times. He has become an essential patron saint of the Crescent City desperate, with votive candles, oils and other sacramentals sold to help along the prayers of his faithful. Huddled in evening pews, believers venerate statues of the long-dead warrior as their flesh-and-blood leaders, dressed in robes and awash in candlelight, lead their chants:

"Black Hawk is a watchman! He will fight your battles!"

New Orleans grass-roots black churches in the 1920s served, as now, a soup comprising Catholicism from the French, Native American spiritualism from the slaves of the French, the music and dance of freed Africans, as well as voodoo brought by Creoles from Haiti. Despite the obvious involvement of the dead in the rituals of the black churches, the Spiritualistic aspect was kept undercover for years. And despite the many women mediums who came to prominence during the heyday of Spiritualism, the leaders of these churches were men.

It was into this world, however, that a woman named Leafy Anderson came from Chicago. Founder of the Eternal Life Christian Spiritualist Churches—the oldest of which she founded in Chicago in 1913—Anderson was a medium who undoubtedly enjoyed a buoyant charisma, drawing many to follow her lead. Whites and blacks all gathered around her, visiting her home for readings and inspired by her unapologetic embrace of Spiritualism, which had been "in the closet" in the New Orleans to which she had come. From early on, Anderson specifically counseled her followers to pray to a man named Chief Black Hawk, who would aid them in all of their needs. "That's your saint, chillun," she was known to tell her flock.

Exactly how Anderson came to preach her religion of Black Hawk is anybody's guess. Her obituary placed her birth in "Balboa, Wisconsin," which may have been a misspelling of Baraboo, a city near Prairie du Sac, where Black Hawk's story would have been vibrant legend in Anderson's youth. She may, too, have devoured the chief's autobiography, which became a popular seller in the Midwest after its publication and remained so throughout the nineteenth century. Some say that Anderson also claimed to be an Indian herself, part Mohawk.

Anderson herself said she found Black Hawk while living in Chicago. Like many who tell their stories of encountering the overwhelming spirit of the chief, perhaps it was during a séance in her Spiritualist Chicago church or—like others—while walking along a crowded street. Like others, too, her "Black Hawk moment" hit her like the proverbial ton of bricks—and never left her.

As for explaining the hold of the chief on so many followers even today, many theories have been offered. Some point to a "co-suffering" of African and Native Americans, both marginalized communities throughout America's history. Others believe it is the chief's unflinching fearlessness—not his suffering—that holds the appeal. Still others wonder if Black Hawk's appeal—largely to women—was as a guardian, a watchman, in the lives of many women who had been abused, abandoned or unwanted by fathers and husbands.

Journalist Jason Berry, who discovered the cult of Black Hawk on a 1979 trip to New Orleans, wondered:

> *Perhaps summoning an Indian spirit to inspire a burgeoning African American church was Leafy Anderson's expression of solidarity, linking two defeated peoples of colonial America. Perhaps Black Hawk's legend of bravery and resistance made him a protective spirit to her followers. Mostly black, mostly women, saddled with hardship and humiliation, they embraced her, and him, as spirit guides and saints guarding the rock of ages.* [12]

THE WATER STOP

In August 1873, eleven people were killed and more than thirty horrifically injured in one of the most atrocious railroad wrecks in American history.

It was late in the evening on the seventeenth when a southbound passenger train on the Chicago-Alton Railroad collided with a northbound freight train near Lemont, almost completely destroying the former and leading to eleven deaths and more than thirty-five almost indescribable injuries.

The passenger train had left Chicago for St. Louis at its regular 9:00 p.m. departure time. On the run were a baggage car, an express passenger car, three coaches and two Pullman cars. At about 10:20 p.m., when the train was three miles north of Lemont, it came around a bend to discover a coal train coming north on the same track at about twenty miles per hour. A dense fog had come over the Sag Bridge area, and the passenger train engineer had had a rough time of it already. The fog and the bend combined with the lax actions of the coal train engineer led to disaster:

> *The two trains came together with fearful force. Being on the curve, however, both engines left the track and passed each other, that attached to the coal-train striking the baggage car a few feet from the end, breaking the coupling between it and the smoking-car, which the engine struck square in the end, and with such force as to throw the forward end in the air, so that the engine ran under it, tearing the floor completely out and hurling the fifty or sixty unfortunates who were in the car in a struggling mass to the lower end,*

Rail car of the Chicago-Alton Railroad, circa 1900. *Library of Congress, Detroit Publishing Company.*

where there was no chance for escape, and then ensued a scene of horrors which cannot adequately be described.

The smoke stack and dome of the engine were knocked off by the collision, and broken timbers of the smoking car penetrated the boiler, letting loose a dense volume of hot steam, which poured into the car, blinding and scalding the helpless inmates, who with shrieks struggled vainly to extricate themselves. Meantime Russell of the passenger-train, who was unhurt, and a number of passengers from the rear coaches, came forward and endeavored to assist the poor victims, but there was little left to do beyond taking from the wreck the dying and wounded, many of whom were fearfully scalded.[13]

Surviving passengers and crew, stunned at first by the scene, quickly went to work to aid the injured. One passenger observed:

In the meadows on either side of the track were lying human beings, yelling in agony, their flesh boiled off them. The freight engine had run clean underneath the smoking-car, and there exploded, shattering the car into little pieces, and blowing the occupants high up into the air, and over the fence into the meadows. The other engine burst at the same time. A man I don't know who it was ran up to me, shrieking with agony, and threw himself into my arms. I tried to hold him, but his clothes tore off him, and the flesh came off with them. I was nearly stunned at the sight. There were a dozen or more, stripped stark naked, running up and down, crazy….They were tearing at their bodies, and tearing off great handsful of flesh.

The surviving passengers immediately tended to the victims, tearing off pieces of their clothing to bind up wounds and trying to make the injured comfortable in the coach seats and sleeping berths.

At dawn, the train crawled into Chicago, hauling its mangled cars, the dead and wounded its ghastly cargo. It was determined that the cause of the accident was the "criminal recklessness" of the conductor and engineer of the coal train. His duty was to hang back at the Lemont station until the evening passenger train had cleared. The conductor of the freight train was considered a solid driver, with no strikes against him in the year and a half that he'd operated for the line. After the accident, he panicked and fled. The railroad company offered a $1,000 reward for his capture; a relative turned him in and split the money with him. No prosecution, however, was ever started, and he went on to drive for years to come.

James O'Neill, engineer of the passenger train, had both legs broken in the crash but escaped the tragedy with no blame for it whatsoever. Bizarrely though, five years after the accident, the exonerated engineer was shot by a man named Dwight Wheaton, yard master of the Chicago-Alton Railroad at Bloomington, as O'Neill walked home from the yard there on the night of December 28, 1878. Wheaton had suspected O'Neill of having an affair with his wife. After the murder, Mrs. Wheaton told police outright that her husband had killed O'Neill and that, moreover, her husband had told her to take his pistols and discharge them in a cemetery field in Bloomington. She also claimed that her husband had a wife out west.

In 1904, another deadly accident occurred at the same site where the 1873 tragedy had occurred. A Chicago-Alton train had stopped for water at the old Sag Bridge water tower, which stood near the Cal Sag Bridge. The engine of the second train plowed through twelve coal cars and thrust an oil tanker into the air, causing a massive fire.

The violence of the Sag Bridge collisions—and the drama surrounding James O'Neill—led to whisperings of a "Curse of Sag Bridge" and tales of hauntings at the site of the disasters.[14]

Not long after the 1873 collision, Engine 122 returned to duty on the Chicago-Alton Railroad. The first night back in service, the train's cab lamps and headlights were mysteriously

extinguished by some supernatural agency, just as the train passed the eventful point [of the accident]….At first the enginemen thought but little of it, except as a singular coincidence, but as time rolled along and the circumstance continued occurring at the same point upon all night runs, it became evident that there must be some invisible agency that marked engine 122 because of her connection with the great disaster.

According to one report, the night watchman stationed at Sag Bridge resigned, saying he could "stand it no more." His superiors asked what he was referring to. "The ghosts," he replied. He went on to state that every Saturday night when he went down to the watchman's shack near the bridge, he saw the ghosts of a couple who had been killed in the collision of 1873. It was soon common knowledge along the railroad that Sag Bridge was haunted.

This was no small matter, as the site included a water tank that supplied most of the passing trains with water. A water stop here was made for most trains passing through the area. As time progressed, tales of ghostly encounters during water stops mounted. Legend says that another trainman resigned: a freight conductor who was plagued with sightings of "forms flitting to and from, ahead of him and behind him, as he clambered over the freight cards comprising his train."

Engine 122's engineer would frequently see a man and woman climb on the pilot of the locomotive as the train neared Sag Bridge, jumping off the moving train when the engineer approached.

One night, two brakemen on a night trip saw a "ghostly looking object" seated on the steps of their train's caboose when they stopped for water at Sag Bridge. The figure fled the scene, and the men followed, watching the ghost climb a nearby farm fence and disappear. Another brakeman talked of the ghosts of Sag Bridge, who were "plenty. Often, when walking by the train, examining the running gear, I could hear the chattering of teeth, the outcries of someone, as if in anguish, 'til the chills would penetrate my very bones." Retreating to the train's comfort, however, he would be met with "faces peering into the windows at me." The same man claimed to have shot at one of the figures, which "looked like a boiling mass of burning Sulphur" and which, upon being shot, "with a fiendish laugh…sank into the ground."

QUARTERS 63

When in the early 1980s Jim Stonecipher began working on the restoration of an old pioneer cemetery at Great Lakes Naval Training Station, along Chicago's North Shore, he had no idea of the questions that would be unearthed as the project progressed. As the group of volunteers sought permission to extend their explorations, fearful of future building over Native American and military burial sites, a curious theory began to take shape.

As Stonecipher began to explore the first settlement at Fort Dearborn and its relationship to the fort's outpost at Waukegan, known then as "Little Fort," he became aware of obvious discrepancies between written accounts of the second Fort Dearborn's geography, which describe deep ravines suggestive of the North Shore, and the actual topography of the Chicago site, an expanse of prairie on a lake-bound river. Stonecipher asks, would the government build a second fort on a site like the one at Chicago, especially after the location was proven by the first fort's destruction to be ineffective for such use?

A tour of Great Lakes with Stonecipher gives form to his remarkable hypothesis. Above the barracks and classroom buildings, officers' residences and administration buildings, the bluffs of Waukegan tower over the tree-choked ravines, inspiring Stonecipher's oft-repeated question: Wouldn't this have been a much better place for a fort? Picturing the flatlands flanking the Chicago River and the predictable fate of the troops at the first Fort Dearborn, one must agree. Yes, this would have been a better place for a fort; and now that you mention it, why would the government build a second fort on the site where the first had failed?

If these initial arguments stop short of persuasion, Stonecipher presents a perplexing piece of evidence, a "General's Map" dating to the time of the second Fort Dearborn. That map, charting the stretch of shoreline from Chicago to Wisconsin, clearly marks the site where an observer would place Waukegan. When Stonecipher pulls a hand away, however, and dramatically reveals the name written across the site, his enthusiasm becomes understandable. Affixed to that unmistakably North Shore site is a clear label: "Fort Dearborn."

The topographical argument placing the second Fort Dearborn at Waukegan certainly presents some appeal to reason, which the General's Map might reinforce. Stonecipher has other arguments to offer as well, though some of these would be called downright unreasonable by his critics. For the North Shore resident and ex-navy man believes that a stretch of property on the base could provide the most compelling evidence of all for his hypothesis: a house on the property is believed by some, including Stonecipher, to harbor the ghost of a West Point graduate who died in a farmhouse-turned-hospital at the second Fort Dearborn. For Stonecipher, the ghost's presence at Great Lakes would prove that the second Fort Dearborn was originally here at Waukegan and not in Chicago, as current history maintains.

Quarters 63 sits on a lot between Ross Theater and Quarters 64, bordering the parade grounds at Great Lakes. Over the years, a resident of Q63 would often stand at the window ironing between one and two o'clock in the afternoon. During these hours, she would sometimes be surprised by a man walking back and forth in the front yard as if on sentry duty. Friends of hers from Japan reportedly saw the same man combing his hair in an interior room. Both parties described a man in a gray uniform, although the officer who lived in the house was in the air force, which has a navy blue uniform. When the family of Q63 was preparing to move, they needed the previously executed power of attorney to authorize the transfer of property. Searching the house, they were unable to find the document. Finally, after expressing their anger over the missing paper, the family found it mysteriously stuck behind a picture hanging in the house.

In addition to the relatively recent happenings at Q63, Stonecipher believes that the haunting of the structure may have already been apparent to residents some time ago. John Philip Sousa, who lived at Great Lakes in 1918, supposedly spoke of his house there as haunted. Stonecipher has reason to believe that Sousa's haunted house may have been none other than Q63.

To one side of Q63, in a house numbered Quarters 64, the marvelous has likewise become mundane. Dogs shy from the basement stairs, lights and windows appear to do as they please, a toilet seat refuses to stay up or down. On one occasion, a table was found moved from one room to another. Most startling of all, a resident awoke one night to find herself staring into the bearded face of a six-foot-tall, 170-pound man in uniform. Before she could fret, he disappeared.

Stonecipher believes that the activity occurring on these properties may be attributed to one or more officers buried in the area stretching from Ross Theater, across Q63, to the end of Q64. As for the officer in uniform seen by occupants of both residential units, Stonecipher wonders if this might be a second lieutenant by the name of McDuffy, a West Point graduate who died at the second Fort Dearborn two weeks after graduation. Pointing out the ravine directly behind the frame structure dubbed Q63, Stonecipher tells of descriptions of the hospital at Fort Dearborn, which "was in the basement of a farmhouse, across a ravine." Stonecipher doesn't stop there, however. If the fort hypothesis fits, then, according to his research, the property under the three buildings is the military cemetery current research places outside the farmhouse hospital at the Chicago fort.

The unusual goings-on at Ross Theater may also suggest that Stonecipher is on to something. The building is supposed to host the "typical disturbances" associated with poltergeist cases, including noises, movement of objects, problems with technical equipment and so on.

Moving away from this supernatural stretch of land, ghost hunters will want to make a beeline for Building 18, which was once the base hospital. More than one hundred persons died inside this imposing structure and at least one just outside, when a nurse reportedly committed suicide by jumping from an upper window. Over the years, the building's occupants have reported seeing and even speaking with a major who turns out to be less than tangible and with a nurse believed to be the suicide victim. Behind the hospital building, strollers on the bluff overlooking the ravine may distinguish "footers" in neat rows, as well as sunken portions of grassy earth that workers like Stonecipher believe to be evidence of another burial ground.

Another suicide has been tied to Quarters A, that of a maid in a corner house. The cause of death was questionable; some claim she was killed. Believers in her murder have told tales of a Woman in White who is seen

Training exercises at Great Lakes Naval Training Station. *Library of Congress.*

on the top floor of the house. During his teenage years in the house, the son of an admiral told his parents that he had seen "Satan" in his bedroom. Stonecipher wonders if the boy in fact saw the disheveled and destitute spirit of an early settler.

For researchers, the USO Building sets yet another plate of phenomena on the smorgasbord of psi that is Great Lakes. No families were ever quartered in this building. Nonetheless, one night a public works person distinctly heard the sound of a little boy's giggling accompanied by recurrent knocking. Thinking that one of the sailors was playing a joke on him, the worker went to his car to get a hatchet, hoping to turn the tables and scare the culprit. When he returned, he found the room empty and the bathroom door swinging wildly. No one had come out of the locked building, nor was anyone hiding inside. Over the years, several similar incidents were reported to have occurred on the premises. Accompanying such reports were claims that furniture and other objects had sometimes moved by themselves.

Even if further research validates Jim Stonecipher's theories about the history of Great Lakes, this impressive institution will never run short of mysteries. Remembering, and often replaying, the experiences and memories of the thousands of men and women who have lived, worked and died here, Great Lakes will long remain a popular port for wayfarers into the unknown—especially in Quarters 63.

THE BEACH PEOPLE

In early September 1860, the steamer *Lady Elgin* headed out of the port of Milwaukee bound for Chicago. Most of the passengers were members of Wisconsin's Union Guard, traveling to Chicago for a campaign rally featuring presidential hopeful Stephen Douglas. Though foul weather was forecasted, the short trip to Chicago passed without incident. On the return trip that same evening, however, just before midnight a fierce gale erupted, causing a nearby, diminutive schooner, the *Augusta*, to approach the *Lady Elgin* for assistance. Out of control, the *Augusta* collided with the steamer, driving a hole into the port side and causing all of *Lady Elgin*'s lights to fail.

Terrified, the crew of *Augusta* headed for the safety of Chicago, not realizing the damage that the *Lady Elgin* had suffered. On that steamboat, all hands rushed to throw cargo overboard to raise the gash above water level. Even live cattle were hurled into the lake in a panicked effort to save the ship and its passengers, the latter bound to the vessel—for better or worse—when the *Elgin*'s lifeboat drifted away.

Shockingly, within a half hour, the *Lady Elgin* had sunk. Shortly thereafter, the sun rose on hundreds of bodies in the freezing water—many, many dead, some fighting for life. In the end, more than four hundred death certificates were issued to victims who either drowned in the wreck or died from being tossed against the rocky shoreline. The loss of the *Lady Elgin* would remain the second-deadliest disaster in Great Lakes history, second only to the horrific *Eastland* Disaster, which took more than 840 lives in 1915 on the Chicago River—in nineteen feet of water.

The site of the *Lady Elgin* wreck lies today under sixty feet of water, several miles offshore from Highland Park, along Chicago's North Shore. More than two hundred artifacts have been brought up from the site by a diver, Harry Zych, whom the Illinois Supreme Court declared owner of the wreckage after a long court case. Zych, who wanted no part of selling the *Lady Elgin* artifacts, instead seeks a museum willing to restore and display them in a full exhibit. He has been unsuccessful.

The disregard for their tragic end may be part of the reason why so many tales of the *Lady Elgin* dead still circulate. For, according to sailors, the vessel has sailed Lake Michigan each anniversary night since its demise. Though the ship is silent, its passengers are not. In fact, seamen have long told tales of picking up castaways from the autumn waters who claim to have abandoned a steamboat en route to Milwaukee. While crews search vainly for the distressed vessel, the rescued passengers vanish without a trace, further panicking the bewildered rescuers.

Strollers along the North Shore, too, have told of similar encounters with wild-eyed stragglers who have literally walked out of the lake in the wee hours, soaking wet and begging for help for their distraught vessel. Interestingly, passengers of the *Elgin* who made it to shore had, in fact, been aided by just such strollers—predominantly students from the lakeshore campus of Northwestern University—whose efforts inspired the founding of the university's student-run U.S. Life-Saving Station in 1876, the first installation of federal lifesaving resources on the Great Lakes, which has since orchestrated more than five hundred rescues.

Without a doubt, the most compelling story of a *Lady Elgin* haunting is the story told to reporters by a Highwood carpenter who lived near the beach when the steamer went down in 1860. The man told a reporter the tale of the ghost of a "beautiful woman gowned in black and wearing a gold chain with a heavy pendant about her neck, with diamonds in her ears and on her fingers, and with the water dripping from her robes."[15] He said the woman had first appeared when a housing development began to go up in the area—which was the site of a makeshift cemetery for some of the *Lady Elgin* dead. He claimed that whenever this "beautiful ghost" came around, she seemed to be waving her hands as if to drive away the builders.

The development was never completed.

The carpenter knew well who the woman was, as he had made four coffins for the *Lady Elgin* dead, including the woman's, and had helped to bury their caskets in a makeshift gravesite that still stands today, unmarked, between Highwood and the bluffs of Lake Michigan.

The man had been on the beach immediately before the wreck of the *Lady Elgin* occurred. He had seen the boat go by the old lighthouse (a long-vanished structure predating the Grosse Pointe Lighthouse),[16] as it was common for locals to go out in the evening to watch for the steamer to go by, the vessel being one of the most famous on the Great Lakes:

On that night it was brilliantly lighted, for it had many excursionists on board. After watching it pass, I went away from the bluffs but heard of the wreck a few hours afterward and went south to that point of the beach where the people were gathered. The sight was something awful. On what appeared to me to be the roof of the pilothouse there were floating certainly more than forty people. All at once a big wave engulfed them and they were all lost. For days afterward bodies continued to be washed up by the sea on the beach just below the lighthouse.

I'll tell you of one specific case which to me was at once the most pathetic and the most horrible of all. A woman clad in black silk and showing, despite the fact that she had been wave-tossed and beach beaten for several days, that she had been a woman of beauty, was finally thrown up by a wave of sufficient strength to give her body lodgement on the sands below the bluff on which stands the old lighthouse. We found her there and carried her to a building some distance from the water. An examination showed that on the body was a handsome gold watch, a thing somewhat rarer than it is now. While about the neck was a fine gold chain, to which was attached a gold piece of the value of $2.50. On the fingers were several rings, two of them containing large solitaire diamonds. The effects were left upon the body and the proper officials were notified. They arrived, but as it was late in the evening they ordered that the remains be left where they were until the next day. The jewelry was left upon the body. I locked the door myself as the party left. The next morning when the officials arrived the door was opened, but there was neither ring, watch, nor necklace upon the body of the woman. They had been stolen in the night.

Now I know what I am talking about, and I have the courage of my convictions. I saw the chain with its gold piece pendant hanging from the neck of the wife of a prominent Lake County official not six weeks afterward.

THE MISSIONARIES AND
THE ACOLYTES

Extending skyward from the corner of Roosevelt Road and May Street on the city's Near West Side is the impressive spire of Holy Family Church, the centerpiece of one of Chicago's oldest Catholic parishes and a seemingly indestructible monument to the unmoving faith of its ever-changing congregation.

Erected in 1857 as the core of a Jesuit-guided parish, Holy Family Church was, according to late Chicago folklorist Richard Crowe, built over the site of an Indian battlefield and, incidentally, over the running waters of the Red Creek. When the Chicago Fire failed to destroy the church just fourteen years after its completion, the parishioners attributed the apparent miracle to the intervention of Our Lady of Perpetual Help.

The night of the fire, the parish's founder, Father Arnold Damen, was in New York City doing missionary work. Hearing confessions at Brooklyn's St. Patrick's Church, another priest passed a note to Damen in the confessional, telling him that Chicago was aflame and his parish in the direct line of its destruction.

Father Damen quietly finished hearing confessions then walked up to the altar. He knelt down and prayed, staying on his knees the whole night through. He prayed for the intercession of the Blessed Mother, Our Lady of Perpetual Help. He promised the Blessed Mother that if God would save his parish, he would build a shrine to her honor at Holy Family and keep seven candles burning there forever.

The mysterious Father Arnold Damen is at the center of numerous ghost stories, as are his fellow Belgian Jesuit missionaries. *Loyola University Library, Chicago.*

Back in Chicago, as the fire raged through the city, it seemed intent on ravishing Father Damen's parish and the homes of his flock. But then, something extraordinary happened. The wind changed without warning, and the flames skirted the Near West Side neighborhood while Damen's parishioners waited with bated breath, on their knees too, inside the church Father Damen had built. After the fire, the shrine was built. Today, seven (now electric) candles still blaze at all hours of the day and night, the kept promise of the faithful Father Damen.

Father Damen was one of a dozen Belgian Jesuit missionaries who were brought to America by the Jesuit missionary to the American Indians, Father Pierre-Jean De Smet. Like his brothers, Damen first went to Florissant, Missouri, just outside St. Louis, living at the Jesuit monastery of St. Stanislaus. He was ordained in 1843, three years after his arrival in the United States, and his first assignment was as a parish priest in the city.

In the summer of 1856, while Father Damen served as pastor of St. Francis Zavier Parish in St. Louis, he traveled to Chicago to preach a string of missions. The missions were an overwhelming success, leading Chicago's Bishop O'Regan to invite the Missouri Jesuits to establish a parish in Chicago, where the order had no existing community. That fall, O'Regan wrote to Damen in St. Louis, urging the project:

> *I know I cannot do a better work for religion, for the diocese or for my own soul than by establishing here a house of your Society, and this is the reason I have been so very anxious to effect this. It was on this account, as also from my personal regard and affection for your Institute, as for many of your Fathers individually, that I so urgently and perseveringly tried to see this good work accomplished.*[17]

The church building Father Damen erected is something of a miracle in itself. No one could quite understand how this massive and exquisite structure had risen from literally nothing, as Father Damen's parishioners were the poorest of the poor, and most of the funds for construction he had to raise on his own. The secret was Damen's charisma, a magical power that compelled hundreds to give literal nickels and dimes from their scant incomes—and caused the occasional wealthy neighbor to hand over great sums of money at Father Damen's request. For Damen's love of the Church—and particularly of *his* church—was contagious. Soon, the parish of the Holy Family was the pride and joy of thousands: a shining oasis of faith and hope in Chicago's west side ghetto.

The familiar black robes of the Jesuit can be found on various statues displayed at Holy Family; many of the saints venerated here are the men who inspired and worked with Father Damen. A curious addition to these is a pair of wooden statues depicting two altar boys in old-fashioned cassocks. The statues immortalize two youngsters who have played leading roles in the mysterious history of this spiritual community. Indelibly etched in parish memory is the story of the tragedy that befell the two brothers when they were drowned together in 1874 and of their subsequent appearances to fellow parishioners.

In 1890, Father Damen was awakened by what was later believed to be the deceased brothers. Dressed in cassocks and bearing lighted candles, the children led the priest to the dying mother of the departed boys, then promptly vanished. Along with this original account, later parish legends developed around the story. Some reports hold that even several years before their deaths, phantasms of the boys appeared to would-be victims of the Chicago Fire to warn these parishioners of their imminent danger. But while the presence of the boys has faded in recent generations, that of Father Damen has been infused with greater energy than ever.

But if Arnold Damen was always there for his church and his flock, protecting both from earthly, and otherworldly, harm, it was his beloved school that won his undying passion. St. Ignatius College Prep is an anomaly, a school unmatched for Chicago prestige, but open through scholarship to the super-rich, the dirt-poor and everyone in between. The result is a student body that's an education in itself; those lucky and smart enough to gain admission live daily with a cross-section of society, forming friendships with young people from Hyde Park to Homewood, Bronzeville to Beverly, Garfield Park to the Gold Coast. St. Ignatius alums, then, are among the most sophisticated and successful of all Chicagoans. Father Damen would be proud. During his lifetime, the Jesuit strove for the school's superiority in all things: the curriculum, the culture and, most notably, the spiritual life of the students it served. Some say that after his death, Damen continued to

Holy Family
Church and St.
Ignatius College
Preparatory
High School,
formerly
St. Ignatius
College—a
haven of history
and hauntings.
*Loyola University,
Chicago.*

serve as the school's headmaster of sorts, overseeing the campus in his usual, ever-loving way. Along with the well-being of the students, he keeps close watch on the physical property, ensuring that all is in tip-top shape and that Ignatius's future is secure.

When, in the early 1980s, the board initiated a massive renovation for the century-old school, elaborate plans were drawn up for the near-gutting of most of the structure, an updating of all the electrical and plumbing systems and the installation of new floors and ceilings where water damage and wear had taken their toll. As with all such projects, a director was assigned to oversee the remodeling through to its completion. Not on the payroll, however, was another far more authoritative boss: Arnold Damen, the project's self-appointed foreman.

Since the founder's death, a number of students and faculty had spotted Damen casually patrolling the halls of Ignatius, going about his rounds as he always had, but by the dawn of the 1980s, sightings of him had all but ended. With the beginning of renovation, Damen reappeared with a vengeance, startling those witnesses unschooled in his legacy.

One 1985 graduate tells the story of his own run-in with the ghost of Damen during an after-hours pledge drive for the renovation in progress:

In the mid-1980s, the school began a fundraising campaign to raise money for badly-needed repairs to the school. Some of the urgent work had already begun: replacing rotten flooring and tuckpointing. Students would work late into the night on this project, calling former students to raise money for the campaign. The calling center was set up in an old, musty library on the top floor of the school, known then as the Cambridge Room. It was a dark and dreary place, with old, dusty books and sheets of plastic covering the windows. Outside employees who had been hired to manage the campaign often times worked late, too (past midnight), preparing letters and managing the records. They often felt strange sensations, like another person was in the room with them, when there were only two employees in the building. The school had a very sophisticated alarm system installed, since it was in a very bad area of the city, and several times this alarm went off while the fundraising campaign was being conducted—the keypad had an LCD display that would ominously flash the word "Intruder" when the alarm went off. Though the system had been in place for several years it had never before experienced a false alarm, so every time the alarm would go off the Chicago police would respond with canine teams, and the school would be searched, with negative results. There were never any indications of forcible entry, and everything was always found locked and secured.

One night, I was standing in the library talking to one of the management people, when I glanced through the set of large, old wooden doors that led to an unused hallway. The hallway also served as a foyer for two old curved stairways, an old elevator, and a large storeroom. I watched an old man about five-foot, six-inches tall and very thin, with white hair, balding, extremely pale, and dressed all in black clothing (a long-sleeved black shirt and long slacks). The person moved very quickly and lightly on a diagonal across the wide hallway, and it was odd, since the floors were very old wood and creaked badly; even so, no sound was made by this man I saw.

I said to the manager, "There is someone in the building," and I pointed out to the hallway and told him what I'd seen. He told the other manager, and they were concerned and went to investigate. As the stairwell was closed off and the elevators not in service, the only place the old man could have gone was into the storeroom on the south side of the hallway. The room was, surprisingly, locked, and when the manager unlocked the door, we found that the floor and ceiling of the room had already been removed by construction crews working on the renovations. We looked down nearly twenty feet to the classroom below and up nearly twenty feet into the pitch-black ceiling of the attic of the school.

We were terrified. A hasty meeting was called, and the students were sent home several hours early. The managers—who had, of course, had their own experiences in the building—left with us, and no one was willing to look through the upper floors of the school that night, or to call the police, who had come in vain more than once before to apprehend "intruders" who couldn't be found.

Later, when I told older priests at the school what I'd seen, there was no question in their minds that I'd seen Father Damen, the founder of the school, to whom the physical maintenance of the building had always been of the utmost importance. Although I knew well of Damen, as he occupied the most prominent of places in the school's proud history, I had never heard the stories of his haunting of the place. Still, everyone I spoke to who knew of the priest's ghost asserted at once that he had likely come back—as he had many times before—this time to keep an eye on the renovations.

Aside from his love for Holy Family and St. Ignatius—seemingly defying the grave—there may be another reason for Father Damen's lingering presence. After his death, he was interred in the cemetery on the grounds of St. Stanislaus Seminary in Florissant, Missouri—where Damen had first arrived so many years before as a young missionary monk before his ordination and where the bodies of his brother missionaries (including Father De Smet) also rested. In recent years, after the closure and sale of the seminary to a Christian school, the bodies of the Jesuits who had been laid to rest there were slated to be moved to Calvary Cemetery in St. Louis. In a story that seems a broken record now, bystanders during the days of the removals claim that no remains were removed—only the headstones. When pressed, authorities insisted that whatever remains were still present were indeed reinterred—but that there was not much to be found after so many years.

Today, visitors make their way to the memorial site of the Belgian missionaries in St. Louis, but are the remains of these great missionaries really here?

St. Stanislaus Seminary, Florissant Missouri, burial site of the Belgian Jesuits. *Library of Congress, Historic American Buildings Survey.*

Ghostly goings-on at the old seminary grounds since the "reinterments" in Florissant seem to question the official record, as paranormal investigation teams have made this a regular point of pilgrimage on their evening outings. Strange lights, shadowy figures and even the sounds of chanting are experienced on the site of the old cemetery at St. Stanislaus, causing one to wonder about the wanderings—after death—of at least one of the old faithful.

THE HANGING MAN

In his "Five Months After" essay, which appeared in the *Chicago Times* in April 1872, editor Everett Chamberlain reiterated an American joke that had been enjoyed in recent months, especially by Chicagoans: the joke wherein a citizen of some far-off town was represented as rushing with mad haste to the railway station…because, as he said, he must reach Chicago…or they would have the whole town built up again before he could get a view of the ruins.[18]

And it was true.

The swift, phoenix-like emergence of the post-fire city—stronger, bigger, better than before—gained Chicago a permanent and worldwide reputation as an unstoppable metropolis: "The City that Works." Yet, while Chicagoans quickly dismissed the disaster in favor of the future, the first few days after the Great Conflagration found Chicagoans filled with despair and the nation and world desperate for details.

Full of the monstrous news and eager for sympathetic ears, stunned Chicagoans wrote to friends and relations around the world, sending much-anticipated news of the state of the city. Without photos or newsreels to provide a vision of the disaster, out-of-towners relied on the vivid descriptions of the fire's own witnesses. Chicagoans' letters regarding the disaster remain some of the city's most precious historical resources, providing as they do keen and colorful witness to the great conflagration. Many of these letters' authors document their own destruction, tracing in a rush of words their overnight falls from wealth and luxury to impoverished homelessness. The loss of family and of friends. Others, luckier, report on the misfortune of others.[19]

Anna Higginson, wife of George M. Higginson, real estate broker, lived with her husband on Dearborn Street, just north of Chicago Avenue. While the city still smoldered, she sent word of the fire to her friend Mrs. Mark Skinner, in Europe with her husband at the time, including literary pictures of the fire's attendant madness:

> *Mrs. Winston saved a pink silk dress trimmed with lace, but very little else; one lady had a carriage full of party dresses & another a half dozen bonnets. One man was seen running from the fire with two immense turnips & another with a piece of broken furniture.*

But while these snapshots peppered the city's memory in the days after the fire, most of the lasting remembrance was vivid film, destined to replay itself forever in the city's mind:

> [T]*he fire worked up gradually along the North Branch & the instant the wind caught it the fire was hurled the whole length of the city; in that way our house was burned at last. As I went out of it & saw the vine-covered walls & the windows filled with flowers all shining so peacefully in the moonlight, it seemed impossible to realize that in a few moments the smoke & flame I saw all around me would seize that too & that I was looking upon my home for the last time.*

This destitution would be, for most, a temporary condition, yet an unquestionable blanket of loss was fixed forever:

> *We…rode to the West Side in company with thousands of other refugees like ourselves—dusty, smoky, forlorn in every way…the air full of blinding dust & smoke & behind us our ruined homes, with all their years of accumulated treasures & associations of every kind. It is for those I grieve…my Mother's Bible, the clothing & toys of my dead children.*

As the once formidable temples to commerce, trade, worship and art—wonders of the modern world—lay in ruins around him, the mayor of Chicago had but one desolate dispatch to the nation:

"Send us food for the suffering. Our city is in ashes."

Incredibly, the unspeakable destruction left behind by the "memorable conflagration" written of by Chamberlain five months after the fire was not exclusively attributable to the fire itself. In fact, a significant portion of the

Left: Ruins of the Great Fire, October 1871. *Library of Congress.*

Below: Men swimming behind the Chicago Water Tower and Pumping Station about twenty years after the Great Fire. *Library of Congress; Baker, R.S., photographer, 1893.*

damage was the work of looters and thieves, who took advantage of the chaos and the preoccupation of police forces to plunder the burning city.

"The like of this sight since Sodom & Gomorra has never met human vision," wrote Jonas Hutchinson, lawyer and notary. "No pen can tell what a ruin this is." But he tried. To his mother in New Hampshire, Hutchinson penned his own testimony of the fire and the blackness that described far more than its charred ruins:

[T]he city is thronged with desperadoes who are plundering & trying to set new fires. The police are vigilant. Thousands of special police are on duty. Every block has its patrolmen and instructions are explicit to each officer to shoot any man who acts suspicious and will not answer when spoken [to] the second time. Several were shot & others hung to lamp posts last night under these instructions....The roughs are improving the time to sack & pillage. The city is in darkness.

When I first studied the ghost stories of the Great Fire many years ago, I wrote: "Least evident here today is the lawlessness of autumn, 1871, when looters swung from the lamposts, desperately subdued by attempts at law and order during a reign of absolute terror." But times are different now. Current newspapers regularly carry stories of the "wilding" carried out by gangs of youths assaulting random tourists and locals in this historic district and throughout the central part of the city. As the world knows, chaos has returned to Chicago, and it is an everyday chaos.

But our history remains, with its own ghosts. Just as the Water Tower itself forces the fire's memory on all who pass its castellated remains, so too do some of the players in that drama. In an upper window of the old tower, before its renovation and even now, passersby have occasionally seen the figure of a man, limp and pallid, dangling by a rope around his neck or sitting quietly, staring from the window. Workers in the information center profess ignorance of the sightings, testifying that memory alone haunts this structure.

On October 21, 1875, a young man named Frederick Kaiser had lunch with his family in their home on Pearson Street. He usually sat and read with his family after lunch, but that day he said he was going out for a walk. He crossed the street, climbed to the top of the water tower and sat for some time looking out of the window, where numerous passersby saw him. At about half past two o'clock, he jumped.[20]

In June 1881, a young shop clerk named Hugo von Malapert jumped too.[21]

Today, many historians claim that the execution of the Great Fire's looters is a myth. Accidental deaths did occur, of course, in the course of law enforcement. But the wide-scale and officially approved hanging of criminals is, many say, the stuff of legend.

Still, the letters remain, their authors' descriptions of the hangings as vivid now as ever. And even those who disregard them may someday catch a glimpse of the proof they need: one hapless witness to the rule that crime doesn't pay, paying his own dues forever in the city's signature tower.

THE CUSTOM HOUSE

By the year of the Great Fire, the U.S. Custom House had operated in today's Printer's Row area for a little over fifteen years. The building housed not only the collector of customs but also the equivalent of the IRS, the steamboat inspector, the U.S. commissioner, the U.S. marshal and the postal clerks' offices. On the top floors were the federal courts, district attorney and clerks of court. The Custom House was one of several so-called fireproof buildings that would be decimated by the Great Fire in 1871.

After the Great Fire destroyed the Custom House, the U.S. government moved the various orphaned offices into Congress Hall, an old hotel at Michigan Avenue and Congress Boulevard that had survived the fire. A decade later, the building would be razed to build the new Auditorium Annex Theater (today's notoriously haunted Congress Plaza Hotel) for visitors to the World's Fair of 1893. But just after the fire, by December 1871, the old hotel site was already known as haunted.[22]

Soon after the government workers' tenancy began, stories of phantom footfalls and other strange sounds began to be reported by employees, and—not long after—a chilling story surfaced to explain the strange events, which were tied to a porter who had worked in the old Congress Hall Hotel.

The dead porter's former roommate told the tale of an evening when his friend had gone out to bathe in the lake. When the porter came back later, his friend saw that he was pale and distressed, and he got into bed with his clothes on, falling asleep without a word.

In the morning, the porter was gone. Later that afternoon, while his friend stood chatting with an associate in the lobby, the body of the porter was brought in on a stretcher. He had drowned the evening before in Lake Michigan.

Not long after the man's death, the housekeepers at Congress Hall Hotel began to report strange noises in his former room and a feeling of unease. Then, one night about three months after the drowning, several people saw the dead man appear, dressed in soaking-wet clothing, standing in the doorway leading to the yard of the hotel. The night watchmen at the hotel also reported hearing the sound of walking between 9:00 p.m. and midnight most nights, and the engineer claimed to have heard someone snoring in his room when he was quite alone. On another occasion he went into the basement, where the porter used to nap on his duty nights, and found the chairs turned upside down, inkstands overturned and papers and other items strewn about the room.

Another night watchman was driven nearly crazy, reporting that he was constantly followed by phantom footsteps while making his rounds, the footfalls walking when he walked and stopping when he stopped.

Today, the site where the Congress Hall Hotel once stood is occupied by the looming Congress Plaza Hotel, known as one of the most haunted hotels in the world and—for my money—the most haunted building in Chicago. Myriad spirits roam these halls, the victims of so many tragedies that occurred here over many, many years, including those of numerous accidental and purposeful drownings in the lake. Whether the porter who suffered here so many years ago is part of today's gathering of ghosts is anyone's guess.

If he still walks the halls, however, he has a lot of company.

Room for One More

So much is experienced by travelers. Open to new experiences and cut free for a day, a week, a month from routine, those away from home seem somehow open to truly alternate realities, especially at the site where they lay down to sleep.

In Chicago, the Sheraton Gateway Suites Hotel is an eleven-story atrium hotel in O'Hare Airport's Rosemont convention hub. Like in many such buildings, a number of past guests have reportedly committed suicide by throwing themselves over the atrium railings; since one such incident in the fall of 2001, the victim has been seen—in suit and tie—gazing over the east side of the atrium rail. A number of drug overdose deaths have also occurred here, and in such rooms, guests have reported dark figures, disembodied voices and the dishevelment of their clothes and belongings, often while they are in the bathroom.

The nearby O'Hare Hilton, directly across from the airport entrance, was long rumored to have an "uninhabitable" room—one that just made guests so inexplicably uncomfortable that they literally couldn't sleep.

There's the Baymont Inn and Suites in Aurora, where employees have witnessed balls of white light in the lobby area and where guests are repeatedly driven from room 208 by a spirit who seeks to strangle them in their sleep.

There is the old Leland Park, also in Aurora, haunted by a number of guests who have reportedly checked in, not to stay the night, but to throw themselves into the Fox River from this, one of the tallest buildings in the city.

Noxious odors and disembodied voices are reportedly rife in the building, now an apartment development.

The Hotel Florence, in Chicago's historic Pullman district, is rumored to be haunted by a woman who lived in the hotel at one time, and the hip House of Blues Hotel is home to a number of phantoms in the larger ghostworld of Marina City, including that of a young girl believed to have died in the hotel structure when it was an office complex.

The Drake Hotel, jewel of Lake Shore Drive, is home to the famed "Woman in Red"—a tragic young woman who jumped off the roof on the hotel's opening night in 1920 after discovering her fiancé in the arms of another woman.

Among the multitude of haunted hotels in Chicago, however, none—or even all of them together—can touch the granddaddy of them all: the Congress Plaza.

One of Chicago's largest and oldest hotels, the Congress Plaza was originally named the Auditorium Annex when it was built to house visitors to the Columbian Exposition—the transformative World's Fair of 1893.

The Congress Plaza Hotel (*left*), originally named the Auditorium Annex, circa 1900. The hotel, built to house travelers to the World's Fair of 1893, has gone on to become one of the world's most haunted hotels. *Library of Congress, Detroit Publishing Company.*

The name referenced the Auditorium Theater across Congress Parkway, an acoustically magnificent structure designed by blockbuster architectural duo Dankmar Adler and Louis Sullivan. The Annex's original North Tower was designed by Clinton Warren, but Adler and Sullivan oversaw its development, including the addition of "Peacock Alley" (now shuttered), an ornate marble tunnel that runs under the street, joining the theater and the hotel. Later, in the early twentieth century, the firm of Holabird & Roche designed the South Tower, completing the current structure, which houses more than eight hundred rooms.

The South Tower construction included a magnificent banquet hall, now known as the Gold Room, which would become the first hotel ballroom in America to use air conditioning. Another ballroom, called the Florentine Room, was added to the North Tower in 1909. These two famous public rooms combined with the Elizabethan Room and the Pompeian Room to host Chicago's elite social events of the day.

On June 15, 2003, members of the UNITE HERE local staff at the Congress began a strike after the hotel froze employee wages and revoked key benefits, including health insurance and retirement plans. Through the long months and years, the strikers won countless supporters, their cause garnering momentum around the world. Even future president Barack Obama and Illinois governor Patrick Quinn walked their picket line, while the skeleton crew that continued to punch the clock was reported to have pocketed wages of more than 30 percent below the national standard. The strike went on to claim the unfortunate honor as the longest hotel strike in history, leaving in its wake a hotel haunted by pulled proms, boycotted conventions and an estimated loss of $700 million in revenue.

And many, many ghosts.

Indeed, the ghosts of the Congress are everywhere. And no wonder. Grover Cleveland, William McKinley, Teddy Roosevelt, William Howard Taft, Woodrow Wilson, Warren Harding, Calvin Coolidge and Franklin Roosevelt all made the Congress their base of operations while in Chicago, leading to the hotel's longtime moniker, "The Home of Presidents." In 1912, President Theodore Roosevelt announced his new "Bull Moose" platform in the Florentine Ballroom, and in 1932, the hotel served as headquarters for Franklin Roosevelt and his hopeful Democratic Party. A few years later, Benny Goodman broadcast his wildly popular radio show from the hotel's Urban Room, a posh nightclub that drew the city's most coveted clientele, and in 1971, President Richard Nixon addressed the Midwest chapters of the AARP and National Retired Teachers Association, speaking before no fewer than three thousand members and guests in the hotel's Great Hall. For years, Al Capone played cards every Friday night in a meeting room overlooking Grant Park, and rumors abound (though most certainly false) that he even owned the Congress for a while. What is true is that Jake "Greasy Thumb" Gusik phoned Capone in Palm Island, Florida, from a phone in the Congress Plaza—before and after the St. Valentine's Day Massacre.

But the ghosts of the Congress are not generally those of headline-grabbers. Rather, they are wisps of memory, glimmers of the hundreds of thousands of ordinary guests who have glided through its halls for more than a century, often embroiled in personal drama, heartache and tragedy.

Endless, it seems, are the stories that echo the tale of James Kennedy, a New York man who checked in, alone, in May 1910. He went to his room, cut the dry cleaner's identification tags out of his clothes, burned his papers, walked to the lake and shot himself.

Later that same year, an insurance salesman—Andrew Mack—called on a friend at his Congress Plaza hotel room before also walking to the lake and apparently drowning himself at the foot of Van Buren Street.

There was the salesman who threw himself down an elevator shaft, the drifter who jumped off the roof of the north tower and the troubled family man who hanged himself from a cupboard hook.

In the summer of 1916, mining investor Morse Davis and his wife were believed to have formed a suicide pact when Davis was found dead in room 312 of cyanide poisoning. His wife was at death's door but alive. She claimed they had taken the cyanide by accident, having confused it with Epsom salts. A few days later, however—broke and staying at St. Mary's Mission house on Peoria Street—she tried to throw herself out a third-story window and was promptly sent to a psychiatric hospital.

In August 1939, Adele Langer, a Prague native, threw her young sons, Karel and Jan, from an upper-floor window in the Congress Plaza. Langer's widower described the family's despair at being forced to flee Nazi influence in their homeland, leaving behind home and family.

In August 1950, a guest shot a Congress employee and then himself when the staff member came into the guestroom to collect on a $104 hotel bill for the jobless and distraught boarder.

In May 1966, Rockford attorney Frederick Haye was found naked and strangled with his shirt, his wrists and feet bound with his own socks.

Accidents, too, have left their mark here. In 1904, an elevator operator at the Auditorium Annex fell seventy feet to the subfloor, dying on impact. In July 1926, a Galesburg woman, Harriet Harrison, staying at the Congress with her husband before a planned European excursion, took a wrong step and plunged six stories down an elevator shaft to the hotel basement.

Since 1989, I have participated in more than three dozen investigations of the Congress Plaza, documenting no fewer than forty-seven distinctively haunted rooms and at least two ballrooms, as well as common areas such as employee workrooms and public guest areas. The sheer variety of phenomena reported and experienced at this massive structure is mind-boggling. Truly, there seems to be no end to the historic tragedy or of its supernatural manifestations.

The Florentine Room, an ornately painted ballroom, was originally also used as a roller rink when the hotel opened to World's Fair visitors in the 1890s. Security guards say that, on their wee-hour rounds, cheerful organ music can still be heard from outside the locked doors, as well as the sound of old wooden skate wheels against the wooden floors. The piano is known to play by itself, and a woman may be heard screaming outside a staff door on the east side of the room. The women's restroom is likewise haunted by a female presence, who appears in the mirrors, staring at the living and following them out down the hallway.

In the lavish Gold Room—a hot spot for Chicago wedding receptions—bride and groom are often chilled by photographers' photos. Those snapped around the grand piano tend to develop with one or more people missing from the pictures, and the doors tend to be found unlocked no matter how often they are securely shuttered.

In the South Tower, there is the phantom who lingers at the fifth-floor passenger elevator, where moaning is frequently heard by guests awaiting its arrival. The third-floor hallways are home to a one-legged man, often reported to the front desk by guests who think a vagrant has found his way inside. One former hotel operator who worked the property in the 1940s remembers a resident with a wooden leg who always had a big smile and a big tip; he suffered a heart attack at breakfast during his residency and died.

Also in the South Tower, a young boy of about ten has been a prolific presence, running up and down the halls in knee breeches and high buttoned boots. Guessing at his identity, some tie him to one of the many families who made their homes at the hotel in years gone by and the all-too-common deaths from then-incurable illnesses like tuberculosis and pneumonia.

As for sleeping rooms, only one guestroom in the South Tower is reported to be haunted: room 905, where constant phone static has bedeviled guests for years.

But the North Tower? That's a different story.

In room 474, a once resident judge eternally changes the channels on his cherished television set. In room 759, another erstwhile resident pulls the door shut from inside when guests try to enter. It is said that he was an elderly gentleman—a longtime resident—whose son had come to take him to a nursing home many years ago. Wanting to stay put at the hotel, he mustered the strength to try to keep his son (and security guards) from opening the door. Even now he remains, determined to live at the Congress forever.

And then there are the rooms that I promised the management not to number: the room where the pictures on the wall rotate 360 degrees before the eyes of astonished residents, the room where an impromptu exorcism was held, on some unidentified Chicago winter's night not so long ago, before the victim was moved to a local convent. There is the room fled by two Marines in 1989, running through the lobby in their boxer shorts at 3:00 a.m., with the later explanation that a towering black figure had entered the room from the closet and approached their beds, and the room where a woman slit her wrists in the bathtub after a night on Rush Street in the 1970s. She has been glimpsed during the night by weary boarders.

And then there is *the* room.

Rumors have long flown that it was a room here at the Congress Plaza that partly inspired writer Stephen King to create his short story "1408," a gripping tale of a professional—and skeptical—ghost hunter who meets his match in a mysterious hotel room (1408) said to be too haunted to lease. Unbelieving, the young man convinces the hotel's manager to let him have the room for a night, though the previous tenants all took their own lives during their stays in it. The real-life 1408 was always believed to exist on the Congress's most haunted floor: the twelfth floor of the older North Tower. Some point to a room that is padlocked and say that's the one. Others say it's the one that's been boarded up. Still others claim you can't even place it anymore: it's been papered over to remove any sign that it was ever there. This room does, in fact, remain. But it's not on the twelfth floor.

If it still had a number, the room would be—believe it or not—number 666. At some point in time, the spot where this room's door should be was drywalled over, a piece of baseboard patched in to connect the wood where the doorway once stood. The lintel above the old doorway is, indeed, still quite visible. Some have ventured that this room was simply put out of use because of its stigmatized number, but there is definitely more to this story. Though no staff member claims to remember why this room was sealed off forever, window washers tell us it was closed up with the furniture still inside, almost as if even the objects in the room were believed to be cursed.

Over the past thirty years, I've had my own harrowing moments at the Congress Plaza. There was the morning I was awakened by the sound of the shower blasting full force, steam filling the bathroom, though I could get barely a trickle and little warmth when I'd tried to take a bath. There was the night my worst fear as a ghost hunter came true: the sheets and blankets were peeled off me by unseen hands as I slept. Then came the Night of Incessant Knocking, as we came to christen it. More than a dozen times through the night, someone rapped three times on our door, but no one stood by. And there was the night my daughter and I were kept awake, chillingly, by the sound of two men whispering at the foot of our bed: "Are they still awake?"

Whatever the beliefs of others, my own experiences have firmly rooted this enigmatic spot at the pinnacle of my "Most Haunted." Escorting in thousands of tour guests over these fifteen years, I have observed that, whether they walk in believing or not, most who enter the Congress today are struck by a peculiar feeling: something "not quite right," something "menacing" or "sinister" as it's variously described. Most leave agreeing that they would rather be alone almost anywhere but in the hallways of this storied monument to Chicago's troubled past, full of sorrow and secrets, with always room for one more.

THE SOLDIERS' LOT

Few Chicagoans today are aware that the body of Senator Stephen Douglas, the "Little Giant" who campaigned against Abraham Lincoln, is interred on its own on Chicago's South Side—under a towering monument outside a condominium complex. In fact, Douglas and his wife had made their home at this very spot, on their estate called Okenwald, near Twenty-Fifth Street and Cottage Grove Avenue, and it was here that Douglas was buried after his death in 1866. Plans for the tomb, however, did not come to fruition for more than fifteen years; in the interim, one of the most notorious prison camps in history grew up around it.

Camp Douglas was first founded as a training camp for Union soldiers in the early days of the war, when Chicagoans were chomping at the bit to participate in the conflict. After the capture of Fort Donelson in February 1862, however, more than twelve thousand captured Confederates had nowhere to be housed, and Camp Douglas became a prison camp.

Death was a daily occurrence at the camp, most from diseases like smallpox and scurvy. There was no cemetery on the grounds, and the dead were hastily piled in makeshift burial grounds near the camp or sold to a local undertaker who promised to give them proper burials at Chicago's City Cemetery in Lincoln Park. Greed on undertaker C.H. Jordan's part, however, led to the burial of more than three thousand of the camp's Confederate soldiers in the cemetery's potter's field. By the time the order

Unidentified Confederate prisoners at Chicago's Camp Douglas, circa 1865. *Library of Congress.*

came to close the cemetery and relocate the graves, a good half of them had disappeared in the shifting, sandy loam of the field. In addition, desirable Rosehill Cemetery refused to reinter the Confederate dead within its property. Oak Woods, instead, stepped up to receive the unwanted soldiers for burial on its south side grounds. Earlier, Oak Woods had arranged for reburial of the smallpox victims who had been interred outside the walls of the camp. Two aldermen were awarded the contract to rebury the soldiers from City Cemetery. Witnesses on hand at the reburials claimed that a large number of caskets seemed to be empty. It is now generally believed that the majority of Confederate burials at City Cemetery remain there today, under the ball fields near LaSalle and Clark Streets. Both that expanse and the park built on the former site of Camp Douglas are today rife with ghostly encounters, including tactile sensations of being grabbed by one's arm or hand, the smell of tobacco and intense spots of cold and feelings of dread or sadness that come and go without reason or warning.

The "Soldiers Lot" at Oak Hill went on to suffer myriad problems with drainage at the site, leading to reports of sunken graves, disappearing markers and, worst of all, claims that buggies and wagons were driving over a portion of the occupied land. In 1893, a monument was erected by former Confederate soldiers, families of the dead and other supporters of the "Lost Cause." The site continued to deteriorate from drainage problems, and just after the turn of the century, the monument was removed, a mound of dirt piled on top of the graves (including many of the markers) and the monument replaced. The "Confederate Mound" still stands today, a tribute to the bravery of the Confederate dead and their legacy of unrest in their final resting place of Chicago.

After the war, the drive to complete Douglas's tomb resumed. Despite a hearty wave of support at the laying of the cornerstone in 1866, the needed funds were not forthcoming for the planned structure. When the tomb portion was completed, the body of the "Little Giant" was put in place, but the site soon languished for want of money to complete the monument, the foundation cracking and the surrounding grass overgrown. Douglas's widow begged authorities to move her husband's tomb to a more fitting location where it could be cared for, but her pleas went unanswered. Finally, after years of failed funding efforts, the tomb and memorial were completed. But the site would forever retain its reputation as unattended, uncared for and unnoticed.

Sightings of a shadowy male figure in period dress sitting on the ground near the tomb began almost immediately after its completion, causing Chicagoans to wonder if the lack of respect shown Douglas by the funding problems had brought him back from the dead. But the truth was that there were at least two other possibilities for a ghostly visitor here. In November 1877, W.F. Coolbaugh, a well-known Chicago bank president and close personal friend of Douglas's, shot himself at the monument. He was found prostrate in his own blood with a pistol at his side. Coolbaugh's family told the press of their patriarch's long ill health and periods of despondency. He had been cheerful enough lately, they said, but when he did not return home the night before, the men of the family had gone out in search of him until the wee hours.[23]

Two years later, a second man shot himself at the Douglas monument: Martin Arndt was a tailor who had asked for a raise at work on the morning of June 29. The raise was denied and Arndt dismissed from his position for asking. Out of his mind with fear and filled with self-doubt, Arndt realized in a moment of insanity that his union provided suicide benefits to families of its members. He decided to kill himself and, after writing a letter of apology to his wife, made his way to the Douglas monument and shot himself in the chest. He did not die from the first wound and shot himself in the temple.[24]

Occasional tales of that shadowy figure at the monument are still told today.

THE OMEN

A "mournful cry" haunted the nights of the villagers of Highwood in the spring of 1896, echoing along the dark lakefront and waking residents from their sleep. The sound was reported to resemble the wails of a suffering human, and many locals got up and dressed to go out to find and aid whoever it might be. No source of the cries, however, could be found.

After several days, it was discovered that the "heartrending moans and shrieks" were coming from a strange bird, which was seen swooping over Highwood in the moonlight, close to the tops of the houses—a bird the likes of which no one had ever seen. "The body is a sooty black, and the head a dingy white....Instead of being composed of feathers, it is evidently of flesh and bone. In shape it is like that of a beaver broad and flat, and it has much the proportions of a paddle."[25]

The bird was reported to be making nightly visits to a barn on the outskirts of town, and soon villagers were taking turns keeping vigil there in order to capture the bird, as it was quickly agreed that the bird was, in fact, an omen of bad fortune. It must be removed, but it could not be killed, as treacherous luck would then surely follow.

Some believed the bird was the so-called Lake Michigan Loon that had been captured by sailors on the lake four years earlier in 1892, a bird that had long been connected with the onset of dangerous storms. Captain Ambrose LeFevre, head of the crew that had caught it, had then reported that he had seen the bird numerous times over the years—always before a terrible storm.

He even claimed to have seen it the night of the Great Fire of 1871, when high winds secured the terrible fate of Chicago:

> *The storm we had that night, you remember, was a snorter from the southwest and the whole town burned up. I made up my mind after the great fire that the bird was a sort of ill-omened devil and decided to kill it.*

LeFevre had gone on to spot the bird many times during his travels on the lake, shooting at it whenever he did, his crew joining in at times. But no one could ever quite fell it. It would seem to fall and disappear under the waves, only to resurface again and take off over the water, even after the captain believed to have broken its wing with one of his slugs.

> *Thanksgiving Day, 1891, the bird was watched by a crowd of people as it circled over the Lake Michigan shallows. A small yacht took up chase, but the bird led it in circles until the vessel suddenly...was put about, thus coming head-on toward the loon. At this instant a violent squall struck the little craft and capsized her. Two of the men, father and son, lost their lives. The others clung to the overturned yacht and were rescued by Capt. Ed Napier and his tug.*[26]

On the afternoon of its capture in 1892, the loon had eerily flown right onto the deck of the captain's schooner. All on board were deeply concerned about what harbinger this could be, and the crew tried to find someone to take the bird away. Several offers came in, including one from a Lieutenant Baker, the director of the marine exhibit for the upcoming World's Fair of 1893, but all involved were wary of exchanging money for the creature—or even holding it at all. Several days after the bird's capture, the crewman who had caught it let it go.

Since its release from Captain LeFevre's boat, the bird had appeared twice, first to the crew of a lumber schooner the evening before an infamous gale in May 1894. Then, during the summer of 1895, it was seen near Summer Island in the Poverty Passage route to Green Bay, Wisconsin, by the men on the schooner *E.R. Williams*, which sank the coming night off the coast of Escanaba, Michigan, drowning the entire crew.

One of the most memorable of the Lake Michigan loon sightings also occurred off the coast of Chicago, witnessed by Captain John Elea of the Chicago Towing Company while his tug was lying outside the harbor late one afternoon waiting for a tow to come along:

Just at nightfall, the crew caught sight of the loon and resolved upon a chase. Around and around went the loon. swimming and flying, always making the circle smaller. They tired him out, and Captain Elea had a pike-pole ready to strike, but something occurred to change the mind of the whole crew in an instant—Suddenly raising itself in the water, and stretching out its long neck, that bird gave out a cry of distress and anguish that seemed human and at times supernatural, ascending to the very clouds. A squall swooped down on the lake from the north just at this juncture and our tug being five miles down the lake we made a run for the harbor. We made bad weather of it, the tug shipping several seas, but we finally got into port sally. Just as we rounded the piers that loon circled around the pilot-house with a solemn croak and then winged its way back to sea again.

THE VAMPIRE HUNTERS

PATTON'S CLAIRVOYIC VARNISH FOR GLASS
Develops a finer sight that enables a person, when looking through it,
to see objects which are invisible…
Specimens sent by mail on receipt of 10 cents.
Address Samuel Patton, 1297 N. Paulina-street, Chicago, Ill.

Intrigued and unnerved was the overwhelming response of the small crowd gathered in Judge Thalstrom's bookshop when the quiet mechanic of Paulina Street passed around his business card on a cool night in September 1888. The group had listened intently to Thalstrom's gripping tales before a local lumber mill worker slammed his fist down on the table, calling it all a "Humbug!" The others were not so sure, especially after Patton the mechanic shared his chilling personal tale of being stalked by a vampire in Chicago after evil spirits had killed his own children.[27]

Patton went on to pass around small pieces of glass that had been coated with the mysterious glaze of his own invention, which he claimed transformed ordinary glass into spirit detection glass, through which anyone could see invisible entities, including the vampire he claimed roamed, invisibly, the desolate corners of nineteenth-century Chicago. Patton lived near the corner of Milwaukee and Paulina, and it was here that he labored at night, making his varnish. He told the men he had developed a sense of premonitions when he was a child growing up in rural Virginia, which had led to a lifetime of torment.

The "Lake View Vampire" caused a short but fervent panic. *From the* Chicago Tribune.

Patton had returned from the Civil War and married. He and his wife had five children, all of whom perished, including the most recent, Willie, just five years old, who reportedly "came out of his grave" a week after he was buried, appearing to loved ones. Like many of the time, Patton had sought solace by attending Spiritualist séances, hoping to contact his dead children. "I had no faith in the holy books," he stated. "I wanted facts." In spirit photography and séance manifestations, he'd found those facts, and he continued to pursue more knowledge of the spirit world wherever he might search for it.

One night, in his Paulina Street cottage, the spirit world came looking for Patton. "I felt a stinging sensation on my forehead. The letter 'W' was imprinted there as if with a needle. The name 'Willie Patton' was then formed in about the style of letters that Willie had learned to make before he died. After that the spirits wrote messages on my forehead. I understood that the spirits had killed Willie and tortured my other children."

Patton said that, after a time, he found that these spirit visitors were "made of cones and bubbles." One of the entities would sing as it wrote on the man's forehead, which he'd tried to protect at night with a thick silk covering, to no avail. Night after night, Patton's head would be pierced with some otherworldly instrument, the messages coming and coming, as the spirit's voice sang:

Over there
Where all is prayer
I'll sit and swear.
Whoora for me, Whoora for me.

After much of this torment, said Patton, "they put a vampire on me."

The vampire took human form, sucked at Patton's nostrils and mouth and followed him when he visited the graves of his children. His forehead, he claimed, began to excrete a poisonous substance, causing havoc in the lives of all who touched it. Some who did so had even committed murder, claimed Patton.

Patton's glass varnish became a reported sensation, with many of the people of Lake View purchasing it so as to be aware of vampires who might be stalking nearby. The varnish was especially popular among the community of men who worked at the Harvester Works. When they went out at night, they told their wives upon return of their colleagues' efforts to see Patton's vampire, which he claimed stalked the streets of the North Side and the then suburb of Lake View. Unease reigned among believers, but Patton told them they could protect themselves by sleeping feet to feet with the other members of their households, as he had met some vampires who sucked blood and energy out of the soles of victims' feet.

When the vampire failed to appear through anyone's treated glass, the vampire fervor began to die down. It returned, however, with a vengeance two months later when, in November, Claes Larsen went missing, failing to return home one night. The local barkeep told Larsen's wife he'd been there the night before but had been despondent, as if in fear of some impending doom. Neighbors, filled with trepidation, immediately wondered if the Lake View vampire had gotten the beleaguered man, suggesting also that the new houses being built in the area were doomed to be plagued by the vampire and by ghosts. This time, the newspapers were less gentle, sparing no expense in the mockery of the local fears. The *Tribune* wrote that the Lake View Historical Society was conducting interviews with locals for a paper on vampires and runaway husbands, among other jabs.[28]

Larsen's wife—and a good number of neighbors—were not so flippant. After a long night of fretting, Mrs. Larsen went to police to report that her husband had been accosted by a vampire. When police did little to respond rather than take a report, it was said that a local group of boys, none of them older than ten, banded together to find and destroy the creature. Calling themselves the "Vampire Hunters," they trekked through Lincoln Park all day Sunday, searching the City Cemetery for the casket of a slumbering ghoul, egged on by their leader's tales of St. George and the Dragon.

Nightfall had brought no capture, and Mrs. Larsen had nearly given up hope. Then, with a creak of the door, her husband appeared on the step of their Otto Street home, hat in his hands and apologetic for his absence. After his wife's tearful tale of the great Vampire Hunt to save him from destruction, her husband confessed that he had merely been out drinking all night and had passed out and slept off the bender all day.

While no one but Samuel Patton ever saw the Lake View vampire whose reputation briefly terrorized the people of Chicago in 1888, this would not be the last time, amazingly, that a group of children would form a vampire-hunting posse. Years later, in Glasgow, a vampire frenzy would break out, causing nearly one hundred children to converge on a local cemetery, armed with rocks and sticks, searching for a vampire with iron teeth who had reportedly strangled and eaten two little boys. As the *Boston Globe* reported:

> *Swarms of grimy-faced urchins scaled the walls around the cemetery in the Gorbals slum area. A group of children, slowly growing into a crowd of hundreds, pushed through the streets to the cemetery to "kill the vampire."*
> *…Once there, they poured over grave mounds in a yelling, excited throng. Police were called in to clear the cemetery, but bands of youngsters still roamed outside the walls "hunting the vampire" until dark.*[29]

THE FORT

Illinois can claim only the scantiest handful of American tall tales, but what the region lacks in quantity, it makes up in quality, especially in the forested coastal areas surrounding north suburban Fort Sheridan. For it is this wild and rocky region that is supposed by American folklore to have been part of Paul Bunyan's logging territory, the Great Lakes themselves having been gouged out by a fall taken by Bunyan's Great Blue Ox, Babe. Even without the whoppers, however, the history of Fort Sheridan remains fully American, richly anecdotal and often eerie.

Fort Sheridan was built along the Indian trail connecting Green Bay, Wisconsin, a French trading post and mission established around 1670, and the Native American hunting grounds and villages in and around Chicago. Tribes of mostly Illinois and Potawatomi would travel northward along the road from what is now Diversey Avenue in Chicago, hugging the lakeshore and heading up what is now Clark Street. With the nineteenth century came a series of treaties between the white settlers and the Native Americans. The last was negotiated in Chicago on September 26, 1833, in which the Potawatomi ceded to the United States all of their remaining Illinois land.

Not long after, the trail was employed increasingly by traders and settlers traveling between Green Bay and Chicago. Because of the trail's use as a passage for military-escorted pioneers traveling from Fort Dearborn, it was also known as the Military Road. Eventually, the road became the central highway connecting Chicago and Green Bay and was officially named Green Bay Road.

Fort hospital at Fort Sheridan, circa 1880. Though the fort is no more, its plentiful ghosts are said to walk the old fort roads and its historic buildings (now homes and public structures). *Library of Congress, Detroit Publishing Company.*

By the late 1860s, Chicago had become a regrouping point for eastern pioneers headed westward. The Division of the Missouri, quartered in Chicago and led by Lieutenant General Philip Sheridan, played a large part in these pioneers' protection. Sheridan's special burden was to make sure they obeyed the law in the frontier regions (in other words, most of the land west of Chicago). From the division's headquarters at Washington and LaSalle Streets, Sheridan met the challenge and established himself and the division as indispensable to the peace and safety of Chicago and vicinity. In the days of looting that followed the Chicago Fire of 1871, Mayor Roswell Mason responded to the chaos by declaring martial law and putting the city in Sheridan's hands.

Although Mason's decision caused an outrage in the governor's office, Sheridan carried out his commission, gaining esteem in the eyes of the city's administration and in the hearts of its citizens. A dozen years after the Great Fire, Sheridan was reassigned to the War Department, leaving in tears a Chicago that would remember when "all eyes were turned to him" in those chaotic days "when men's hearts failed them, and ruin and desolation stared us in the face."

With such a strong reputation, it was natural that Sheridan came to mind several years later when Chicago businessmen, concerned about the violent potential of labor unrest, met to discuss plans for a military installation near Chicago. With fresh memories of the Haymarket Riot of 1886 overshadowing the city, the moguls recalled the power of the military to restore order on that devastating day. Accordingly, they decided that a ready source of military force would be crucial if business were to proceed without serious future threat from workers.

On November 8, 1887, Companies F and K of the Sixth Infantry Regiment pulled into Highwood from Utah. Eighty soldiers were commanded by Major William J. Lyster, who set up camp near the wild shoreline set aside for the fort. With five men to each tent, the companies started out poorly, with no vegetables, undrinkable water and the looming realization that the elite of Chicago were relying on the soldiers' readiness to take on urban unrest.

Major Lyster nonetheless persevered in his duties, and by the time he ended his command in late summer of 1890, the erection of permanent buildings had begun. Nearly ten years later, Congress appropriated several hundred thousand dollars for permanent structures to house six companies of infantry and four troops of cavalry, as well as a wharf, water tower, cemetery and rifle range. The construction proved tedious, if ultimately successful. Water had to be pumped from the lake and driven to the building sites by horse-drawn tankers. Construction materials had to be transported through ever-present mud. Adding to all the frustration within the fort were still more problems outside of it.

With the establishment of the fort came the development of the village of Highwood. Originally planned in 1868, Highwood's settlers came from Chicago after losing their homes in the Chicago Fire, hoping to establish farms on the North Shore. Less than a year after Lyster's arrival, Highwood had become inextricably tied to the military post and was renamed the village of Fort Sheridan. Although the town and the fort suffered few conflicts of interest, one was enough to test their relationship—the question of liquor.

Worried that the town would become a "den of iniquity" and pointing fingers at the dram shops (taverns) that catered to soldiers and construction workers, residents banned the sale of liquor, though "blind pigs" remained in business peddling alcohol in defiance of the law. Finally, liquor licenses were established, at $1,000 a pop, and issued to anyone who was willing to pay the price and to promise not to sell to "lunatics, idiots, insane persons, minors, and habitual drunkards." Not surprisingly, illegal liquor sales continued, as did the arguments. Finally, in 1908, taverns were closed and stayed shuttered until state laws took over liquor sales.

Amid such squabbling, the physical fort was quietly and admirably taking form. Designed by the pioneering Chicago firm of Holabird and Roche, the fort would eventually attain status as a National Historic Landmark. After a movement that began in 1979, a Historic American Buildings Survey found ninety-four of the fort's buildings, beginning with its massive 150-foot water tower, worthy of designation as a National Historic District. These buildings deserve reverence, but not merely or even mainly for their artistic or military significance. As silent witnesses to the struggles of countless individuals, these structures are venerable ultimately for the stories they shelter.

Among the hundreds of thousands of anecdotes grown dusty in these landmarks, the most motheaten are the humdrum tales of day-to-day army life. But even the strangest realities inevitably became typical, the most bizarre of personalities just another among hundreds of buzz-cut heads. For example, a mess sergeant assigned to the Anti-Aircraft Military Training Center (AATC) ate razor blades, nails, tacks, buttons and even drinking glasses before enlisting in 1941. After he swallowed a wristwatch, doctors predicted an imminent demise. Instead, the sergeant went on to a great career with Ringling Bros. and Barnum & Bailey Circus.

Although most of Fort Sheridan's more colorful characters have since passed away, a few still linger. Curiously, the most famous do not seem to be military. Instead, the fort's two most active spirits are working-class un-enlisted going about their respective business. Best known is the so-called Woman in Orange, seen during random sunrises at Building 31, the Community Club Building. Building 31 previously housed the officers' mess hall and the El Morocco Lounge, an officers' club that once hosted George S. Patton. The Woman in Orange, so dubbed for the stunning orange dress she wears, seems perpetually concerned with the perfection of her catering skills. She, by the way, is rumored to resemble Mamie Eisenhower.

Meanwhile, at Building 1, the old fort hospital, a custodian eternally tends to his duties, stoking the furnace and tapping the pipes. Across the road out back, the hospital morgue, nicknamed the "Dead House," still stands, although its ivy-covered walls and skylights have disappeared. The tiny, solid structure, bearing blind windows and crosses in relief, housed a neat interior with sink, sewer and a room for autopsies. It is interesting that the Dead House was designed by Holabird and Roche, while the fort hospital itself was built from standard plans.

Other phantoms at the old fort included a nineteenth-century chaplain named Charles Adams; a drill sergeant who scared the dickens out of witnesses by hollering orders to his long-dead enlisted; the galloping shade of a horse on Patten Road; and the festive strains of accordion music from the site of a former German POW camp.

Just after Christmas in 1893, the news erupted at the fort that the ghost of one captain had been confronting men at the base. The bizarre murder of Captain Alfred Hedberg on October 30, 1892, was just one of many disturbing incidents that had occurred at the fort under the sitting commander, starting with the sighting of a sea monster on Lake Michigan by two officers (which you'll read about later in this book), which had led to more than one hundred soldiers taking an oath of abstinence. The murder of Hedberg, however, was generally regarded as a service to society in general and the army in particular. He was known as an arrogant, demanding, controlling loon to his men, constantly punishing them for perceived failures to show him the proper reverence. Most famously, a private one afternoon rowed out on the lake with Hedberg and a boy who was visiting the fort with his father. When the boat capsized, Hedberg and the child were saved by enlisted men, while the private died. The moment he was back on shore, Hedberg placed one of his rescuers under guard, reportedly because he felt the private had addressed him as an equal during the rescue. Ironically, hidden by Hedberg's unforgiving insistence on protocol was his own shady history of court-martial, most for misappropriation of government property—a fact that came to light during a hearing over one of the many perceived "offenses" of Hedberg's own men against him.

As Hedberg's past came to light, more and more of his men wrote to Washington to beg for his removal from service. One of the complainants was a lieutenant named James Maney. Either by circumstance or arrangement, the men met one evening outside the water tower at Fort Sheridan, near the infantry drill hall. Two men, a private and a sergeant, watched what happened next. Hedberg, his arms full of bundles, pulled out one arm from his load to hit James Maney directly in his face. He then reached for his hip as if reaching for a firearm. At that moment, Maney shot him. Hedberg died of his injuries.

The headstrong Hedberg, whose murder filled the headlines for almost three years after his death, did not go gently into that good night, as they say. Two days after Christmas 1893, the Chicago papers reported that the captain was still making his hateful rounds at Fort Sheridan, where the most recent sighting of his vicious ghost was only the latest in a string of encounters:

> *The ghost of Capt. Hedberg, who was killed by Lieut. Maney last October, has, it is said, been seen by a number of soldiers near the scene of his violent death. An effort has been made to keep the matter quiet. Officers do not say a word about it, and privates change the subject whenever a civilian comes within earshot. But so large a sensation as that caused by the bloody apparition that stalks about the picturesque grounds of Fort Sheridan cannot be kept within the lines of a military reservation. One man*

has spent two weeks in the hospital as the result of the appearance of Capt. Hedberg's disembodied spirit, one man has deserted, it is believed for the same reason, and it is with the greatest difficulty that a sentry can be kept upon a certain post after midnight.

The ghost was first seen on a bright moonlit night just two weeks after Capt. Hedberg's death. Private Johnson of Company B was on picket duty near the cavalry stables and pacing along the very path traversed by Capt. Hedberg on the day he walked to meet his death at the muzzle of Lieut. Maney's pistol. It was shortly after midnight. The moon was shining brightly, there was not a breath of wind stirring, and everything was so still that the sentry might almost have heard the beating of his own heart if he had not been too busy thinking of the cups of hot coffee he was going to have as soon as he was relieved.

He had reached the extreme end of his round and had faced about to retrace his steps when he suddenly saw the figure of a man approaching not twenty feet away. It was Capt. Hedberg's spirit. Private Johnson was startled, for no footfall had disturbed the death-like stillness.

"Halt! Who goes——" The rest of the challenge froze in the speaker's throat, for as he spoke he recognized distinctly in the intruder the face and figure of Capt. Hedberg. The apparition approached slowly—so slowly that Johnson could scarcely see it move. His starting eyes noted that the apparition was dressed exactly as Capt. Hedberg was when he was killed. It had some parcels under its left arm just as Capt. Hedberg had shifted them from his right arm to strike Lieut. Maney in the face. Blood was trickling from a little hole in the breast. All this Johnson noted. Then he observed further that while he could distinctly see all these seemingly material things, yet the approaching figure appeared to be only a pale, bluish white shade, through which he could distinctly see a tree and the outlines of a stable line beyond. His gun dropped from his nerveless fingers. He tried to run, but some unseen force seemed to tie him to the spot. He tried to shout, but his tongue refused to move. The apparition approached until it almost touched the terror-stricken sentry. Suddenly his hat was stricken violently from his head, his benumbed muscles assumed the attitude of attention. Then, with a blood-curdling moan, the apparition vanished.[30]

Today, a drive through the roads of Fort Sheridan, now a glorified subdivision on awesome Lake Michigan, is a bittersweet trip. The repurposing of such an opulent array of architectural gems remains a puzzling reality even in the face of all the facts, figures and logic that explain the fort's closing. Explorers should not be deterred from seeking out its secrets. For while this richly historical setting has been emptied of most military life, a warm welcome awaits from at least some personalities who remain eternally present and accounted for.

THE OLD STACKS

On December 7, 1871, just two months after the Great Fire decimated Chicago, a Londoner named A.H. Burgess proposed a project he called the English Book Donation, which called for the creation by Englanders of a free library for the city of Chicago, as a "mark of sympathy now, and a keepsake and token of true brotherly kindness forever." The donation collected eight thousand volumes, from commoners as well as prominent citizens like Alfred Lord Tennyson, Robert Browning and Queen Victoria herself.

Chicago's mayor, Joseph Medill, led a meeting to establish the Chicago library, leading to the Illinois Library Act of 1872, an important measure that allocated government funds for the establishment of local libraries. On January 1, 1873, the Chicago Public Library opened, situated in an abandoned fifty-eight-foot-diameter iron water tank at LaSalle and Adams Streets.

In October 1873, William Frederick Poole was elected the first head librarian by the library's board of directors, and he quickly went on to procure more than thirteen thousand volumes for circulation and an additional four thousand or more volumes available for reference by late 1874. The library moved often during its first two decades, including eleven years on the fourth floor of city hall.

In 1887, Poole resigned from the Chicago Public Library to establish the Newberry Library, which would go on to become one of the world's greatest research library foundations. His resignation made way for the man whose name would become synonymous with Chicago's library system: Frederick H. Hild.

From day one, Hild's main goal was to find a permanent home for Chicago's wandering library. It took ten years after his appointment, but in 1897, Hild realized his dream when Chicago's first central library opened in a mammoth structure on Michigan Avenue, between Washington and Randolph Streets. Designed by the esteemed Boston architectural firm that had built the city's Art Institute, the library was erected on land donated by the Grand Army of the Republic, a Civil War veterans' group led by a U.S. senator from Illinois, John Logan. In donating the land, Logan and the GAR had but one demand: that a Civil War exhibit would remain on display in the library until the last Union soldier died.

In 1909, after more than twenty years of service to the Chicago Public Library, Frederick Hild was forced to resign due to controversy over his policies. Some say he was never the same. Hild died of pneumonia in his

The Chicago Public Library, now the Chicago Cultural Center, where the city's premier librarian still walks. *Library of Congress, Detroit Publishing Company.*

native Virginia at the age of just fifty-five, though legend says he died of a broken heart over his separation from the Chicago Public Library.

Some say Hild still walks the halls of the jewel in the crown of his life: the grand library building at Michigan and Randolph that served as Chicago's library for ninety-six years. Today it is Chicago's Cultural Center—a hub of free concerts, art exhibits, lectures and more. One former employee of the building claimed that numerous visitors with spiritual perceptiveness have picked up the presence of a sad man near the entrance to Frederick Hild's old office in the building. Others have talked about seeing the figure of a man disappearing through that old doorframe. Still others have seen not a man but a woman or have reported poltergeist-style activity such as chairs for events rearranging themselves or important exhibit pieces going missing, only to return again under mysterious circumstances.

Today, Chicago's central library is housed in a mammoth structure on the south end of Chicago's Loop. The Washington Library—named for Chicago's African American mayor Harold Washington—comes complete with escalators and elevators and a gleaming Winter Garden event space on the top floor, replete with skylight and seemingly countless volumes, in addition to state-of-the-art digital systems serving millions of people each year. Despite the progress, however, "Chicago's librarian" Frederick Hild seems to like the old stacks.

GHOSTS OF ENGLEWOOD
AND THE CURSE OF H.H. HOLMES

E nglewood is troubled with periodical visits by ghosts," reported the *Inter Ocean* in 1878. "It is an utter impossibility for her people to settle down to business and go along in the humdrum fashion of their fathers." The reporter bemoaned the tendency of Englewood residents to flit from one ghost story to another, from a female phantom one year to "the old devil himself…with glaring eyes and flaming tongue."[31]

In fact, perusing the papers of the late nineteenth century, it is hard to avoid the fact that much of the ghost contagion that had consumed Chicago emanated from this single area.

Though the settlement that would become Chicago was established in the very earliest years of the 1800s, it was not until 1840 that the U.S. Government Land Office officially declared the city's present-day Englewood area as "habitable land."

The sprawling swampland (which would one day border the massive White City of the 1893 World's Fair) was hardly desirable ground for settlers, but when the Great Fire of 1871 leveled the town, Chicagoans moved en masse to the closest unharmed grounds—the outskirts of the victimized metropolis. Englewood became a goal of such exodus, and by 1889, more than one thousand trains passed through Englewood in a single day. But while the area became one of the most desirable in the burgeoning city, it also became the stage for some wild ghostly happenings—some credible and some not so much.

In the summer of 1892, Chicago's First Methodist Church of Englewood was the scene of a ghostly practical joke when the church organist and an accomplice staged a "haunting" during a young man's organ practice in the gloomy building. Speaking in hushed voices from the depths of the shadows, the conspirators' work sent the young boy fleeing down the stairs and out into the neighborhood. The tale soon spread of the infestation of the church, but the truth of the matter and the "merry laughter" it inspired in the culprits was soon discovered and the full story published to allay the fears of the living.

Less "merry" was the situation on South Loomis Street in November 1906, when a John and Reverend Morean Schumacher disappeared from their Englewood home, a note left behind by John saying he'd killed his wife with an axe. In the days that followed the disappearance, neighbors reported faces at the window of the empty house and mysterious bundles "thrown upon the sidewalk from a window," only to vanish when they hit the front lawn.

Sensational could be the only word used to describe the supernatural situation that had erupted at the Englewood home of Dr. Louine Hall just weeks before when a series of relentless knockings—always in threes—began on the front door and side windows of the residence. The sounds were described by police as "at times loud enough to shake the whole house." As was typical of the time, there were often hundreds of spectators who would gather at the scene after word of the knockings hit the street. The disturbances had the entire Englewood police force up in arms. There were reports of shots being fired at fleeing "phantoms," and a flock of "ghost experts" and "spook chasers" turned up at the house to offer their services after a call for help was published in the Chicago papers.[32]

Mrs. Hall told reporters that the knockings began while her husband was away and that upon her relating the incidents to him, he

> *scoffed at our stories…..Next night he was home, and the rappings continued. We tried every means possible to find the cause and failed. Some nights the knocking was omitted; then again it would return. I am no believer in ghosts and would care nothing about the matter, but it has worked on the children's nerves until I am anxious for their sake. I can't get them to go to bed for fright. I think it is some one that wants to be bothersome, but can't understand how they do it.*

Police standing watch around the house would also hear the knocks, always in threes, *firmly on the front door. Upon opening the door four detectives had gathered from all corners of the yard. They, too, had heard the sound, but declared that no one had approached or left the house. Search lights proved that there were no secret devices by which the noises could be made.*

Eventually the knockings ceased, and the disturbances were written off as the work of a prankster (possibly one of the teenage daughter's suitors), though no one is quite sure this was where credit was due. Could this have been a poltergeist incident? Such outbreaks generally occur around an adolescent or teenaged family member and start and stop with equal seeming randomness. Also typical is the charge of fraud. We will likely never know if the pranksters who received credit for the events actually initiated them or simply took credit for them to gain attention, as is also common in numerous authentic cases.

The harrowing events in Englewood inspired a rash of talk among police officers about phenomena encountered on duty. The next year, the *Chicago Tribune* published an extensive article about haunted police stations in Chicago, among them the one at Englewood.[33] A reporter related how, the previous summer, one of the plainclothes officers had been pushed out of his bed by a ghost in the second-floor station bunkroom. The officer had been told by colleagues that a Polish laborer had been killed on the Rock Island railroad tracks in back of the station and had moved into the bunkroom. The ghost was known to carry a bag filled with brick bats, which it used to attack anyone who came near it.

Electing to spend the night alone in the bunkroom to prove the falsehood of the story, the officer turned in for the night on one of the cots. A few minutes later, he was alarmed by a thumping sound on the floor beneath the bed. He claimed: "Peering out from under the covers to learn the nature of the disturbance, he was startled out of his wits to discover in the corner of the room a life-sized ghost with fire balls for eyes and equipped with the bag of brick bats, just as the other men had described him." The officer claimed to have been chased out of the station and down Wentworth Avenue by the specter, which hurled bricks after him until he reached his own house.

Today Englewood is a very different place than it was when local pranksters and the "Englewood Spook" turned the enclave upside down and when police officers had time to play tricks on one another. Most of the posh digs of the once fashionable settlement have fallen into decay or disappeared altogether, the landscape morphing into one of the most notoriously crime-ridden neighborhoods in Chicago.

Still, haunting tales survive.

Two A-frame brick houses on the 6000 block of South Loomis Boulevard have captured a lot of attention over the years. The houses were designed by a Russian immigrant, architect Carl Shparago, who was commissioned to build them in the early 1930s by a local single woman named Bobbette Austin, who sold them soon after their completion. Chicago Historical Society records show no trace of the peculiar ornamentation on the houses: swastikas.

A couple who lives in one of the houses—6011—says that not only the architectural ornamentation is haunting: the house itself has a ghost. Plagued for years by the sound of footsteps upstairs, the tenants took to actually padlocking the door to the stairwell at night and unlocking it in the morning.

Some believe the entity is the house's former owner, Dr. Walter A. Adams, the city's first black psychiatrist. After an illustrious career (he was head of the psychiatry department at Provident Hospital and a champion of drug rehabilitation), in 1959 Adams fell down the stairs of his Loomis Avenue home, developed a blood clot on his brain from the fall and died.

Adams's wife remarried and lived in the house with her new husband before selling it to the current owners. Ever since, they have heard the heavy tread of footfalls in the upstairs rooms and hall, and the couple's son once saw a man in a plaid jacket sitting near his upstairs bed.

Not far away, on Yale near Seventy-First Street, stands the house where singer Jennifer Hudson's mother and brother were shot to death in October 2008. Just a few days after the tragedy, Hudson's seven-year-old nephew was also found dead in a car on the city's West Side. William Balfour, the ex-husband of Hudson's sister, was sentenced to three consecutive life sentences for the deaths. Neighbors attest that, despite the "free for all" tenor of the neighborhood, the boarded-up house has remained shut tight and undisturbed, with even local troublemakers so spooked by it as to remain at bay.

Along the Sixty-Third Street shopping strip in this still-dynamic district, pedestrians have glimpsed the figure of a man dressed in clothing evocative of the 1940s, believed to be the victim of a violent attack that occurred in a now shuttered former clothing store near Wentworth Avenue. Without a doubt, however, the most truly haunted tract of land in unfortunate Englewood is the small block along Sixty-Third Street where H.H. Holmes—"America's Serial Killer"—once built his "Castle for Murder."[34]

When, in 1887, Herman W. Mudgett (alias H.H. Holmes) was hired as a shopkeeper in a drugstore in Chicago's Englewood neighborhood, he had been officially "missing" for two years. Still a very young man, the not quite thirty-year-old Holmes had already substantially ruined his life. About a decade earlier, he had married local girl Clara Lovering and settled down in New York for a time, where he worked as a schoolteacher before hearing the call of higher education. Holmes moved with Clara to Michigan, where he began medical school. The couple's time together was brief, however. Holmes sent his young wife home to her New Hampshire family; soon after, he was thrown out of school for stealing cadavers from the college anatomy lab and criminally charged for using them in insurance scams. He then "disappeared."

A year later, Holmes was hired in Englewood by a Mrs. Holden, who operated a local pharmacy, and soon purchased the business as well as some nearby property.

Holmes wasted no time in finding a second wife, ignoring the fact that his pending divorce from Clara Lovering was stuck in the legal system and, thus, not finalized. His new fiancée, Myrtle Belknap, was the daughter of North Shore big shot John Belknap. Two years after their wedding, Belknap left Holmes. Their marriage had been an odd one at best; Myrtle lived in Wilmette while Holmes continued to live on the city's South Side.

After his second wife's walkout, Holmes began construction of an enormous "hotel" on the property he'd purchased across from the old Holden drugstore. With money from further insurance scams, Holmes raised his Englewood "castle" to awesome heights. Plans for the hotel, however, resembled a funhouse of some sort: the triple-story wonder contained sixty rooms, trapdoors, hidden staircases, windowless chambers, laundry chutes accessed from the floors and a stairway that led to a precipice overlooking the house's back alley.

In only a year, the "World's Fair Hotel" was completed, and its owner sent out word that many of its plentiful rooms would be available to out-of-town visitors to the Columbian Exposition. And so the horror began.

Detectives and later scholars surmised that a good number of the fair's attendees met gruesome ends at the hands of Holmes in the "hotel" he built as a giant torture chamber. It was later discovered that the building contained walls fitted with blowtorches, gassing devices and other monstrosities. The basement was furnished with a dissecting table and vats of acid and lime. Alarms in his guestrooms alerted Holmes to escape attempts. Some researchers believe that many were kept prisoner for weeks or months before being killed by their diabolical innkeeper. Others believe Holmes was not really "into" killing—that it was all for the money.

Along with his hotel of horrors, Holmes had other ways of attracting victims. Placing ads in city papers, he offered attractive jobs to attractive young women. Insisting on the top-secret nature of the work, the location and his own identity, he promised good pay for silence. In the competitive world of turn-of-the-century Chicago, there were many takers.

Far from satiated, Holmes also advertised for a new wife, luring hopeful and destitute girls with his business stature and securing their trust with what must have been an irresistible charm.

After disposing of numerous potential employees and fiancées in his chambers of terror, Holmes decided to seriously find another mate. In 1893, he proposed to Minnie Williams, the daughter of a Texas realty king. Williams shared Holmes's violent nature and lawless attitude. Soon after they met, Williams killed her sister with a chair. Her understanding, empathic fiancé dumped the body into Lake Michigan. Yet the two were not to live horrifically ever after.

Holmes employees Julia Connor and her daughter, Pearl, were distraught at the news that their boss would be taking a new wife. Julia had been smitten with Holmes at the expense of her own marriage, and she and Pearl had

Holmes preyed on many young women in the context of the World's Fair of 1893. *Library of Congress.*

worked with their employer to pull off a number of his insurance swindles. Not long after objecting to the coming union, Julia and Pearl disappeared. When Julia's husband, Ned, came calling for them, Holmes told him that his family had moved to another state. In reality, Julia's alarm over Holmes's imminent marriage stemmed not only from mere longing but also from the fact that she was pregnant with his child. Her death was the result of an abortion that Holmes had performed himself. Stuck with Pearl as an annoying witness, he poisoned the child.

In 1894, the Holmeses went to Colorado with an Indiana prostitute in tow. Georgianna Yoke had moved to Chicago to start afresh and had answered one of Holmes's marriage ads in a local paper. Introduced as Holmes's cousin, Minnie and Holmes saw the same thing in Yoke: a girl with wealthy parents and a substantial inheritance awaiting her. In Denver, Minnie witnessed her husband's marriage to Yoke, and from there the trio went to Texas, transferred Minnie's property to Holmes and conducted a few assorted scams.

Not long after, the group returned to Chicago and Minnie and Yoke disappeared. Around the same time, Holmes's secretary, Emmeline Cigrand, was literally stretched to death in the castle basement along with her visiting fiancé.

Finally, in July 1894, Holmes was arrested for mortgage fraud. Though his third wife sprung him with their dirty bail money, Holmes had used his short time behind bars to launch yet another scam. Holmes planned to run a big insurance fraud at the expense of early accomplice Ben Pitezel, who had served time for one of their swindles while Holmes had walked away. Hoping to eliminate the possibility of Pitezel's squealing on their earlier capers, Holmes planned to get richer by rubbing the man out. With a shyster lawyer in tow, Holmes killed Pitezel in his Philadelphia patent shop after taking out an insurance policy on Pitezel's life.

When Holmes neglected to pay a share of the winnings to his old cellmate, Marion Hedgepeth (who had helped him plan the swindle), Hedgepeth turned in Holmes's name to a St. Louis cop, who made sure the tip got to Pinkerton agent Frank Geyer.

While Geyer dug up the dirt on Holmes, Holmes was digging graves for fresh victims. After Pitezel's death, Holmes had told his widow, Carrie, that some of Ben's shady dealings had been found out and that he had therefore gone to New York incognito. Holmes then took Carrie and the Pitezel children under his dubious care. The family did not know their husband and father was dead.

While on the road with Georgianna Yoke and the remaining Pitezels, Holmes decided to send Carrie back east to stay with her parents. The Pitezel children were left in the hands of Holmes, who first killed Carrie's son, Howard, in an abandoned Indiana house and then gassed her daughters after locking them in a trunk while the group was staying in Toronto.

Next, Holmes returned to his first wife, Clara, and, after explaining that he had had amnesia and mistakenly married another woman, was forgiven.

Whatever devilish plans Holmes had for his first love were thwarted when he was charged with insurance fraud. Holmes pleaded guilty while Frank Geyer searched the castle with police. What they found was astounding: the torture devices, the homemade gas chambers, the shelves of poison and dissection tools, the vats of lime and acid—all revealed the true criminality of the man being held for mere fraud. Evidence of the purpose of the grim house was easy to find: a ball of women's hair was stuffed under the basement stairs, Minnie's watch and dress buttons remained in the furnace, bits of charred bone littered the incinerator. Through the hot summer of 1895, crews worked to unearth and catalogue all of the building's debris. Then, in late August, the Murder Castle burned to the ground in a mysterious fire, aided by a series of explosions. A gasoline can verified arson, but no one could tell if it was one of Holmes's many adversaries or the man himself who had done it.

Holmes was sentenced to death in Philadelphia, where he had killed his old accomplice. On May 7, 1896, he was hanged, to the relief of a nation and, particularly, Chicago, the city that had unknowingly endured the bulk of his insanity. Some claimed that at the moment of his hanging, Holmes cried out that he was the notorious London butcher Jack the Ripper. Others swear that when Holmes's neck snapped, a bolt of lightning struck the horizon on the clear spring day.

The fact that Holmes remained alive with a broken neck for nearly fifteen minutes after the execution fueled the belief that his evil spirit was too strong to die. Rumors of a Holmes curse abounded during the months and years that followed.

Dr. William Matten, a forensics expert who had testified against Holmes, soon died of unexplained blood poisoning. Next, Holmes's prison superintendent committed suicide. Then, the trial judge and the head coroner were diagnosed with terminal diseases. Not much later, Frank Geyer himself fell mysteriously ill. A priest who had visited Holmes in his holding cell before the execution was found beaten to death in the courtyard of his church, and the jury foreman in the trial was mysteriously

H. H. HOLMES, THE ARCH CRIMINAL OF MODERN HISTORY.
From the latest photograph of the murderer. A flashlight taken in jail for the Journal.

Holmes's confession
was unlike anything the
modern world had heard.
From the Chicago Tribune.

electrocuted. Strangest of all was an unexplained fire at the office of the insurance company that had, in the end, done Holmes in. While the entire office was destroyed, untouched were a copy of Holmes's arrest warrant and a packet of photos of Holmes.

The eerie string of Holmes-related deaths stretched well into the twentieth century, ending with the 1910 suicide of former employee Pat Quinlan, who many believed had aided Holmes in his evil enterprises at the Murder Castle. Those close to Quinlan told reporters that the death had been long in coming; for years, they said, Quinlan had been haunted by his past life with Holmes, plagued with insomnia, driven at last to the edge and over. Some still say that it was Holmes himself who had haunted the boy and that the Monster of Sixty-Third Street had finally gone away, taking with him the one person who could reveal all the secret horrors of Holmes's brutal heart.

While the Murder Castle is long gone from the Englewood landscape where H.H. Holmes once walked, his evil spirit seems to inspire the bad seeds scattered in his old neighborhood. While the working class and the woefully poor struggle to make a life here, others continue Holmes's gruesome tradition, carrying out the serial murders and random slayings that have long plagued the south side Chicago neighborhood and its bordering areas. Those Englewood residents familiar with the area's dark history may pause at the corner of Sixty-Third and Wallace and wonder about one man's legacy. Chilled by half-remembered rumors and all-too-real headlines, they may hurry home, looking behind and listening, remembering the old neighborhood and the secrets it keeps.

AFTER HIS CAPTURE, HOLMES confessed to killing twenty-seven people in his Murder Castle, only a fraction of which police were able to confirm. Many historians, however, believe his brief claim of killing more than one hundred victims was closer to the truth: there are some who believe his victims may have numbered as many as two hundred or more. No excavation of the site was ever done.

During the filming of *The Hauntings of Chicago* for PBS Chicago's station WYCC, our team interviewed postal employees on staff at the Englewood branch of the United States Postal Service, which was built directly adjacent to the Murder Castle property after it was torn down in 1938. Several employees attested to strange goings-on in the building, especially in the basement, which some believe shares a foundational wall of the original castle, which stood on the corner next to the current post office structure. One employee shared a chilling story of hearing a sound in the basement and poking her head around a corner to see if her colleague was there. She called out to her but heard no answer and saw nothing down the hall but a row of chairs lined up against the wall. A minute later, when she returned to the hall, the chairs had all been stacked up. Other employees have seen the apparition of a young woman in the building or on the grassy property where the castle once stood, and the sound of a woman's singing or humming has also been heard in various parts of the current building.

Most compelling of all have been the experiences of Holmes's descendant Jeff Mudgett, who has visited the site numerous times since discovering the gruesome ancestor in his family line. Attempting to make peace with this dreadful reality of his life, Mudgett wrote the book *Bloodstains*—a heartfelt journey through his revelations and remembrances and his hopes to help heal the family lines of his grandfather's victims.

Mudgett went on to pursue the truth behind his ancestor's chilling, death row claim that he was London killer Jack the Ripper. The beginnings of his search are documented in the History Channel's miniseries *American Ripper*, which culminates in the exhumation of Holmes's body from its grave in Holy Cross Cemetery in Lansdowne, Pennsylvania.

Jeff Mudgett is not finished with his search for answers from his ancestor's shrouded story. Part of his plans include the exhumation of the Murder Castle site and the placement of a memorial plaque there, where an untold number of victims died during that matchless Chicago year of triumph and tragedy.

When Jeff first visited the site of the Murder Castle, employees of the Englewood post office told him of the basement: "Don't go down there. It's a terrible, haunted place." Mudgett experienced severe physical and emotional effects from the visit. He recalled:

> *Before I walked down those steps I was a non-believer. Absolutely non. I would have walked into any building in the world. An hour later, when I came out, my whole foundation had changed. I was a believer.*

THE HAUNTED PALACE

Only one building remains standing on the old 1893 fairgrounds in Chicago's Jackson Park today: the former Palace of Fine Arts, which now houses the spectacular Museum of Science and Industry. After the fair ended, the building first became the Field Columbian Museum, today's Field Museum of Natural History. While most of the fair buildings, some of them much larger, were built of something called staff—a medium composed of concrete, woven jute and plaster—the Palace of Fine Arts had been built with a base of stone to protect the priceless masterpieces inside, which had come from collections around the world.

Along with the Palace, the rest of the fairgrounds decayed after the close of the fair. Most of Jackson Park—including its "White City" and carefully chosen trees, shrubs and plants—had been destroyed by fire the winter after the fair, the wreckage left to deteriorate on the South Shore while the rest of the city developed, inspired to staggering achievement by the fair that was no more.

When in 1920 the Field Columbian Museum moved into its new quarters farther north, artist Lorado Taft led a movement to establish a new art museum in the old Palace of Fine Arts, featuring works of sculpture—his own medium. In fact, Taft had been the head of sculptural detail when the White City was created. He and students from Chicago's Art Institute worked around the clock to complete the buildings in time for opening day. Included among the artists was a group of female students known as the "White Rabbits," as fair architect Daniel Burnham—in a panic because

Above: The Palace of Fine Arts, World's Fairgrounds in Jackson Park. Today, the structure houses Chicago's Museum of Science and Industry, or MSI—where ghosts walk. *Library of Congress, Detroit Publishing Company*.

Left: Daniel Burnham, architect of the Columbian Exposition of 1893, believed to still walk the fairgrounds in Jackson Park. *Wikimedia Commons, via Arcadia Publishing*.

of the work left and the impending opening—had instructed Taft to "hire anyone, even white rabbits if they'll do the work!"

Despite much community and financial support for Taft's vision, it was decided that a science museum would instead be created. This decision was largely made because Julius Rosenwald, then president of Sears, Roebuck and Company, pledged $3 million to such a project after visiting the Deutsches Museum in Munich. The façade of the building was recast using limestone, the designers carefully preserving the 1893 heritage but creating an ultra-modern interior design. When it opened, Rosenwald did not want his name on the building, but Chicagoans still called it the Rosenwald Industrial Museum. In 1928, the institution was christened the Museum of Science and Industry. Today, in our world of abbreviations, it is often called simply "MSI."

Several years ago, I was invited to tell ghost stories on the terrace of the museum, which overlooks the Jackson Park Lagoon, where a lively phantom, dressed in topcoat and fedora, is said to walk. Indeed, this ghost is one of the most prolific haunters in Chicago, long believed to be the shade of famed defense attorney Clarence Darrow, whose ashes were scattered over the lagoon after his death. (I have come to believe, however, that the spirit is that of Daniel Burnham, the great mastermind and architect of the World's Fair, discussed further later in this volume.) At any rate, I was asked to tell the tale of the resident phantom and other popular ghost stories of Chicago, suitable for the children who were gathering for a pre-Halloween evening at the popular museum.

During the course of the evening, a security guard came up to me and pressed into my hand a piece of folded-up paper. I looked up at him quizzically, and he just nodded. I unfolded the paper, and on it, the guard had written, "They told us not to talk to you, but you need to call me."

The next day I called the man, and he explained to me that the staff had been instructed not to share with me any of the strange happenings regularly experienced at the museum, but that there were many that I "needed to know about" as a researcher of the unexplained.

He told me about the ghosts of the Burlington Railroad's Pioneer Zephyr, the beautiful diesel stainless-steel train that was brought in for permanent exhibition and still hosts sounds of hushed voices, laughter and music. My mother always talked about walking to the tracks in the evening with friends and siblings to wait for the beautiful Zephyr to come through like a rocket. Later kids like me even remember the Zephyr ice cream parlor at Wilson and Ravenswood Avenues next to the tracks, a gorgeous art deco tribute to the train's sophisticated era.

He told me about the apparition of a young girl who lost her life several years ago in the Blue Stairwell; she died while trying to slide down a railing.

He told me about the many appearances of Darrow's ghost, both outside on the terrace and inside the building.

And he told me, most chillingly, about the bowler-hatted, mustachioed man seen walking the Yesterday's Main Street exhibit: a gaslit, shadowy re-creation of a turn-of-the-nineteenth-century street scene. That figure, the staff firmly believed, is the ghost of none other than serial killer H.H. Holmes, who would have walked very similar streets in his day—and the halls of this very building—during the World's Fair of 1893.

Yet no story in the museum is more notorious than that of the haunting of the *U-505*.

The *U-505* was one of the terrifying German submarines (or U-boats) that ruled the seas during the early years of World War II. U-boats cruised the seas above the waterline, stalking merchant ships. Only after a sighting would the U-boat captain order submersion, in order to approach with stealth aided by periscope. Once the U-boat got close enough to attack, a torpedo was launched to sink the merchant ship by blasting a hole in its hull.

After their introduction, U-boat attacks on merchant ships soon numbered in the hundreds, causing merchant crews to dread travel on the open seas. Allied merchant ships began to travel in convoys of up to two hundred vessels for protection, but a U-boat attack still called off all bets, disrupting a convoy's formation and undermining the safety of all members. Often, the convoys were escorted by powerful destroyers that would launch depth charges in response to U-boat offensives, but fear still reigned, as many deaths typically occurred during these exchanges.

Furthering the fear was Adolf Hitler's response to the convoys, his own fleets of U-boats—the so-called Wolfpacks—sent to pummel the Allied convoys. In the worst month of the Atlantic conflict, March 1943 brought an attack by more than three dozen U-boats on more than one hundred Allied craft, resulting in the sinking of a fifth of the Allied vessels.

By the time of this attack, the American navy had had enough. As assaults increased, the Allies took action, forming the hunter-killer task groups to hunt and destroy the U-boats, ship by ship. The task groups restored a great deal of peace to the minds of Allied seamen, and their formation increased as the war progressed, aided by advances in anti-sub intelligence

One of the most effective hunter-killer task groups was 22.3, whose escorts included the aircraft carrier USS *Guadalcanal*, home base for fighter planes whose pilots spent their days at sea monitoring the waters for U-boats and alerting 22.3's four destroyer escorts of the subs' positions.

Commander of the *Guadalcanal* was Chicago native Captain Daniel V. Gallery Jr., a decorated pilot whose elegant and forceful direction in an earlier task group had led to the sinking of the *U-544*, the *U-68* and the *U-515*. While the sinking of the earlier U-boats had been a boon to the United States Navy and the Allies, Gallery had other plans for the new task group: capture an enemy sub.

If the navy were able to do it, such a capture would put into Allied hands priceless intelligence, including U-boat ammunition technology; insight into the Axis code system, Enigma; and precious communication logs. When the *Guadalcanal* set sail in the spring of 1944, capture was the mission.

The Tenth Fleet was the American antisubmarine intelligence command, headed up by Kenneth Knowles, and Gallery was debriefed by Knowles himself before setting out with Task Group 22.3. Knowles put Gallery and his group on the trail of a U-boat that had cast off two months earlier from France, headed toward the coast of Africa.

Task Group 22.3 bore for the Canary Islands on May 15, 1944, where Wildcat pilots joined the sea vessels in the hunt for the elusive sub. For nearly three weeks, search efforts dragged on, seemingly in vain; then, just as the search was abandoned, the destroyer USS *Chatelain* radioed sub contact—of the *U-505*.

Judging the sub's location, the *Chatelain* unleashed two dozen Mark 4 hedgehogs, missing the target. While the destroyer prepared for a second launch, *Guadalcanal* fighters tagged the sub's submerged location by firing rounds into the water. The *Chatelain* then fired more than a dozen Mark 9 depth charges—with success. Moments later, the sub burst to the surface.

Boarding the sub minutes later, the Allied party worked against time to dismantle the scuttle charges, time bombs that would have been set by the crew during abandonment of the sub in order to sink the vessel and prevent its capture. On the *U-505*, the crew had also tried to flood the ship by opening a pipe that allowed the inrush of water, but the boarding party was able to secure the opening and prevent further submersion of the craft.

While the boarding party carried out its dangerous work on the *U-505*, German sailors from the sub were rescued by Task Group 22.3 and taken prisoner aboard the *Guadalcanal* to await transport to a POW camp in Louisiana where they would remain until the end of hostilities.

FINALLY, THE AMERICAN CREWS prepared for the overwhelming task of towing the semi-submerged *U-505* to Bermuda—under U.S. Navy orders.

Though the sub eventually toured American cities as part of a bond drive, its days were numbered. After picking the sub apart for intelligence's sake, the U.S. Navy slated the sub to be employed in target practice, but retired Commander Daniel Gallery, as usual, had other plans.

Still moved by the import of the *U-505*—and his own experiences of its capture—Gallery sought the sub's survival and aimed to bring it to his own city of Chicago for permanent exhibition. Gallery found open ears to his plea at the Museum of Science and Industry, an astounding Chicago institution housed in one of the sprawling exhibit halls of the 1893 World's Fair. Then president of the museum Lenox Lohr shared Gallery's hopes of acquiring a submarine for his inimitable museum, and he quickly approached naval authorities with their desire for the *U-505*. The navy approved but would not front the monstrous expense of the actual transfer—a quarter of a million dollars.

Almost miraculously, the City of Chicago and the Museum of Science and Industry joined a slew of private organizations and individuals to raise the needed funds, and on May 15, 1954, exactly ten years after Task Group 22.3 had left port to find it, the *U-505* began the long tow from Portsmouth to Chicago, where it took more than a week to haul it out of Lake Michigan, across Lake Shore Drive and across the museum's great front lawn of Jackson Park. That fall, the *U-505* became a memorial to the fallen of World War II; soon, it would obtain the status it retains as one of the museum's most popular exhibits.

When it was first installed as an exhibit, the *U-505*'s home was actually outside the building, and visitors accessed the craft from an exhibit hall passageway inside the museum. Half a century of brutal lakefront weather,

The *U-505*, pictured here, was one of the terrifying German submarines (or U-boats) that ruled the seas during the early years of World War II. *Library of Congress, Detroit Publishing Company*.

however, took its toll, and in 1997, curators decided the sub would have to be moved indoors to remain safe for boarding.

After two years of repairing and refurbishing the *U-505* with the aid of antique photographs and eyewitness memories, the unthinkable task of moving the sub was again at hand. Luckily, experienced NORSAR signed on for the job, designing an elaborate system of dollies and jacks for the move into the museum and down into the *U-505*'s new, underground exhibit hall. But is all quiet on deck?

Nein.

Since the sub's arrival at the museum, staff and visitors have been aware of an unseen sailor on the submarine. Surprisingly, the invisible crew member is not believed to be one of the vanquished of the infamous capture but former commander Peter Zschech.

In October 1943, a year before its capture by Task Group 22.3, the *U-505* found itself enmeshed in battle with an Allied destroyer hailing from Britain, which attacked the sub with numerous depth charges. Believing his ship was near the end, Zschech took his own life, shooting himself in the head with his pistol as he stood, white-faced, at the controls. Even more horrifically, the shot didn't instantly kill him, and as Zschech lay on his bunk, crying out, crew members muffled his cries with his pillow to keep his voice from detection by the enemy and, as the men admitted, to quicken the inevitable end.[35]

Docents and security guards have both experienced unseen forces on the sub. In 2005, one security guard told of hearing voices on the *U-505* every single night she was on duty, and another reported sightings of a most unusual sort: the apparition of legs, feet or shoes in the door of the commander's cabin and the strong feeling of being watched while inside the room. Interestingly, in his autobiography, *U-505* submariner Hans Goebler writes that it was only when the crew saw the "lifeless legs" of Zschech being "dragged into the Olymp, our nickname for the area around the Skipper's cabin," that they "realized that something was very, very wrong."

Author and ghost hunter John Kachuba visited the museum before the move of the *U-505* and discovered that, while on the sub, one docent had felt an invisible presence attempt to enter his own body. Kachuba described his *U-505* visit in *Ghosthunting Illinois*, noting that

female docents especially seem to be having a tough time with the commander's ghost. One young woman had just made a rather insulting joke about the commander…when a steel door suddenly slammed closed on her hand, injuring her. Another woman felt a hand come out of nowhere and grasp her shoulder. Of course, there was no one else in the room.

Before the move of the *U-505* to its new site inside the Museum of Science and Industry, I spent many hours inside the sub, talking with guards and docents and taking environmental readings of the interior. Unusual effects abounded, from skewed compass readings in the 1980s and, later, spikes on my EMF meter to inexplicable pounding sounds and indistinguishable whispers near the commander's cabin.

Since the opening of the new exhibit hall and the refurbishing of the *U-505*, I've made several trips to see the sub in its new digs. Discreetly brandishing my digital thermometer, I was lucky enough to capture a fourteen-degree temperature drop in the doorway of Zschech's old cabin, a change not tremendously impressive but, indeed, totally inexplicable. I was also fortunate in another respect. During one of my visits, I was the only visitor on the sub, so I was able to make a reasonable attempt to collect samples of EVP (electronic voice phenomena) or possible spirit voices. Throughout the sub, I asked standard questions, such as "What is your name?" "Where are we?" "What year is it?" and "What time is it?"

Well, they say the third time's the charm, and on the third try of the last question, outside one of the bunks, I got the most distinct EVP answer of my twenty-year career. I am familiar with simple German phrases, as my daughters attend the Saturday morning German language school at Chicago's DANK Haus in Lincoln Square, and so, when I played back the tape I'd made on the *U-505*, I was quick to decipher the clear words of a slow, low, male voice affirming, "einundzwanzig hundert," that is, "twenty-one hundred."

No small matter. At just after 21:00 hours on October 24, 1943, a blunt entry was made in the *U-505*'s logbook, stating only, "Kommandant tot," that is, "Commanding officer dead."

A few hours later, just before dawn according to the privately published autobiography of *U-505* crew member Hans Goebler, "Zschech's body was lifted up to the bridge and dropped over the side without ceremony. We continued running on the surface at high speed in order to put as much distance between us and the destroyers as possible."

Though the days ahead were racked with additional depth charges and close calls, Zschech's first officer, Paul Meyer, was able to save the *U-505*, maneuvering it out of Allied view. On the morning of November 7, the *U-505* surfaced and entered Lorient Harbor—and safety. "As we entered the harbor," writes Goebler, "we fell out to assemble on bent knee on the upper deck....It was quite an experience....We had made it home, all of us, safe and sound."

All, that is, except one.

Though the men under Zschech's command admitted little sorrow at the incompetent commander's passing, the pall of his end has ever hung over the craft. Goebel writes:

> *I was never one to be frightened much by superstitions, but whenever I passed Zschech's cabin, I got goosebumps. We kept the curtain to his cabin closed, and no one had dared to enter it since the day of his suicide. Even Oberleutnant Meyer felt more comfortable staying in his junior officer's bunk. Seeing that closed curtain reminded me of the way Zschech would hide in his cabin, alone with his tortured thoughts. It was as if his ghost still haunted the little room.*

NIGHT AT THE MUSEUM

O riginally founded as the Columbian Museum of Chicago, the city's Field Museum of Natural History was born in conjunction with the World's Fair of 1893, the Columbian Exposition, where the city displayed massive collections researchers had gathered into anthropological and biological displays.

After the fair, the collection was moved into the old Palace of Fine Arts—the only fair building that remains on the old fairgrounds. In the early 1920s, the museum moved its collections from its exposition site in Jackson Park to its current home on the lakefront, where it fixes one point in the triangle of institutions composing Chicago's popular "museum campus": the Field, the Adler Planetarium and the Shedd Aquarium, all connected by landscaped pedestrian pathways. With more than twenty million specimens crammed into its many halls and storerooms, the Field has retained, many times magnified, its original power to thrill the audiences that stream through the museum's exhibits season upon season.

Part of the mystique of the Field can be explained by the cultural diversity of its collections, artifacts dripping with ancient intrigue and reeking of esoterica. Another part can be traced to the army of staff members that toils behind the scenes and around the clock in countless labs and workrooms. Here, biologists, anthropologists, geologists and zoologists carry out their research, registering anywhere from uneventful to earth-shattering.

The move of the Field Columbian Museum collections from the old Palace of Fine Arts buildings at the World's Fairgrounds to the museum's new building, the Field Museum of Natural History near current-day Roosevelt Road and Lake Shore Drive. *Library of Congress, Detroit Publishing Company.*

This double-edged intrigue has led to the telling of many tales about Chicago's Field Museum. When, in 1996, the film *The Ghost and the Darkness* was released, chronicling the history of the so-called man-eaters of Tsavo, a pair of African lions that killed more than 130 railroad workers in the late nineteenth century, longtime rumors resurfaced regarding the lions' carcasses. These have been part of the Field's collections since the mid-1920s, when they were sold to the museum by Lieutenant Colonel John Henry Patterson, who shot the lions in 1898. Patterson, chief engineer of the British government's project to build a railway bridge over East Africa's Tsavo River, wrung his hands for nine long months as scores of his men reportedly fell prey to the lions, which were guessed to have resorted to man-eating out of sheer hunger when an outbreak of disease killed off much of their natural prey.

The lions of Tsavo, now highlighted with a detailed exhibit at the Field, are worthy of the story attributed to their name. Though their taxidermized appearance comes up shy of the lions' original statures (one measured more than nine and a half feet at the time of death), their dreadful natures still seem nearly tangible. It is not surprising that the

Opening day at the Field Museum, 1921. *Library of Congress, Detroit Publishing Company.*

legend of the animals, enhanced by the mystique of their African origin and dramatically underscored by their imposing physical presence, has given rise to new stories of strange behavior: peripheral glimpses of movement in the lions' display case, shifting of the animals' positions between viewings, their occasional disappearance altogether and terrifying growls emanating from the exhibit hall.

One archivist at the Field told me in the spring of 1996 that she had seen one of the lions walking through the museum halls while working alone one night. Security guards reportedly called Chicago Police, thinking that a bobcat had somehow gotten into the museum—or perhaps an escapee from the Lincoln Park Zoo. No trace of any live animal was found.

The Field is also home to a piece of a "cursed" meteorite, the Elbogen meteorite that fell to earth in the fifteenth century in Loket in the Kingdom of Bohemia, present-day Czech Republic. Legend held that the meteorite was in fact a much-maligned count of Loket Castle, who had turned to stone after being cursed by a witch and struck by lightning. Citizens and rulers alike maintained such a fear of the object that it was chained up in the dungeon of the castle for generations.

Another of the museum's permanent exhibits, *Inside Ancient Egypt*, has also played host to a number of paranormal reports, namely of the sound of screams coming from the rooms housing the mummy displays that, some claim, inspired the film *The Relic*, an ancient-horror movie set in Chicago's natural history museum. One mummy in particular, a fellow named Harwa, was reported to occasionally catapult his own sarcophagus off the display stand and onto the floor, several feet away, after coming to live at the museum. Security guards were said to discover the movement after investigating a loud, gunshot-like sound that preceded the phenomenon. Though many believe that Harwa took midnight strolls through the museum on the nights when his casket went haywire, few have seen the man behind the mummy in action.

Yet some staff members admit to odd activity around the ancient Egyptian, and employees like Pamela Buczkowske, a circulation clerk at the museum, have their own twilight run-ins with a decidedly Egyptian manifestation in the building's darkening hallways:

I had been at the Field Museum for about two years. One evening after closing I was headed back to my office. I had taken the east center staircase down to the ground level. Off to my left was a short hallway I used to get back to where I worked. The hall is all but gone now. A new elevator was installed there, and the Egypt store was housed in that area.

As I walked down the stairs, I was surprised to see what I thought was a visitor coming toward me. Normal closing time was five o'clock; we had been closed for twenty minutes already. What didn't dawn on me until later was the fact that I could not see the upper body of the person. A shadow covered it at any angle.

I hurried up to the person to tell them that the museum was closed and he or she (I couldn't tell if it was a man or woman) would have to leave. But suddenly, the figure turned into the Egypt exhibit. I was practically on the person's heels, yet when I entered the exhibit, there was no one there. There wasn't even the sound of footfalls. I walked around the dark exhibit for a few minutes and found nothing.

Now, there are three ways to get out of the exhibit, and one gets locked at 4:45, on the first floor. The other two are on the ground floor, and I checked them out. One was locked, and the other would have brought the person right to me.

At first, I didn't really think I saw a ghost, and I wasn't scared. I did a little bit of investigating and found out a few things that I didn't realize at that time. One was the lighting. It wasn't dark enough to cover any part of the person I saw. Two was that the person never even acknowledged my presence. He or she had to have seen me coming toward them. The third thing occurred to me when a guard and I reenacted what I saw. The lighting was the same and, as I'd suspected, there was no shadow over the upper part of his body.

I could see him perfectly.

THE SWAMI AND THE STORYTELLER

In 1866, about three dozen Chicago artists joined together with plans to open a free art school with a gallery for displaying the students' work. Thus was founded the Chicago Academy of Design. The school was originally run out of a studio on Dearborn Street, with classes meeting daily. The free tuition could not be realized entirely, but a charge of ten dollars a month was low enough to enable many aspiring arts to take advantage of the resource—enough, in fact, for the school to build a new, five-story school on Adams Street fewer than four years after the academy's founding.

In October 1871, like much of Chicago, the Chicago Academy of Design burned to the ground, and the school became mired in debt collections. Though members desperately tried to raise funds by striking deals with local business investors, their efforts were not enough. Some abandoned the effort to form a new school: the Chicago Academy of Fine Arts. Later, when the original school went bankrupt, the new school purchased its assets.

The rebuilding bug that had gripped the city in the aftermath of the fire inspired the academy too. Soon after its regrouping, members changed its name to the Art Institute of Chicago and elected a president, Charles Hutchinson. It was a brilliant move, for Hutchinson had led many notable institutions, including the University of Chicago, and during his reign he would take the Art Institute from a local art school to what it is today: a world-class art museum and important international art school. In 1882, the Art Institute purchased a piece of property on the southwest corner of Michigan Avenue and Van Buren Street. There was an existing building there, which was used for the administration of the school, while an annex was added for gallery space, studios and classrooms. Within two years, the school and gallery had outgrown the new digs, and the adjacent property on Michigan Avenue was purchased, with famed architect John Wellborn Root hired to design a new school and museum. The impressive structure opened to an overwhelming reception in 1887.

Not to be satisfied, however, when Hutchinson heard the announcement of a World's Fair to be held in Chicago just six years later, he and the institute's board urged the fair planners and the city to build a completely new and massive art museum and school on Chicago's lakefront. A deal was proposed: use the building for fair activities in 1893, then let the Art Institute move in. The deal was forged.

The new Art Institute of Chicago opened on May 1, 1893, having cost over $625,000 to construct. During the fair, the school and gallery continued operations across the street, while amazing events took place at the institute's future home.

Most notably, the new building hosted the World Congress Auxiliary—including a seventeen-day-long Parliament of the World's Religions. This

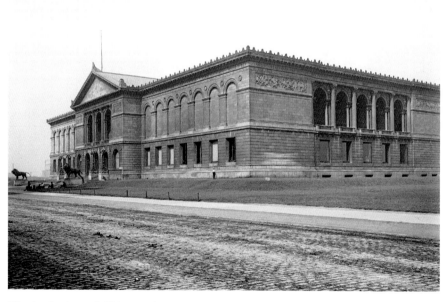

The Art Institute of Chicago, circa 1890. *Library of Congress, Detroit Publishing Company.*

unprecedented event began with an address by a young Hindu monk, Swami Vivekananda, whose speech on religious tolerance shook the foundations of religious understanding and inspired generations to come. In 2010, more than 110 years after the swami's address, artist Jitish Kallat inscribed Vivekenanda's words on the steps of the Art Institute's massive entrance staircase.

ONE OF THE MOST interesting investigations I have ever done took place at the Art Institute of Chicago in 2008. I had been contacted by a graduate student at the School of the Art Institute who had become intrigued by a fascinating question: Do artists, with all of the emotion invested in their pieces, somehow "haunt" their works?

A colleague and I met with Thomas Gokey in his studio space at the school and talked at length about the themes involved in his work, the relationships between the mind and paranormal activity and the artists who inspired Gokey to start thinking about some amazing possibilities.

A few weeks later, Gokey had obtained permission for us to "investigate" a number of pieces in the institute's collection, and we met one afternoon to proceed with the project.

We were a strange sight in the galleries that day, holding electromagnetic (EM) meters and tape recorders to paintings, sculptures and ancient artifacts. Everywhere we went, security guards were more than a little concerned about our intentions. Our explanations didn't do much to ease them. The awkward feelings, however, were well worth the experience, and we did experience several incidents that made us wonder.

The first work investigated was a painting by Jackson Pollock titled *Greyed Rainbow*, which was completed in 1953, just a few years before his death. Pollock, of course, had been one of the major influences in the abstract expressionist movement, and his drip painting or splatter painting, as most describe it, is one of the most recognizable styles of the twentieth century. A man of volatile temperament and a voracious alcoholic, Pollock's paintings seemed to reflect the often chaotic nature of his personal life, and Gokey wondered if there may have been some paranormality involved in his work, reminiscent of the almost spasmodic physical phenomena associated with poltergeist cases, in which a troubled mind is thought to unconsciously influence the movement of objects and other activity. We took temperature readings around the painting and scanned the area to find any fluctuations in the EM fields around the

The author testing for EM fluctuations at Jackson Pollock's *Greyed Rainbow*, circa 2008. *Author's photograph.*

piece, but nothing out of the ordinary was found, at least through our preliminary investigation.

The second piece on the roster was located in the Spanjer Gallery, a collection of artifacts from the ancient Americas and American Indian art. The initial object of our attention was a piece called *The Storyteller*, a figure from the West Mexican State of Jalisco, circa AD 100–800. Though we asked a number of questions at the display case, hoping to capture some audible answers via electronic voice phenomenon (EVP, or the electronic recording of spirit voices), none came. As we said goodbye and thank you to whoever might be listening, however, our EM meter spiked twice, a possible indication of paranormal activity. In the same gallery, mural fragments from the Teotihuacan culture (circa AD 300–750) and a limestone stele seemed to host no unusual activity, so we moved our investigation back to modern times—and interesting results.

Our next stop was an Ad Reinhardt work simply titled *Abstract Painting*, one of the artist's so-called black paintings that he produced in the 1960s, not long before his death. A sudden drop in temperature of approximately fifteen degrees occurred at one point in our monitoring, and there was an EM spike after we said goodbye, identical to our experience in the earlier gallery.

Without question, the most provocative part of our investigation was that of Carl Andre's *Steel Aluminum Plain*, completed in 1969, a pattern of floor tiles typical of the artist's work. Andre's work has received much acclaim, but the most talked-about aspect of his life is not his art but an incident that occurred in his personal life. Andre met artist Ana Mendieta at a New York City gallery in 1979, and the two married in 1985. Tragically, Mendieta fell from Andre's thirty-fourth-story apartment that same year, and her husband was charged with second-degree murder. Andre declined a jury trial, and in 1988, he was acquitted of all charges by the judge of the case. Controversy still rages, however, regarding Mendieta's death, and Gokey wondered if we could tap into the truth by channeling the artist—still living—by approaching one of his works.

Andre encourages the trampling of his floor-level works by gallery-goers, and so I walked onto *Steel Aluminum Plain* with my EM meter and recorder to talk to the man himself and to ask him what had happened that fateful day at his New York apartment. The moment I squatted down to get closer, before I could ask for the truth, my EM meter spiked and the recorder shut itself off.

WILD NIGHTS

As one of the oldest neighborhoods in Chicago, Lincoln Park is also, surely, one of the most haunted in the city. The neighborhood is named, of course, for the sprawling lakefront park, once confined to this neighborhood but now extending much farther along the lakefront.

The home of George "Bugs" Moran, Lincoln Park saw some of the worst gangland violence in American history, including the 1929 St. Valentine's Day Massacre. Occurring in a narrow brick garage at 2122 North Clark Street, the slaughter was part of a Chicago almost as blighted as today's city by turf wars, shootings and death.

Lincoln Park also hosted one of the terrifying deaths that became known as the "Tylenol Murders." On October 1, 1982, flight attendant Paula Prince was found dead two days after buying a bottle of the cyanide-laced capsules at the Walgreen's store at North Avenue and Wells Street, in Lincoln Park's Old Town section.

The famed Second City comedy theater and school makes its home across Wells Street from Walgreen's, in an ornate structure where a murder allegedly took place soon after its erection. According to my old friend, comedian and writer Kevin Dorff, the residue of that violence is believed to still remain, nearly a century later, manifesting to performers and staff over many generations.

Next door to the Second City was the infamously haunted restaurant called That Steak Joynt (later Adobo Grill), an old-school eatery housed in the former Piper's Bakery. This place had one of the meanest ghosts in town, known to drag waitresses down the staircase and manifest as a pair of glowing eyes. Psychics and mediums claimed that a double murder had occurred in Piper's Alley, the cobblestoned pathway that once ran along the building, and that the killer, in phantom form, was still at large on the premises.

Old Town is also home to St. Michael's Church, where the devil himself is said to have appeared in the Communion line one Sunday night in the 1970s, cloaked in a black hood and robe, with hooves instead of feet. And the neighborhood is the stomping grounds of "Candyman." The old Cabrini Green housing project, now gone forever, was the fabled lair of Candyman—the hooked killer of urban legend—and nearby Carl Sandburg Village, the home of the heroine who tangled with his menace.

Without a doubt, one of the most legendary of Lincoln Park's ghosts is that of the late John Dillinger, the swashbuckling bank robber who in 1934 wreaked havoc for months across three states before being gunned down in the alleyway just south of the Biograph Theater. They say you can sometimes still see his bluish form stumbling and falling on the pavement—or feel the icy chill of his spirit move through your own body there.

Despite these plentiful tales of the neighborhood, there is no part of Lincoln Park more haunted than the park itself, which was originally the home of Chicago's City Cemetery, a sprawling burying ground stretching from North Avenue to Armitage and from the old Green Bay Trail (Clark Street) to Lake Michigan. The cemetery, established in 1843, was short-lived. A cholera scare caused residents to fear that the burial of victims would spread the disease to the nearby water supply. Soon, the order was given for the disinterment and removal of the tens of thousands of corpses. The long process came to a shocking halt when, on the night of October 8, 1871, high winds blew flaming debris from the south side inferno across the river. The Great Chicago Fire, sweeping swiftly northward, pushed north side residents to flee into the cemetery grounds and, eventually, into the waters off North Avenue Beach.

The cemetery was almost completely destroyed in the Great Fire. Headboards—the wooden markers that designated most burials of the day—were reduced to ash by the conflagration, rendering plot after plot impossible to identify. With no way to discern where the myriad burials remained, the city simply continued its plans to create a lakefront park, and Chicago moved on. Apparently, not all of the dead did.

Artist and scholar Pamela Bannos, after years of painstaking research, determined that as many as fifteen thousand bodies may remain in Lincoln

Park today, under the zoo, the ball fields, the grounds of the Chicago History Museum and even the posh homes of the Gold Coast; land south of North Avenue was home to an archdiocesan cemetery concurrent with City Cemetery's time here. The mansions built on those grounds later have their own stories to tell.

In addition, grave robbing was an earlier plague on the Lincoln Park burial ground, where as early as 1844, Chicago mayor Augustus Garrett addressed the problem of grave robbing in his inaugural speech, offering rewards for information leading to the arrest of the ghouls.

In May 1851, the local papers reported that passersby had seen a dog in an alley near the post office dragging a mutilated woman's arm, which was assumed to have come from a dissection studio. And in 1857, the great detective Allan Pinkerton set up a stakeout leading to the arrest of one Martin Quinlan—a "resurrectionist" well known by police and locals. Pinkerton's agency would monitor Chicago's cemeteries for decades thereafter, searching for "ghouls."

GHOST HUNTERS HAVE LONG known of the haunting of these old cemetery grounds by the dead left behind after the Great Fire, but while several investigations have been done on the public grounds of Lincoln Park and in some of the private homes and businesses of the surrounding area, no investigation had ever been done of the Lincoln Park Zoo, which spread from its original enclosure over a large acreage, including much of the former cemetery grounds.

Despite the interest of savvy investigators, the haunting of the zoo has been little known to the public in modern times—certainly largely due to concerted efforts to downplay its history. The fact of it, however, was common knowledge in the summer of 1887, when the *Chicago Tribune* published the following darkly humorous poem, titled "The Monkey Sees Ghosts":

> *I am a monkey out at Lincoln Park; I was a cheerful monkey when they*
> *caught me.*
> . *And when, on the great Continent called Dark, A trader bought me.*
> *And I was cheerful when they put me here. In this huge cage amid the*
> *rustling greenery*
> *I had no present dread, no brooding fear, And liked the scenery.*
> *It was a charming spectacle to me. Scenes new and strange recurring*
> *without measure;*

I thought my future life destined to be One constant pleasure.
I liked to watch the curious people pass. To hear the water in the fountains
  spurting,
To note the children playing on the grass, and nurses flirting.
I liked the life, joyed in its merry sum, I thought my lot cast in a field
  Elysian;
Little I dreamed that with the night would come A fearful Vision!
For then, ah, then, appeared before my gaze That which the stoutest spirit
  might have daunted;
Came ghostly Shapes to startle and amaze. The park is haunted! [36]

When, then, the events manager called me in the spring of 2013 about creating a "ghost tour" of the zoo for patrons as part of its public programming, I was beyond thrilled at the prospect, and we immediately set a date for an initial investigation night.

There was so much to think of in planning this project, for the history of the zoo was a staggering one. The institution was founded before the Great Fire, in 1868, when the Lincoln Park commissioners were given a gift of two pairs of swans by Central Park in New York City. Soon after came a puma, two elk, four eagles, three wolves and eight peacocks. In 1874, the zoo made its first purchase: a bear cub from the Philadelphia Zoo. The local Chicago papers were peppered in the months after with stories of the bear's frequent escapes; it was often found roaming the park after midnight. The zoo also acquired a herd of bison, several of which

Bear pit and visitors, Lincoln Park Zoo, 1901. *Library of Congress, Detroit Publishing Company.*

were purchased by the U.S. government and sent to Yellowstone National Park to repopulate the park during its crisis of dwindling herds.

From 1888 to 1919, the director of the Lincoln Park Zoo was Cy DeVry, responsible for building many of its first structures and securing the first elephant and first monkey of the zoo's collection. A beautiful new Lion House was erected in 1912, followed by a Primate House in 1927, which served for years as the home of the beloved gorilla Bushman and was later renovated and decorated by the noted sculptor Walter S. Arnold.

Marlin Perkins, the well-known host of the television programs *Zoo Parade* and *Wild Kingdom*, was director of Lincoln Park Zoo from 1944 to 1962, and it was he who created the Lincoln Park Zoological Society, a citizens' group that still exists today.

Dr. Lester Fisher, Perkins's successor, was famous among Chicago schoolchildren in the 1970s, as he cohosted with Chicago children's television star Ray Raynor a frequent feature of the *Ray Raynor Show* called "Ark in the Park," which filmed Raynor and Fisher meeting with and learning about the zoo's animals. Fisher, one of the world's greatest primate researchers, also cared deeply about the education of Chicago's children, building the first "Farm in the Zoo" where city children could learn about the raising of farm crops and animal husbandry. When he broke ground for the main barn at the zoo, however, Fisher found coffins containing human remains—relics of the former City Cemetery. After numerous requests for instructions from the city regarding their removal, Fisher finally had them returned to the ground and the foundational cement poured for the barn. The coffins and their contents remain today.

The South Pond Refectory—the park's old boathouse—is today known as Café Brauer, a popular site for weddings. It was known not only as the site of numerous drownings but also operated as a swanky restaurant in the 1910s and '20s, with rumors of Gangland hauntings.

Despite the many possibilities for hauntings from this rich history, however, I knew exactly where I wanted to go on our first investigation of the zoo, because over many years I had been approached via letter, phone call and email about close encounters in, of all places, the women's restroom in the Lion House basement. Time after time, women would report having used the facility and, while washing their hands or applying makeup, seeing in the mirrors men and women dressed in Victorian clothing. On the night of the first investigation that summer, another investigator and I entered the restroom and were immediately struck by the layout of the room. Rows of sinks lined the two walls, parallel to each

At the Lion House, Lincoln Park Zoo, circa 1906. *Library of Congress, H.C. White Company.*

other. Above the sinks were rows of mirrors, creating an "infinity" effect from the two walls of mirrors facing each other.

Now, most paranormal investigators will concur that mirrors are one of those things—like salt or water—that have some definite power in the world of the preternatural. Steeped in folklore, these items really do seem to have some importance in the realm of paranormal experience. One theory is that entities can be easily "trapped" in mirrors. Presumably, the spirits enter them to explore the objects they see reflected but suddenly find themselves engulfed in blackness, on the other side of the mirror's glass—essentially inside the mirror.

This works the opposite way as well. My friend Colleen Nadas, a medium, likes to build and use a tool called "The Devil's Toybox," which is a kind of "ghost trap" comprising a cube made of inward-facing square mirrors, securely taped together at the seams. Investigators use contact microphones to record sounds from inside the box, believing that if a spirit attempts to investigate, it will find itself trapped because of the mirrors and start to make a fuss. Sometimes this "fussing" leads to great EVP (electronic voice phenomenon): recordings of the voices of the angry or frightened ghosts or knocking sounds from inside the box. In the zoo's Lion House, we instantly theorized that entities were routinely finding themselves stuck in these mirrors due to the effect created by the rows of mirrors facing each other.

Anecdotes collected from the zoo staff confirmed that staff members had also experienced encounters here, especially hearing a man's voice commanding, "Get out!" Amazingly, when I set up my laptop and began to record for EVP, within a minute I picked up a stern male voice warning, "Get out! There's a woman here!" A future visit by a medium confirmed that one of the male spirits had taken on the task of keeping men—dead and alive—out of the women's restroom.

As we continued our investigation, I took several series of photographs down the row of stalls leading to the end of the facility. During investigations, I like to take fifty to one hundred photos or more of each location to see if any of the frames contain an anomaly. When I played back the recording done during this time, I found that one of the male entities was a bit angry that I wasn't paying as much attention to him as the area I was photographing, because he clearly says, "Will you look at me!"

As is typical with most investigators, I asked if there was anything I could do for the entities who remained in this spot. The same voice, now with a tinge of sadness, answered, "Help me…with leaving." When I asked if there was anything the spirits wanted to tell us about their time on earth, one can make out the sound of a lion's roar and of the same voice saying, "I miss it."

On a subsequent visit to the Lion House bathroom, I was amazed to find that I had photographed a shadowy figure silhouetted against one of the bathroom stalls. This photograph was one of a sequence of sixty I had snapped, one after another in quick sequence. Only this photo showed the image. The other investigators with me attempted to re-create the shadow by standing against the opposite wall, out of view, but could not.

On the first investigation night, after several hours of research and experiment, we decided to call it a night and began to disable and pack up our equipment. I would say that, generally, when an investigator ends an investigation and says "Goodbye!" before turning off a recording device, the entities tend to scramble to say more, especially to give more pleas for help. Not so in the case of this location. At least one of the entities was eager to see us go. In response to my invitation, "Is there anything else you'd like to say before we go?" the sound of—perhaps anxious—footfalls can be heard, along with the words, "Turn out the light. Goodnight!"

THE WOOD WALKERS

While the overwhelming majority of Chicago's sidewalks and streets are today paved with concrete and asphalt, there remain numerous sections of the city where one may still walk and drive on Belgian block—which most of us refer to as "cobblestones." When we think of old-fashioned streets, we certainly think of these. Yet before Belgian block became a widespread paving material, wood—named "Nicholson pavement" for its innovator—was favored for paving, due to its abundance, durability and affordability. Amazingly, wooden pavement held up very well against the Great Fire of 1871 because it was treated with a chemical preservative.[37]

No wooden streets remain in Chicago, but at least three sections of wooden alleyway do. The most famous one is in the Gold Coast neighborhood—the old Catholic cemetery grounds on the lakeshore south of North Avenue—in the alley behind the cardinal's mansion between State Parkway and Astor Street.

When, in 1885, Archbishop Patrick Feehan set up housekeeping in the lavish mansion on State Parkway, a large acreage surrounded the dwelling. For decades, the Chicago Gold Coast had kept its dead here, interred in the old City Cemetery just beyond North Avenue. When the question of disease threw lakefront residents into a panic, the cemetery was closed and the bodies relocated to outlying sites along the Chicago and North Western rail line. Catholics went to Calvary, on the border between Chicago and Evanston, a town directly north of the city limits. The others were buried in Rosehill, bordered today by Ravenswood, Peterson, Western and Berwyn Avenues.

With the corpses gone, the abandoned expanse was open for suggestions. After the fire, the cemetery grounds eventually were overtaken by Chicago's existing recreational ground, Lincoln Park, and over the next decades, the Lincoln Park Commission sought to push out the memory of the cemetery with massive improvements to the area including a bathing beach; panoramic, illuminated bridges; and expansion of the growing Lincoln Park Zoo. The rest—that part south of North Avenue—was sold off for residential development.

Yet while the lakefront and its adjacent neighborhood would become beautiful over the next half century, little did the earliest squatters know that this area was destined to become one of the swankiest neighborhoods in America. Little, too, did they realize that bodies from the empty cemetery would continue to turn up here for the next one hundred years.

Fourteen years after the opening of Lincoln Park, Potter Palmer, Chicago's most influential businessman of the day, moved into a million-dollar castle at 1350 North Lake Shore Drive, fleeing the elite community of Prairie Avenue, south of the city center. In a short time, Palmer's former neighbors followed suit, and the old burial ground began to really glimmer. From then on, Chicago's old and new money would consider the Gold Coast as the ultimate in city living.

Many of the sumptuous residences that arose from this former swamp still stand today, relics of an age of overkill. Living in them are a number of descendants of those first Chicago "haves" and a host of relatively new millionaires as well. Though their origins may vary, many have at least two things in common: they're loaded, and they're haunted.

Since the neighborhood's earliest days, Gold Coasters settling down on Dearborn Parkway, State Parkway and Astor Street have been aware of a sort of shadow population living with them in these haunts of the rich and famous (a population hailing, presumably, from the old City Cemetery) and the remains that, despite the cemetery's relocation, remained right here, often under the foundations of their houses.

After the first run-ins with partially decomposed corpses during the groundbreaking of the early homes and the hasty disposal of the evidence, residents complained of strange goings-on in their dream homes. As these hauntings arose time and again, would-be builders listened well. Soon, an unspoken understanding prevailed among future homeowners: when

NORTH END OF DEARBORN AVENUE.

North end of Dearborn Street, Lincoln Park. Houses built on old Catholic cemetery grounds. *Library of Congress, S.L. Stine Publishing Company.*

remains were unearthed, no expense or effort was spared in properly burying the grisly find.

Even today, this silent pact holds true.

In recent years, a landscape company stated that every single time it has been hired to install underground lawn sprinklers, workers have found bones.

A contractor, hired to do work on a Chicago celebrity's Gold Coast home, was startled to find dried leaves on the bathroom floor where no one had trekked. The owner told him, then, about the resident ghosts. If he was not a believer when he first arrived, he became one before he left, witnessing a light sconce rotate 360 degrees before his eyes, untouched by hands.[38]

In the late 1990s, when a wealthy businessman began the total renovation of a grand old structure on State Parkway, he was hardly surprised at the discovery of an early team of contractors and well prepared with an old neighborhood solution. One worker explains that when the renovation of the elegant brownstone began, the basement floor had to be opened up for plumbing, electrical and ventilation work. The job had to be dug by hand, by pick and shovel, and the men digging the trenches unearthed human remains.

The general contractor on the job had a Native American laborer, a very spiritual man. When the men working on the trench would disturb any remains, they were told to go upstairs and get this employee, who would then come down and remove the remains to the side of the trench and say prayers over them.

They say that Native American laborer ended up having a business card made because of all the calls he began to get for similar services—all in the homes of the old wood walkers.

THE BRIDGE OF SIGHS

It is an interesting coincidence that the bronze monuments in Chicago's Lincoln Park—one of the city's most haunted places—compose a sort of "supernatural sculpture garden," where one may learn a good deal of the paranormal history of America by strolling through the walkways.

The Lincoln Memorial, behind the Chicago History Museum, commemorates the man who was famously connected in life to a spiritual world through dreams and premonitions, and whose phantom funeral train still pulls into Chicago as May dawns each year, as the real thing did after his assassination in 1865. Each year, around the first of May, train spotters, Lincoln enthusiasts and others congregate along the Illinois Central tracks or on the Roosevelt Road bridge to watch for the infamous specter, said to be manned by a literal skeleton crew and with a phantom Union guard standing by. They say that if you see the train, time stands still—literally. If you are wearing a timepiece of any kind, it will stop and never work again.

Benjamin Franklin is commemorated in Lincoln Park by a memorial that stands on the north side of the pedestrian tunnel between the museum and the ball fields. When Spiritualism was in its heyday, Franklin's spirit was a frequent guest in séance parlors; believers were convinced that the famed inventor had forged a "spiritual telegraph" to communicate across the veil of death.

General Ulysses S. Grant's statue commands the vista over the south pond on the west and Lake Shore Drive on the east, towering over a city that greatly lauded him in life. Few know, however, that Grant was known to have

The future Lake Shore Drive in Lincoln Park. By the late nineteenth century, the park and the lake had become popular places for suicides. *Library of Congress, Detroit Publishing Company*.

had numerous "presentiments" during his lifetime, including precognition of his becoming head of the American army. His wife, Julia, shared his gifts, even successfully urging her husband to leave town with her on Good Friday 1865, when they were scheduled to attend a performance of *My American Cousin* at Ford's Theatre with President Lincoln.

On the other side of the drive, near the lakeshore, a monument to Swedish spiritual philosopher Emmanuel Swedenborg commemorates a man who many call the father of paranormal research, directly influential in the founding of the Society of Psychical Research and its offshoot, the American Society for Psychical Research.

If you read the previous section, you would understandably assume that the haunting of Lincoln Park and its zoo is wholly the result of the destruction of the City Cemetery by the Great Fire and the abandonment of the more than ten thousand bodies, left behind in unmarked graves in its aftermath. But you might be wrong. For it is estimated that, from before the Great Fire until 1919, over one hundred people lost their lives in Lincoln Park, the majority of them the victims of accidental drowning, acts of God or—most often—suicide.[39]

On the evening of Saturday, June 16, 1892, thousands of visitors thronged Chicago's pristine Lincoln Park, the city's favorite place for recreation. Though thousands of bodies still slumbered below, the former City Cemetery had long been redeveloped as a lush expanse of manicured gardens, boating ponds and walkways, highlighted by popular zoological gardens and a light-filled plant conservatory, and on any given day, Chicagoans came out by the thousands to enjoy the lakefront air and cheerful scenery.

The sun had been particularly hot that Thursday afternoon, and even after 6:00 p.m., its rays drove dozens to seek shade under trees, in the boathouse and under the cool, dark, arched edifice supporting the park's monument to General Ulysses S. Grant—which can still be seen today towering between the park and the lagoon just west of Lake Shore Drive.

Some gathered had sought shelter under the statue, the base of which is a long corridor with arched, open windows overlooking the park to the west and the lake to the east, with stairs leading down to the lagoon.

Just before half past six o'clock in the evening, a sudden storm came up, dense clouds rolling in from the west toward the water. As the fronts met, faint jags of lightning flashed over the distant skies and a summer rain began to fall, sending more running for shelter under the Grant Monument. They crowded together, awaiting the end of the rain, which had become a torrent in a few minutes' time.

Suddenly, without any warning, there was a blinding flash and a massive boom.

A bolt of lightning had struck the left hind leg of the bronze horse on which General Grant is mounted. The current traveled along the northwest corner of the granite coping and hummed into the corridor beneath. In its silent power, all of those huddled below were knocked off their feet. A moment later, some came to—others did not. In all, thirty-seven were injured and three killed in the freak event.

Officer Murphy was on the beat in Lincoln Park that afternoon and told reporters about the scene:

> *I make a run to my box for my rubber coat. I had started from underneath the monument when the bolt descended. I was still within ten feet of the monument. Involuntarily I turned around, and where, a second before I had seen a crowd of 37 people in conversation, I found forty unconscious figures strewn about the stone floor. It was an awful sight. I was fearfully*

dazed myself, but I hastened in to see if all were dead. Close beside where I had been standing a moment before had stood a young man and woman. He was lying dead at the south end of the second arch and she was making an effort to crawl to his side. [10]

Officer Duddles was on duty that day as well and called the scene "the most terrible sight…ever witnessed."

The people who were least affected by the lightning were making painful attempts to get upon their feet. Some had succeeded, some were crawling about in an aimless way, and four were entirely motionless and apparently dead. In the southeast corner of the north arch was Mrs. Schele the old lady. She was sitting up against the granite wall, and, with the exception of a dark hue about her cheeks, she was apparently unscathed by the lightning. She, however, had suffered the worst of all by its mad freak. Her clothing was torn in shreds from her shoulders in many places, as if it had been cut with a knife. Strangely enough, her shoes had been torn from her feet, and they lay nearby, ripped and broken. She had evidently been instantly killed. At the time that the lightning struck her she held in her arms the little child of her and William Hulluns. It had escaped without a scratch, and when the wagon arrived it was laughing in its father's arms. Mr. Hulluns had arrived at the monument just a moment before the flash came to take his family home in his carriage. He fortunately escaped injury. Meyer's body was lying in the third archway, prone on its back. He was right in the path of the lightning, and, if there could be such a thing as first, he was the first to be killed. Like the rest, his face and hands had turned to a dark color. His coat was badly torn and his right trouser leg was split from top to bottom. His right shoe had also been torn from his foot. Near Meyer's body lay Miss Louisa Schmidt, and she was vainly endeavoring to make "her sweetheart speak to her."

On our nighttime walking tours of Lincoln Park, there have been numerous guests who have had strange experiences in the dark corridor where tragedy touched down that summer evening of 1892. Shadow figures are sometimes seen peering from behind the arched openings as visitors approach from the west area of prairie flora surrounding the South Pond. Others are seen leaning on the openings on the east side, gazing over the lagoon and the lake and then vanishing. Zoo and park personnel will speak of similar encounters, and one zoo security guard

Left: The General Grant monument in Lincoln Park. In the summer of 1892, three people were killed and many more injured by lightning. *Library of Congress, Detroit Publishing Company.*

Below: The bathing beach at Lincoln Park, seen here in 1900, was the site of great days of recreation but also great tragedy. *Library of Congress, Detroit Publishing Company.*

shared that at times when he's riding near the monument, strange voices will break into his golf cart's two-way radio: voices saying "Help me" and "Help us."

Though the incident of June 1892 was tragic to be sure, and though it seems to have possibly left a supernatural imprint at the site of the tragedy, even this singular sorrow was deeply overshadowed by the many other deaths—accidental and willful—that would occur at Lincoln Park from 1893 to 1919. It was during those years, despite its beauty, that the park became the final destination for many who would accidentally die here—and many more who came here to take their own lives. In fact, it is estimated that during those years, over one hundred people lost their lives in Lincoln Park.

From its early days, most of the deaths here were of those—mostly children—who met their deaths on the Lake Michigan shore off the park or in the lagoon, which stretches between the park and the lake, just west of today's Lake Shore Drive. Others made their way to the relative tranquility of the park in desperate straits to poison themselves, drown themselves in the lake or one of the park ponds, shoot themselves or otherwise pass from their weariness by their own hands. Most who died by self-inflicted means, however, were the estimated fifty to one hundred souls who jumped—or otherwise did themselves in—from the top of a panoramic steel "high bridge" built over the lagoon in 1893: a walkway that quickly became known as "Suicide Bridge."

Though suicides and drownings had occurred in Lincoln Park before and after the Great Fire, a rash of deaths hit the headlines the year before the building of the High Bridge. Along with the lightning strike tragedy, a girl named Caroline Wolper, a domestic, disappeared from the home of her employers, complaining of headaches. Her body was found in November, badly decomposed on the Lincoln Park shoreline of Lake Michigan.

That same summer, a man walked to the park on an August night and swallowed a bottle of strychnine. He recovered, later telling police that a wound in his head was from attempting to mortally shoot himself the year before.

The following summer, at least three deaths occurred in Lincoln Park, including that of an unidentified woman, aged about fifty-five and dressed all in black, found floating in one of the ponds, and a dry goods merchant who committed suicide by shooting himself in the head at the park after losing all of his property the previous winter.

In the midst of this disturbing trend, the Lincoln Park commissioners announced, in the summer of 1893, the building of a bridge to span the lagoon and what was quickly becoming a popular carriageway between the lagoon and Lake Michigan—the future Lake Shore Drive. The bridge would be built at the cost of $20,000 and allow strollers to pass between the park and the lakeshore without walking the mile between Fullerton and North Avenues, the only pedestrian ways to the lake. The dimensions of the bridge remain a mystery, with estimates that it was four or five stories high and anywhere from forty to seventy-five feet in height. Photographs from the top of the bridge suggest that it was at least toward the higher end of those estimates, with today's current pedestrian and bike bridge across Lake Shore Drive a significantly more diminutive structure.

The bridge and other improvements planned for Lincoln Park seem to have been largely inspired by the World's Fair of 1893—which featured lagoons spanned by illuminated bridges, flanked by pristine gardens. I have heard it said that the High Bridge in Lincoln Park was so tall that on fair days, strollers could view the faraway fairgrounds in Jackson Park. Later, after the fair closed, the famed Ferris wheel would be temporarily relocated to Lincoln Park.

Later newspaper reports claimed that the first suicides from the High Bridge began in 1893, soon after its completion and opening. However, I have not yet been able to find any publications documenting these early events. Death did not take a holiday during the bridge building or during the immediate aftermath, however.

In mid-December 1893, probably around the time the bridge was completed, a Russian refugee committed suicide in Lincoln Park after fleeing the czar's army. He had been living in fear of capture, terrified of the punishment that would await. He had been told he would be sent to Siberia for the rest of his life and that his wife and children would be prevented from ever seeing him again.

On June 13, 1894, the body of a man was found in either the lagoon or North Pond near Fullerton Avenue in Lincoln Park. The man turned out to be a Maywood man down on his business luck who had drowned himself.

The next day, a druggist by the name of Mr. Merrill was found near death in Lincoln Park, suffering the effects of morphine poisoning. After Merrill later died at Alexian Brothers Hospital, a coroner's jury returned a verdict of "suicide while despondent."

In early July 1895, the body of a machinist named John Barnet was found in the lagoon opposite the Grant Monument at about 1:15 a.m. The body was discovered by a police officer on his park rounds when he saw something floating on the moonlit water. He rowed out to the object and discovered the badly decomposed corpse, which he towed to shore. The discovery was the end of a search that had gone on for days, after the dead man's wife received a letter, addressed to "My Dear Wife and Children," in which Barnet expressed affection for his family but an overpowering feeling that, due to his business failures, his life wasn't worth living.

Later that month, a man named John Tris was watching the boat races on the Lincoln Park Lagoon, standing on the bank near the High Bridge. At 3:30 p.m., without warning, Tris jumped into the water. Despite its depth of only five feet, his body did not resurface. A number of men who were waiting their turns to race responded to shouts for help from those who had seen Tris jump. The men dove under the surface to locate his body, a feat that took nearly thirty minutes. When he was finally recovered, Tris was long dead.

The next month, on August 10, 1895, little August Schaefer, eleven, fell into the lagoon and drowned while watching some workmen dig a trench near the boathouse. Later that month, the body of a man, identified as that of John Peterson, was found in the lagoon, a bullet wound in the center of his forehead. The man had been missing for days from the boardinghouse where he lodged. On the banks of the lagoon, police found his coat and hat and a revolver with one empty chamber. A recent immigrant, he had been unable to find work.

Less than a week later, Ella Olsen, a twelve-year-old girl, was found floating in the lagoon on a Friday afternoon. The previous day, the girl and her mother, along with another woman, had gone to the park to enjoy a picnic. The girl had run away from their picnic spot toward the High Bridge, intending to view the park from its summit in search of a better site for their lunch. She was not seen again until her body was discovered on the water the following day.

After a year of relative quiet, 1897 brought another epidemic of deaths in Lincoln Park—most suicides but some accidental. In May, three boys were walking along the Lincoln Park Lagoon when one of the boys, Johnnie Scott, tumbled in. His companions attempted to drag the boy out but were startled by the approach of a police officer and fled, dropping the boy back into the water in their retreat, after which he drowned.

In July, in view of dozens of spectators, a man paused at the top of the High Bridge, took off his coat and hat and then leaped to his death in the water below. In the pocket of his coat was a note reading, "Tired of life; no money; no work; no home."

Two days later, a twelve-year-old girl named Annie Schrelber was playing at the lagoon's edge when she slipped and fell, drowning moments later.

Later that year, several took their lives in Lincoln Park, including a woman named Maude Jennings, who jumped from the High Bridge in November after a small quarrel with her mother.

On the last day of the same month, a man named W.A Clark drowned himself in Lincoln Park after desperate attempts to find work failed. His wife later said that on the morning of his disappearance, he left the house with tears in his eyes.

Barely a week later, in early December 1897, a man named John Schwinen leapt from the High Bridge to crash through ice that had formed early in the season, drowning below the surface.

The day after Schwinen's death, the *Chicago Tribune* reported that the Lincoln Park Commission was discussing what to do about the rash of suicides from the Lincoln Park High Bridge, which distressingly had gained the nickname "Suicide Bridge."[41]

"The last suicide," remarked a reporter, "has called the attention of the Park Commissioners to the unusual favor that their sight-seeing structure seems to afford people searching for a spot to end their lives." One of the commissioners remarked that the number of suicides was relatively small compared to the number of people who enjoyed the bridge, but the commission's secretary said that something had to be done. There had been talk of boarding up the bridge entrances until "this peculiar mania…died out" or of tearing down the bridge. No one seemed to think these measures would stop those bent on killing themselves, but they did believe they would do it elsewhere and "save the reputation of the park."

It wasn't only political leaders who voiced concern over the suicides in Lincoln Park. The next Sunday after the commissioners' meeting, a local pastor preached on "The Fatal Bridge." In his sermon, the Reverend James of the Pilgrim Temple Baptist Church drew lessons from the sensational span, proclaiming:

> *Many of you have walked over it and admired its artistic features and its solidness. And yet persons have used that bridge for their own destruction. So it is that the gospel, which was ordained to be a savior of life, is used*

by many people as a savior of death unto death. You are horrified at the thought of that beautiful young girl throwing herself from that fatal bridge to a watery death. The country is shocked at the news of that gray-headed man who plunged himself upon the ice below amid the youth skating on its surface. Their physical suicide is horrible, though it is not to be compared with spiritual suicide. But does not a fatality attach to that high bridge? Witness the lives that have been thrown away from it. It is surely rightly named the "fatal bridge." [42]

The bridge suicides were taking another kind of toll as well: a supernatural one. By February 1898, sightings of ghosts were so common in Lincoln Park that the phenomenon was reported in the local papers, one reporter writing that cops on the night watch in the park were asking for transfers because of the strange experiences they were having on duty, both with the ghosts of the High Bridge suicides and others who died before the bridge was built. [43]

A park officer named McCarty was patrolling the zoo grounds one night when he came upon a small park enclosed by a fence. McCarty stopped dead in his tracks and watched as every swing on the playground swung violently back and forth in the wind and two white figures, human in form, glided between them without being struck, their hands waving wildly over their heads.

After his initial shock, the officer jumped the fence to confront the figures, who floated through the park and out of his grasp, over the frozen South Pond and past the statue of Benjamin Franklin, then out toward the High Bridge over the lagoon, disappearing.

Another park officer named Blaul talked about encountering a man robed in Mexican dress, including a wide sombrero, who had "two eyes…like sparks." When Blaul spoke to the figure, he received only a chilling laugh in return. The figure advanced toward the officer and was greeted with gunfire from Blaul. The shots, even at close range, failed to faze the figure, which then disappeared.

Reporters were quick to point out, however, that the ghosts at the park were not necessarily those of the bridge suicides:

The high bridge, with its haunting memory of unfortunates who from its top have flung themselves to death in the lagoon below, is held responsible by many for the appearances which have made the park at midnight an uncanny tramping ground. Other people say that Lincoln Park in all its parts has been a favorite suicide ground for years, especially a favorite dying ground for people who were discouraged because they could not find work, and that there is no more reason for believing the midnight wanderers are the disembodied spirits of high bridge victims than that they are the ghosts of those who have perished by their own hands in different places from the big hill on the north to the Lincoln monument on the south.

That spring, things reached an absurd level at the High Bridge when Paul Tustln, an acrobat, climbed up onto the bridge rail and tumbled backward into the water, performing a series of somersaults before striking the water. Bystanders, unaware of his identity at first, thought this the latest in the epidemic of suicides. In fact, Tustln had performed the feat as a stunt; when he swam to shore after his dive, panicked parkgoers told him they thought he was trying to kill himself, at which Tustln laughed and said, "In blue tights?" He was arrested for disorderly conduct.

Two months later, a laborer named Louis Rockne jumped from the bridge in front of hundreds of onlookers. In his pocket was a library card and a pawn ticket for his overcoat, which he'd pawned for one dollar.[44]

Not four days later, an unknown man walked through the park gate just north of the Grant Monument and threw himself into the lagoon. It took several hours of grappling to recover the man's body.

That September, a woman named Mrs. A.C. Sagert was found floating in the lake at the east end of the High Bridge. No motive was found for the apparent suicide; her husband believed the recent hot weather had made her delusional.

More strangeness developed at the bridge that winter when, in January 1899, a woman named Helen Case was found at the top of the High Bridge after disappearing from her home on the South Side. Friends claimed she was under the influence of hypnosis by a spiritualistic medium, though the man denied having put the woman under his power.

After a quiet summer, suicide returned to the park in the fall, when November brought news of an unidentified but well-dressed woman who threw herself into Lake Michigan from the Lincoln Park shore.

Just weeks later, in early December, a woman named Ida Washburn attempted to drown herself and her two small children in the lake after seven years of marital problems. A police officer found her kneeling on the shore. She said she was praying for forgiveness for what she was about to do. She later told authorities, "For seven years I have been a slave to the whims of my husband. He has beaten me until I was unable to move….He beat our children and called them the vilest of names."

The "Suicide Bridge" in Lincoln Park, 1900. *Library of Congress, Detroit Publishing Company.*

In late July 1900, a ten-year-old boy named Willie Ashton was fishing with his family on Lake Michigan's Lincoln Park shoreline when, frustrated by his luck, he made his way to the lagoon to try for fish there. His blue-banded hat was later seen floating on the water by his mother when she went in search of him. Her screams brought police, who attempted to calm her, but she refused to believe her child was dead—even after his lifeless body was dragged from the lagoon.

Later that summer, a man shot himself at the Lincoln monument in Lincoln Park, just behind the present-day Chicago History Museum. When he was first seen by a policeman from the East Chicago Avenue Police Station, he was still living, and an ambulance was sent for. He was removed to the German Hospital and died shortly after reaching there without regaining consciousness. In his pocket was found a letter addressed to "Nettie," saying, "I have been unable to find employment. I cannot stand this suffering and suspense any longer. Good-by."

By the summer of 1901, the contagion of suicides in Lincoln Park had become a serious concern, with many of the opinion that the waves of suicide were copycat actions resulting from "psychic suggestion" spawned by reports of the acts in the newspapers. In Kansas City, a place suffering its own suicide epidemic, a "ban" on coverage of suicides was suggested, with many urging publishers to downplay suicides in their coverage or to limit coverage of suicides altogether. In response, the chief deputy coroner of Chicago agreed with the tendency for copycatting, remarking:

> "If I should receive notice of a suicide by drowning today, I would confidently expect at least three more within the week with the same features." He said the same was the case with incidents of poisoning by carbolic acid, asphyxiation by hanging and other means prevail[ing]. "If these ghastly things were not published the Idea would not suggest itself to others who are tired of life." However, he admitted, "I don't think such a ban could be put on the newspapers of Chicago." [45]

A period of quiet followed the concerns of summer 1901, though whether this lull reflected a lack of suicides or a lack of their publication is unknown.

Whichever it was, by the following spring, suicide was back in the news when Howard Miller of Keokuk, Iowa, shot himself through the heart at the Lincoln monument. His body was found in the snow on the cold morning of March 30, his pockets stuffed with handwritten quotes from poems about death.

More followed that spring and summer, including a series of three in August. The last of those was of a man named Albert Samuelson, a Larrabee street tailor whose business had failed. His body was found in the lagoon under the High Bridge; in his pocket a note read, "No friends, no money, no work; better to die."

LATER THAT YEAR, a teenage girl named Salina Peterson walked out of her schoolroom at Northwest Division High School, telling her classmate to "look for the letters…they will explain everything." Her body was found partially embedded in the sand immediately south of the bridge. Among the many notes she had left to family and friends was a letter to her mother reading, "If my body is ever found, my dear mother, bury me in the plainest possible manner, for any magnificence will disturb my rest." Other letters explained that her failure to succeed at school had been too much for her to bear, as her mother had tried so hard to support and encourage her. She wanted, she said, to spare her mother any further suffering over her failures.

The following spring, a well-known high-end realtor named Z.H. Allen walked to Lincoln Park from his North Clark Street home, sat down and swallowed carbolic acid after a period of despondency.

The next year, in September 1904, an electrician named Stanley Ilumason walked to the top of the High Bridge and shot himself in the temple with a revolver.

In August 1905, an elderly man named August Eggers tried to slit his wrists while sitting at the arch of the High Bridge. A widower, it was said he had tired of years of loneliness.

The following spring, Anna Donnenmeyer, a mother of three small children, drowned herself in the Lincoln Park lagoon, despondent over an apparently terminal illness.

Just weeks later, the body of a Michigan man was found under the High Bridge; police could not be sure if his drowning was accidental or willful.

That summer, in mid-July, two girls walking through Lincoln Park found a woman's coat with a note pinned to it, reading, "Dear Ed, By the time you receive this I will be resting in the lagoon. I have kept my part of the pact. Be sure to keep yours. FROM YOUR ELLA." No body, however, was recovered.

That fall, in late October, a man named Alexander Evenoff, just twenty-seven, climbed to the top of the High Bridge and shot himself between the eyes.

The following spring, Adam Brewster, forty, tried to jump from the High Bridge after telling a park police officer he was "tired of life." He was promptly arrested.

That summer, in June 1907, two sisters, ten and twelve years old, drowned in the lake off Lincoln Park. The girls' parents believed one had drowned trying to save the other; however, the girls' grandmother told police she believed the girls had committed suicide because of abuse at home.

A month later, a man and his two daughters drowned in the Lincoln Park lagoon. Bystanders believed the man had died trying to save his children, who had fallen in.

A long span of years followed the summer of 1907 without mention of suicides or accidental deaths in Lincoln Park. One can only speculate if they did not occur or if the papers failed to report them.

It would be five years before the next story, when in July 1912 a man named Harry Meyer climbed onto the rail of the High Bridge with an open razor in his hand, "apparently undecided whether to jump or draw the steel blade across his throat." While he decided, a police officer placed him under arrest.

In February 1912, a man attempted to take his life by jumping into the lagoon just south of the High Bridge. When he hit the water, however, he changed his mind and began to call for help. Though police sent motorboats to rescue him, by the time boats arrived his body had disappeared below.

After 1912, the record goes dark, with no suicides or deaths recorded until 1919.

That June, a woman named Violet Martin was found, crying, near the Lion House in the Lincoln Park Zoo. "Let me alone....Let me die," she told police, who found her writhing in pain. She had taken bichloride of mercury. Family had committed her to Dunning Asylum. "For no reason," she said. The things she had endured there, a place known for its patients' torments, left death a preferable future. A note on her person said, "I hope I die in peace. I have suffered enough."

The next month, in late July, Bertha Keppler took her two baby daughters from their Hermitage Avenue home and led them to the top of Suicide Bridge. She had left a letter at home to her teenage daughter, reading, "I am tired of everything. My husband has been unkind to me. I am going to end it all." After being stopped by police from jumping with her children in her arms, she told police she had spent her last pennies on biscuits for her daughters, herself "consumed with hunger," before taking them to the bridge, determined to end their constant suffering from want.

This attempted murder-suicide of Bertha Keppler seemed to be the final straw for Chicago. A week later, park commissioners announced the closure of the entrances to the Lincoln Park High Bridge. Suicide Bridge was closed off to public access. Park superintendent John Cannon announced that the bridge was no longer safe and would likely never be used again.

Still, this would not be the end. A final suicide was to come. On September 28, 1919, two months after the closing of the bridge, a man scaled the barricade, walked to the center of the span and dove the sixty feet into the autumnal waters below. It took several hours to find his body with a grappling hook. The man had a red mustache. He wore well-beaten shoes. His name was Edward Hadick.

WHEN SUICIDE BRIDGE CLOSED in 1919, many traded reminiscences of the tragedy the bridge had not only seen but also inspired. Stories of love lost, business failed, lives of relentless depression, abuse and violence. Swirling around its dark history were, too, tales of the many accidents and suicides in the lagoon, the lake and Lincoln Park as a whole: the city's former cemetery that had seemed, somehow—to have developed a lust for blood.

Still, as one reporter remarked upon the beginning of the bridge's dismantling:

> *All these episodes are…of yesteryear. The famous arch, which rises forty-two feet above the lagoon, is closed to the happy and the forlorn alike, and the hand of death is upon it. Perhaps it will not even wait for the wrecker. It may heed the whispers of those restless ghosts and disappear, like the house of Usher, into the waters below.*[46]

Incredibly, Suicide Bridge would not go quietly. Devoid of any remaining willing victims, it tried for one more. On November 15, 1919, an ironworker, Frank Watts, was swept into the Lincoln Park lagoon while working on dismantling the bridge. He was saved by Patrolman William Stift, who jumped into the lagoon and bore him to shore.[47]

THE HEAD OF BELLE GUNNESS

Just outside of Chicago sprawls historic Forest Home Cemetery, one of the largest in Chicago's cemetery-studded expanse. In 2008, a fascinating and gruesome exhumation took place here: the disinterment of the headless body of a woman believed to be—or not to be—Belle Gunness, a brutal killer known by many as "Hell's Belle," who is believed to have killed between 40 and 180 people.

Gunness grew up in Norway in a family with few financial prospects. As a girl, she dreamed of following many of her compatriots to better days in the United Sates. As soon as she could, she immigrated to the States, vowing to end her poverty in the land of opportunity.

Reaching Chicago, Belle married Mads Sorenson, her first husband, in 1884. Belle and her husband opened a candy store in the Austin neighborhood and together had four children: Myrtle, Lucy, Axel and Caroline. They were also raising a foster child named Jennie Olsen.

It was during her time in Chicago—possibly inspired by the contemporary crimes of Chicago serial killer H.H. Holmes—that Gunness came up with the idea of committing insurance fraud to attain the wealth she had dreamed of in Norway. It was after this idea dawned that Gunness began to appear to be cursed with very bad luck.

First, the candy store burned down. Then, Caroline and Axel both tragically died of colitis. When Belle's husband then suddenly died of "colitis" as well, a doctor examined him more thoroughly and declared that he had been poisoned.

Belle Gunness seen here with her children before they began, one by one, to mysteriously perish—or disappear. *Library of Congress.*

The family doctor insisted that the man had died of a heart attack, and Gunness cashed in his insurance policies—not one, but two, as he had two policies that overlapped on the day he died, so Belle cashed in twice. She collected on him, the ruined business and the dead children and bought a farm in northwest Indiana, not far from Chicago. It wasn't long before there was another "accident" at the farm and a good deal of it burned in a fire, leading to more insurance funds.

Belle's second husband, Peter Gunness, began to suspect something when one of his own children died. He soon went the way of Mads, but this time, strychnine poisoning was discovered and an inquest held. However, despite the suspicions of many, Belle went free. She cashed in the insurance policy. She was, at the time, expecting Peter's child.

Belle then began advertising for husbands, much the way the like-minded H.H. Holmes had done.

"Bring money," she'd tell her romantic interests in gushing letters, "and don't tell anyone you're coming." Belle then would have these men essentially buy stock in her farm, killing them shortly thereafter. She would thereafter cut up their bodies and feed them to her pigs or bury them on the farm.

Then, in the spring of 1908 the Gunness farm burned again—this time completely. The bodies of Belle's dead children were found in the rubble, along with the headless corpse of a woman.

Most everyone believed that Gunness had been murdered—probably by someone aiming to avenge her evil deeds. But soon after the fire, a man arrived in LaPorte looking for his brother, Andrew Helgelein. He told police of the letters his brother and Belle had exchanged and of his brother's plans to go to his love in Indiana. He begged the police to find what he knew would be his brother's dead body.

Indeed, when police resumed their search of the farm, they discovered eleven bodies in the pigpen, among them Belle's foster child, Jennie. A dental bridge was found, too, among the fire's remains, and the coroner ruled that this proved the headless corpse was that of Gunness.

That fall, however, Belle's old farmhand, Ray Lamphere, was convicted of arson connected to the spring fire. And later, just before his death, he admitted he had aided Gunness in her diabolical schemes. He told of Belle's habit of luring men to the farm, only to kill them and add to her wealth. When she discovered that her scheme might soon be revealed, Belle planned to make an escape. She allegedly asked Lamphere to set fire to the house with her remaining children inside. They had been lovers; he complied. Lamphere claimed that, in order to escape the pursuit of the police, he'd agreed to help Gunness fake her own death. They'd traveled to Chicago and hired a "housekeeper" for the farmhouse. It was that woman, and not Belle, whose headless corpse had been found in the ruins of the farm fire. Belle Gunness—Hell's Belle—was at large. Or so Lamphere claimed.

Sightings of Belle were reported throughout the ensuing years. Many believe that she finally got her due in 1931, when a woman named Esther Carlson went on trial for murder. Carlson, who looked strangely like Gunness, had been charged with poisoning her husband in order to inherit his money. Interestingly, Carlson had no "footprint" before 1908—she didn't seem to exist before then, having no birth, census or other records to document her.

In 2007, Andrea Simmons, a graduate student at the University of Indianapolis, headed a team of forensic biologists through an investigation into the mystery of the identity of the headless "Murder Farm" corpse, which was interred at Forest Home Cemetery outside Chicago. Having received permission from Gunness's family members to exhume her body, the grave was opened and DNA samples taken from the body, in order to compare them to DNA from saliva on an envelope and stamp from a letter Belle had sent before her "death." Unfortunately, the samples taken from the artifacts were too old for a usable sample to be taken. The tests were deemed "inconclusive."

The exhumation led to other questions as well, as researchers found the bones of children in Belle's casket, along with the children—her children—who were buried separately beside her. Were these part of her own children's bodies—or of others she had killed?

In recent years, Markus Griffin, founder of Witches in Search of the Paranormal (WISP), went with his team to the farm to investigate and encountered some interesting things. A neighbor confided that a woman who had lived in the former Gunness farmhouse had found part of a human finger while gardening. And the man who currently owns the house claims to hear strange voices coming from the root cellar and the mysterious disappearance and reappearance of objects at the Gunness family home.[48]

THE OLD RED SHIP
AND A LADY IN BLACK

C hicago's well-storied Maxwell Street neighborhood has never been short on folklore. The jumble of life here has lived harder than most Chicagoans, seeing the place through from its tough days as the city's Jewish ghetto, to its glory days as urban marketplace extraordinaire, to its modern hard times as rickety holdout of all that is good and true in Chicago. Myths, too, are more monstrous here than in the city's other environs, from the legend of the devil baby who showed up in the early twentieth century on the doorstep of Jane Addams's nearby Hull House to the rumored ravings of former prisoners from the shuttered dungeon of the notorious Maxwell Street Police Station.

By the time it was glorified nationwide in the early 1980s, in the opening frames of the popular TV crime drama *Hill Street Blues*, the Maxwell Street Station (943 West Maxwell Street) had already endured nearly one hundred years of notoriety in its own town. From its inception, it ruled over the precinct the *Chicago Tribune* christened "Bloody Maxwell," a turn-of-the-nineteenth-century name that would fit well into the twenty-first. For this was "the crime center of the country," filled with "[m]urderers, robbers and thieves of the worst kind." And in those days of Eastern European immigration, and the later days of African American and Hispanic infusion, the Bloody Maxwell station was known variously as "The Old Red Ship," "The Old Fortress" and "The Rock of Gibraltar." Built to last in 1888, the red and gray stone building towered above the incessant swarm of life here, staking a claim for good at any cost in "the wickedest police district in the world."

Like the facts behind the beatings alleged to have occurred here with alarming frequency until its closing in 1951, the ghosts of the Twelfth District dungeon are hard to lay hands on. Despite their vagaries, however, they are easy to believe in. The dungeon's history is rife with shocking tales: the dozens of prisoners who "fell" down the two flights of marble steps to the front desk, the reported beatings on the kidneys with phone books, the sudden and numerous deaths of perfectly healthy inmates. Whether any of these stories are true, the living hell described by one prisoner was fact: thirty-one cells, four of them women's, were installed in the station's cellar during a surge in crime at the beginning of the twentieth century, during which officers at Maxwell wrote up a murder a day. For half a century, prisoners in the station's near-catacombs urinated, vomited and bled into troughs dug from the floor, the refuse flowing under the cells of a dozen fellow convicts. Rats flourished. The walls grew black and blue with graffiti.

Though the allegations of "lower Maxwell" beatings were halted by the mid-century shutdown of the basement cells, rumors of the cells' continued use abounded, in and out of police circles. Though the station and the city denied such charges, the dungeon bars were sawed down to the floor sometime in the 1970s.

Though the Old Red Fortress has, like much of the Maxwell Street neighborhood, been consumed by the University of Illinois at Chicago, stories of its dungeon prevail, along with reports of bloodcurdling cries seeping from the basement windows. Also alive and well is another neighborhood mystery: a local legend known only as the Lady in Black.

Hailing from the earliest days of "Bloody Maxwell," as betrayed by her period clothing, a silent female phantom has been known to play both guardian angel and prophetess to unsuspecting citizens. I was first introduced to her as a teenager, when I heard from my dad's old police friends a tale of the harrowing rescue of a motorcyclist that had occurred on the Dan Ryan Expressway in the Maxwell Street area. As the biker was lying near death by the side of the road where he had been thrown, a woman in nineteenth-century dress—jet black—with a black covering around her face had appeared beside him, kneeling down and staying with him until paramedics arrived and then vanishing into thin air. Paramedics testified that the man had told this story to them upon their arrival but that no woman was seen by the first responders. His injuries, which he was not expected to survive, quickly healed, amazing the doctors who attended him in the weeks that followed.

IN LATER YEARS, I was astonished when the television program *Unsolved Mysteries* featured the story of a man named Robert Davidson, a motorcyclist who was struck by lightning in June 1980 while pulled over during a storm on the interstate near Acton, Indiana.

Davidson instantly fell to the ground, dead, smoke pouring from the wound made by the bolt. Paramedics were called and tried to revive the man, but they could not coax a heartbeat from his frame. Then, something truly weird happened. The paramedics reported that their ambulance went dead, all of their equipment fizzling into darkness and silence. At the same time, motorists who had stopped to aid the victim claimed that a chill rippled through their bodies. Then a stranger appeared out of nowhere: a small woman, dressed in black clothing of antiquity, with black flowing hair framing her face. "I must touch him!" she cried, as she pushed through the crowd, arm outstretched. A silver cross shone on her breast, and she wore high button shoes and held a Bible in her hand. The woman knelt beside the man and recited Psalm 23: "The Lord is my shepherd, I shall not want."

Onlookers, amazed, noticed that—in the pouring rain—the woman did not get wet. After finishing, the woman smiled at the paramedics and vanished in the crowd, never to be seen again. At once, the ambulance equipment blared to life and Davidson opened his eyes. Later, many at the scene—including one of the paramedics—claimed that they had seen no woman there.

OTHER STORIES HAVE SURFACED over the years, with reports of aid from a mysterious Lady in Black told by residents and passers through Chicago's near west side Italian neighborhoods. One man spoke of being suicidal in the 1970s after losing his job and his wife filing for divorce. He had gone to a park near the University of Illinois with the intention of slitting his wrists. He was sitting next to a tree sometime after midnight when a woman appeared, standing next to him, dressed in black, with a black habit around her face and a crucifix around her neck. She said, with some ferocity, "Go home." The man had attended Catholic schools and, conditioned to obey the nuns who had taught him, got up and did as she said, going to his family home and ringing the bell. There, he told his wife what had happened and about the woman. His wife's face, which had been angry and hard, softened as she listened. She was deeply moved by the story and agreed to continue to work on saving their marriage. They did.

Similarly, in the late 1960s, a Chicago Police recruit encountered a mysterious woman outside a local eatery not far from the expressway where the motorcyclist had met his own mysterious stranger. The meeting would remain with him more than thirty years later:

I was twenty years old. I was enrolled in the Chicago Police Academy, which was located near Maxwell Street and the Dan [Ryan] expressway. I had been attending the academy for several months and was taking lunch with two other academy students. As we entered a small restaurant in this area, I remember a white lady dressed in all black clothes. Her dress reminded me of someone from the 1800s, and the reason I mentioned her color is because the area was basically a black neighborhood and seeing a white lady in this area made this individual encounter even stranger.

Now, as I stood in the entryway to the restaurant with my friends on either side of me, this Lady in Black came up to me and looked right into my eyes. Without a word or hand gesture or even a facial expression, she somehow communicated to me to hand her the pen and small note pad I had in my upper left-hand shirt pocket. I did just that without knowing exactly why. She took the pen and note pad and wrote something into the note pad. Then she looked at me and shook her head in a gesture of no, no, no. She handed me the pen and note pad and left abruptly.

I looked into the note pad and noticed what she wrote: my name and my birth date. But then I also realized that it was in my own handwriting. I quickly turned to my friends and asked them, Did you see what the lady just did? They responded to my question as though I was crazy: What lady? They acted as if nothing unusual happened, and we went into the restaurant and had lunch.

Well, this strange little encounter stayed with me, and [because of it] I always felt that I would have to quit the Chicago Police Department someday.

I felt she was telling me to leave this career in order to save my life.

Happily, this young recruit stayed out of the way of danger, but he had many close calls. And he never forgot—each time one occurred—what the mysterious Lady in Black had done and what she had known.

I have come to believe that encounters with this mysterious Lady in Black of the Near West Side may have their origins in the story of one of Chicago's real-life saints: a dynamic Italian American woman named Frances Xavier Cabrini.

Born in Italy, Mother Cabrini was sent to the United States in 1889 to minister to the swelling immigrant population in New York City. She went on to establish more than sixty institutions, including hospitals, schools and children's homes across the Americas. Mother Cabrini became the first naturalized U.S. citizen to be canonized; she is the patron saint of immigrants.

A great deal of Cabrini's work centered on Chicago, with her base of operations Columbus Hospital in Lincoln Park, where she also lived. Upon her death at the hospital just before Christmas 1917, penitents began to travel to the hospital to visit her former room and pray. A national shrine was erected at the site in 1955. Though the hospital was demolished in recent years, the saint's former room was dismantled and rebuilt as an annex to the shrine, which still stands today.

One night, some twenty years after Mother Cabrini's death, a torrential rain was beating down on Chicago when a cab driver, peering through his windshield, saw an elderly nun, clothed in black, making her way along the street. He rolled down his window and urged her to get in his cab. She did.

The woman said she was going to Columbus Hospital in Lincoln Park, where she lived with the other sisters of her order. The night was dark, and the driver could barely see through the windshield, but he followed her directions and headed through the rain to the hospital.

They were far from the destination and began to talk. They talked about current events: the Ohio River flood and the Spanish Civil War. They talked about the First World War, and then the nun said something terrifying: Soon, she said, another war would come—far worse. Atrocities would eclipse anything mankind had seen. America would be attacked on its own soil by vicious enemies different from any they had fought before. Prayer was of the utmost importance, as was charity to all who would suffer in the terrible days to come.

The driver thought little of the conversation aside from the manner in which the nun had spoken. More of fact than opinion, he would remember years later. Arriving finally at the hospital, the nun thanked the man and bid him goodnight, getting out of the car and disappearing behind the large oak door of the building.

The driver pulled away and soon picked up another rider in the rain. But when the passenger got in, he exclaimed, "Oh sorry! I almost sat on your Bible! Better keep that dry up next to you!"

"Oh! I had a nun before you. She must have left it!" he said.

The man handed the driver a worn black Bible, tattered with years of reading, and he put it on the seat next to him. When he dropped off his fare, the driver returned to Columbus Hospital to return the Bible. He double-parked his cab and went up through the rain to the door, knocking loudly.

In a minute, a young nun answered, smiling. "May I help you?" she asked. "Visiting hours are over, I'm afraid."

"No, no," the man answered. "I'm not visiting. I just wanted to return this. I drove home your Mother Superior this evening, and she left this in my cab." He held out the Bible.

The young girl laughed. "I see," she said. "She certainly is forgetful, even after death!"

The man looked at the girl, bewildered. In answer, she swung the heavy door open, revealing the dim entrance hall of the hospital. She gestured to a large illuminated portrait that hung on the wall before them: a portrait of the smiling nun from his evening trip.

"Is that the woman you drove here?" the girl asked.

"That's her!" he affirmed.

"That's our Mother Cabrini," said the girl. "She founded this hospital—and she died twenty years ago."

THOUGH MOTHER CABRINI LIVED mainly in the Lincoln Park hospital where she died, her countrymen and women—the Italians of Chicago—had always made their homes on the Near West Side, the site where the extension hospital was built. Today, though that hospital, too, is gone—the old building turned into condos—Chicago's "Little Italy" still thrives here, though greatly diminished by the march of history and the University of Illinois, which took over most of the area.

I firmly believe that this powerful woman is still ministering here to her countrymen and women who loved her so in life—but that her intercession and help has sometimes traveled far beyond Chicago…perhaps even to the storm-riddled Indiana roadside of 1980 and the side of Robert Davidson.

THE GREAT GHOST PANIC OF 1908

It is a well-known fact among historians that many great mob actions have occurred in the month of July. Such was the case in the summer of 1908, when on the last day of the month, a house at 181 West Twenty-First Street drew a crowd of what the press reported at five thousand people. They had thronged the house hoping for a look at the specters that had been seen in this "haunted house."

Men, women and children pushed, pulled and fought one another to get close to the place—but not too close, because all seemed just a little bit timid. Mothers with children in their arms and others clinging to their skirts would shove through the throng, scrambling until they were near the ghosts' habitat, then scurry away. Automobiles and wagons lined the streets for blocks and at times got so thick that streetcar traffic in Leavitt Street was tied up until the police opened a passage.

Thirty patrolmen attempted to subdue the crowd, resulting in eight arrests taken to the Hinman Street station and thrown in the lockup on charges of disorderly conduct. The crowd was so unruly that a fire hose was called for from the local engine company:

> *Streams of water were poured into the crowd, which then fled in all directions. Several times the police thought they had the crowd scattered and shut down the water, but the people flocked back and took up more advantageous positions.*
>
> *This ghost panic had been going on for days when this thrilling evening arrived. So disruptive were the reports that detectives were put on the case*

to solve the mystery of the strange reports. This "spook squad," as they were called, was certain that the haunting tales had at their root a simple joke which had been played by a visitor to the home the week before. The Batcheldor [sic] family, who owned the house, had hosted a party and, during the course of the evening, a table was overturned. A guest yelled "Spooks!" which caused some kind of mass chaos and exodus from the house by the women in the next room who had overheard the crash. Intending to play a joke and scare the women further, the guest pulled some pictures off the wall and stopped the clocks, so that when the women re-entered they found a shambles and the eerie timepieces.

The "spook squad" announced plans to arrest the joker, but the woman of the house, Mrs. William Bachelder, refused to enter it. Her brother, too, was convinced of the haunting, claiming to have seen "the table spin about the dining room and…the knocks on the wall."

In short order, the local Spiritualists showed up to the house to attempt communication with the resident phantom, but none succeeded. With the house abandoned by its owners, one of the Spiritualists was allowed to stay in the house overnight, but he had no luck tapping into any ethereal conversations.

The next night, thousands gathered again at the house, leading to the arrest of ten more men and boys, who were first hosed down again by the local fire department, still refusing to leave. The howling mob swirled through Twenty-Third Street from Hoyne Avenue to Leavitt Street, catcalling and challenging the ghost to show itself.

Police stationed themselves around the house but could not keep the crowd at bay and called for reserves. Fifty additional offers were sent to assist, but they "were swept about in the turbulent mob like straws in a Niagara."

After the crowd was finally dispersed that night, the house was locked up, with no more Spiritualists allowed. The Bachelders had fled to the home of Mrs. Bachelder's mother, as none of the family was "willing to undergo the blood chilling, nerve freezing horror of the table rappings, the stopping of clocks, the moans, moving of pictures, and jumping of furniture that has cursed the place."

Mrs. Bachelder reported that her family had bought the house the first week in July and that the former owners seemed eager to move out but would not reveal why. The incidents, she said, began the Sunday after their arrival, and not at the previous week's party as the press had reported. As she told it, the previous owner had died in the house, his sons contesting the will while his body was still cold, and a candle had mysteriously ignited the man's clothing. When her own family moved in, a photograph of the man in the house fell to the floor, and then the chairs in the house began to moan, making sounds like the low keening of pigeons. The clocks began to stop at seven o'clock in the evening, the time the previous owner had allegedly died. Mrs. Bachelder claimed that the occurrences went on consistently, but she was the only one who believed they were paranormal in origin—at first:

> *My husband laughed until a week ago tonight. He had always called it some kind of a practical joke. But a week ago last night…my brother was seated in the dining room. Mr. and Mrs. Charles Hesher and others of my family were in the front parlor. Suddenly Harry, white as paste, came rushing into the room….I hear it! he cried. But there was no need for him to warn us. A long, low moan that ran up my spine like a mouse clinging to the spinal cord came from the room just vacated. The great dining table lifted itself into the air and moved about the room. We fled.*[49]

When all else had failed, Mrs. Bachelder told reporters she was planning to turn to prayer and that she hoped her church would send someone to come and pray in the house and release its ghosts.[50]

It is presumed they were successful. No further reports appeared in the papers about the haunted house of Twenty-First Street—or the Great Ghost Panic of 1908.

THE DEMON OF LEMONT

A t the turn of the nineteenth century, the Willmans farm was one of many that sprawled in Lemont, Illinois, just south of Sag Bridge. Like other surrounding towns, the farming and quarrying town of Lemont had not seen much of any excitement since the time of the building of the Illinois & Michigan Canal many years before. Village life was as peaceful as it could be, and the Willmans farm was one of the collection of typical sleepy homesteads in the region.

Until the day the demon came.

One evening, in the fall of 1901, while the Willmans family was sitting down to dinner—father, mother and four children between the ages of twelve and sixteen—a letter dropped out of the air near the ceiling and landed in the middle of the dining room table. The bewildered family looked at one another, then—after a few long moments—Mrs. Willmans carefully picked up the letter and opened it. The letter was written in a difficult hand, as of a young child, with capital and lowercase letters mixed up and numerous spelling errors. The message, however, was clear: whoever or whatever had written the letter stated that the family had ten days to leave the house or some dreadful tragedy would befall them. Shocked and horrified, Willmans told his wife to burn the letter.[51]

When the family did not vacate the farm, more letters appeared, taking on a tone of viciousness and falling from the air at the feet of the horrified family members. There were numerous letters threatening to kidnap the younger children and a distinctly malicious attack on one of the children,

Anna, whose mother had died at the age of thirty-five. She received a letter that said, "You will live no longer than your mother. You don't know what killed her, but I do!"

The letters increased as the days wore on, as the entity alternated between threatening the family and predicting visits from family and friends and other future events.

The family's cows also became involved. When Mr. Willmans and his son were milking them one day, his son cried out, "Father! My cow is giving cheese instead of milk!" Sure enough, when Mr. Willmans looked into the pail, the milk had turned to cheese when it touched the pail. That same day, Willmans had seen a black cat wandering around the farm and shot at it to chase it off.

That night, the family received a letter stating, "Do you want to know why your cows have stopped giving milk? I did it!…You thought you'd put a shot in me, didn't you?"

Word got around that a black cat had been speaking to the family through mysterious letters, and talk of witchcraft and demons spread like wildfire through the village.

And the letters still came, written on every kind of paper the entity could find, and sometimes in ink, in pencil or even in the bluing Mrs. Willmans used for the laundry. The family's pen, which was kept in a cupboard with writing paper and pads, would disappear just before the family received a letter and then be returned again to its rightful place, though the doors never opened.

The family's dog seemed keenly aware of what was happening. When the dog was outside before a letter dropped, he would begin to bark and howl and claw at the door of the house, desperate to get inside at something. When let in, however, he would run inside and stop dead in his tracks in front of some invisible presence, running back to the door and whining to get out.

The demon or whatever it was also played tricks on visitors, including a family member who came to visit one Sunday. He and the family sat in the parlor to talk. The visitor had hung up his coat and hat on the coat rack in a corner of the room. After their visit, he rose to leave and went to the coat rack, which had been in full view the entire time, to get his things. His hat was gone, and the front of his coat had been smeared with butter. The hat was found in the garden, tattered and filled with dirt and rotten apples. Mrs. Willmans opened the cupboard, which was also in full view of everyone, and took the lid off the butter crock. Inside she found an indentation of fingers as if someone had scooped out a handful of it.

When the family's nerves were close to the breaking point, they turned to the Church.

At the time, Father Westarp was the pastor of St. Alphonsus Church in Lemont, and the Willmans family begged him to come to the house to help them. Father Westarp had not been quick to believe what was happening to the family. He later told a reporter he was "extremely puzzled" by the goings-on at the Willmans farm, as they seemed to have no place in the progressive world of the dawning twentieth century:

> *In this age of the world it appears absurd to talk of ghosts or evil spirits, and so I would have said before investigating what is going on at the Willmans' place. But what I have witnessed there with my own eyes and what has been told me by persons whom I know to be absolutely reliable leaves me no option but to believe that an agency that is not mortal is responsible for them.*

Father Westarp finally complied, obtaining permission from Archbishop Feehan to perform an exorcism of the house. Westarp arrived at the farm several days later, accompanied by another priest, Bibles and holy water in hand. Father Westarp "exorcised" the house, going from room to room giving a house blessing, with a different prayer for each room to rid whatever human or non-human spirits might be there. When he finished, his colleague did the same.

After the exorcism, Father Westarp put a piece of paper and a pencil on the kitchen table, and the two priests and family went outside for several minutes. This was in keeping with the Roman Catholic Rite of Exorcism, which demands that, before departing, a demon must give its name and reason for infesting the human or humans it has troubled. When the family and priests reentered the house, the paper was blank, a sign that the demon—if that's what it was—had no intention of leaving. Indeed, though the house was quiet for three days, the letters and torments began again, starting with a note that mocked the exorcism: "How I did laugh at seeing you all on your knees and praying! What do you think of such a letter? It must be a demon!"

Another letter repeated, almost word for word, the private conversation the priest and Mrs. Wellmans had had outside the house after his visit, laughing at the advice he had given her.

FATHER WESTARP HAD INSTRUCTED Mrs. Wellmans to remove all of the writing paper in the house, and she complied. But the entity was industrious. Soon after the exorcism, a letter written on a piece of Mrs. Wellmans's hatbox fell out of the air. She burned a piece of blessed palm the pastor had given her and blew the smoke into the inkwell, thinking this should take care of the nuisance. Indeed, the demon no longer used the ink but resorted to the pencil.

As for the source of the manifestations, the consensus in the village was that it was obviously demonic. The black cat had spoken, and the entity had mocked the sacred Rite of Exorcism. Word got around that Father Westarp had a theory that the family had possession or knowledge of the Seventh Book of Moses, a book of necromantic knowledge believed to have once been part of the Scriptures, but the priest denied having made such a suggestion.

Some, of course, suggested that the children were responsible for the diabolical letters, but Father Westarp quickly dismissed this theory, based upon the foul language and outright blasphemy many of the letters had contained—and the fact that all members of the family and often visitors were present when many of the letters arrived.

Mrs. Wellmans wondered if, since the farm was supposed to be sold by the owners the next year, a potential buyer might be trying to spoil the value of the property. Still, she said, there was no way to explain just how the letters made their way into view from thin air or how any of the other myriad phenomena had actually been created.

Her only explanation was witchcraft.

MRS. JEKYLL AND HYDE

In October 1907, Dr. Axel Gustafson addressed a lunchtime crowd of members of the Society of Psychic Research at Chicago's Auditorium Assembly Hall. The topic was one with which everyone had been obsessed as of late: a wealthy Milwaukee socialite who had been arrested for multiple jewel thefts in Chicago. These meetings were popular—this one more than usual—and the place was packed. Among the crowd were members of the press as well, including a reporter from the *Inter Ocean*, who reported the next day on the extraordinary claims of the esteemed Dr. Gustafson: that the baffling Evelyn Romadka was possessed by a devil.

Romadka was wealthy—very, very wealthy. But this did not prevent her from burglarizing multiple houses in Chicago and stealing tens of thousands of dollars in jewels. Bizarrely, Evelyn would apply for positions as a housekeeper with wealthy families and then, when hired, set about finding the location of the family jewels, only to swipe them.

After several successful heists, Romadka was arrested and convicted for stealing from the house of a couple she just randomly observed leaving their home without locking the door. She waited until it was all clear, then went through the house and searched for booty, finding it in an alligator pocketbook containing $1,000 worth of jewels.

A detective arrived on the scene after the couple called police, finding evidence of the theft. After visiting the house, the lieutenant visited a local café to think the case over. At the next table sat a well-dressed woman—with an alligator purse on the table.

He followed the woman out of the café and trailed her for some time, until he found himself in a social gathering with her and could ask others in the crowd her identity. He discovered that she was a popular socialite in Milwaukee, the wife of a wealthy and successful trunk maker. He learned, too, about her strange penchant for jewel theft. Further investigation led to Romadka's arrest in October 1907. When police called Evelyn's husband, the shock was almost palpable.

Romadka confessed to the string of previous thefts and, in her confession, told of a Chicago man with whom she had fallen in love. She said that she had committed the burglaries in order to lavish him with these expensive gifts.

Evelyn's devotion to her lover remained true. When they sought to arrest him, she told police she couldn't remember his name. Searching her room, however, police found her list of phone numbers—including that of William Jones, Romadka's lover. Police tracked down the address and tapped the phone line. As a result, they heard the man tell his "wife" to destroy a trunk in the house and hide its contents. The house was raided and the trunk opened; inside were the stolen jewels.

This was where the very high strangeness began. When arrested, Jones bragged that he had an "evil influence" over Romadka, and indeed, she fainted when she saw him. Both Romadka and Jones were sentenced and sent to Joliet Prison. Romadka's husband divorced her. But the story was far from over.

Evelyn Romadka was released from prison in January 1910. By the next summer, Chicago Police were on her trail again, as she was found to have drugged a couple in a bar and stolen from them more than $900 and a diamond stickpin.

After the investigation into this theft, it was revealed that Romadka was the leader of a gang of Chicago "Vampire Women," who charmed travelers to Chicago, only to steal their valuables. Chicago's Vampire Women were eventually found and charged—all but one. Their leader, Evelyn Romadka, disappeared from Chicago and was never seen again.

THE BIZARRE TALE OF the Vampire Queen of Chicago led certain occult practitioners in Chicago, including Gustafson, to wonder if there was some supernatural influence working on Romadka that had led this wealthy and respectable businessman's wife to turn to a life of burglary, fornication and other debauchery. One of the clues was the ominous "power" her lover claimed to have over her, leading some to believe that Romadka had been the equivalent of "possessed."

Romadka was, Dr. Axel Gustafson declared to a gathering of the Society of Psychic Research, inhabited by a "demon, the disembodied spirit of some marauder." The spirit, he guessed, must have been "some blundering Viking or pirate of the seas" or even a modern spirit who had led a life of thievery, working out "its evil desires in her." Gustafson believed this would be Romadka's best line of defense in her trial, and many agreed.

How else, they wondered together, could she have simply walked into the houses of the wealthy, under the most rigorous scrutiny, and walked out again with the family's guarded treasures? And how, too, could she even find them, when the wealthy were known to secret their jewels where no one could? However, said Dr. Gustafson:

> *This ghost could enter the houses of the rich without being suspected, for no one could see him. He would notice that the jewelry was within reach, and then would get her to reach for him, because he, being nothing but ghost, had no hands with which to pick up necklaces and rings.*

Gustafson went on to suggest an interesting theory that still has many proponents today in the world: that the commission of crime can be tied to control by evil forces:

> *The disembodied spirit, earthbound by its desires, will continue to roam over the earth seeking attachment, to some mortal through whose bodily organism it can obtain satisfaction for its cravings....They succeed in this with people, good or bad, who are susceptible, sensitive and possessed of little self-control, changing them temporarily.*[52]

Interestingly, Gustafson spoke to the rapt audience about an event in Romadka's life he felt had been the turning point for her. Back in Wisconsin as a young, married woman, Evelyn had become pregnant. The pregnancy was fraught with difficulty, prompting her husband to bring in the greatest specialists to tend to her. Family and friends observed that her personality underwent a change during this time and that she was never the same. Soon after, she disappeared to Chicago.

Gustafson believed that the trauma of childbirth had created a weakness in Evelyn that had allowed "that thieving spirit to enter and compel her to steal to satisfy its craving for theft....Manifestly, her depredations were not due to criminal motive on her part but to an overpowering evil influence. She is not personally guilty, of course, and should not be held responsible according to criminal law."

After the doctor's speech that day at the Society of Psychic Research, Evelyn Romadka's own doctor—or "healer"—addressed the crowd. Agreeing with his colleague's assessments of the case, Dr. Sheldon Leavitt affirmed that many people of the day were under the same kind of influence his patient had suffered. He pointed out, however, that both bad and good spirits are looking for bodies to inhabit, and both do succeed.

But, he cautioned, one should not open oneself to such possession. After all, he warned, "It is not safe to take chances on the character of a perfectly strange ghost that wants to make friends."

THE DEVIL BABY

As a champion of women's independence and the founder of one of progressivism's most controversial institutions, much was asked of Jane Addams, one of the first social workers and among the most influential of the nation's progressivist leaders. Addams was able to provide most of what she was asked for: shelter to the homeless, food to the hungry, encouragement to the hopeless, protection from abusive injustice. But there came a brief period in the life of her pioneering Chicago settlement house, Hull House, when the needs of its visitors became insatiable—when women began arriving there by the handful demanding to see the "Devil Baby."

Stories of devil children were not new. Other such tales peppered the headlines in the late nineteenth and early twentieth centuries. In 1888, a Polish neighborhood just south of Cleveland, Ohio, was searching for the father of a devil child, "red in color, covered with hair, having incipient horns and tail, and claw-like hands, and wing-like protuberances on the back." Several years later, a Minnesota woman went mad after giving birth to a "devil child" after turning away a Bible salesman who knocked on her door. The woman is said to have proclaimed she'd rather have the devil in her house than such a book, after which the salesman apparently put some sort of hex on her, cursing the imminent birth. Years later, Detroit was rocked by the news of a similar "devil kid" who refused to eat food, instead snatching coals from the stove to munch on with its full set of sharp teeth, between bouts of blaspheming and mockery of its poor parents.

In all of these instances and others, stories of these diabolical children were sensations, leading to alleged offers of carnival and museum operators to "buy" the children, hawkers charging money to see them and bewildered parents fending off throngs of visitors certain that they harbored the children. For each of the stories, there was an attendant backstory: the woman who turned away the salesman or—in another—a woman who scoffed at a religious icon. In still another case, a woman had done no more than view a play featuring a demonic character.

The Hull House baby was different. There was no doubt on the streets of Chicago that the baby had been born in a tenement on the Near West Side and brought to Hull House by its beleaguered parents. But unlike the other stories, the backstory of this child differed, depending on who was telling it. There were different cultural specifics but a moral common to them all: the father of the baby had been punished with the evil offspring for his ingratitude for the expected baby or mistreatment of his pregnant wife and her cultural traditions.

Italian women described a young Catholic girl who had foolishly married an atheist. After she hung a portrait of the Blessed Virgin on their apartment wall, her husband ripped it down, proclaiming that he'd rather have the devil in the house than such a picture. The Devil Baby was his punishment for that preference.

A Jewish version described the sheepish mother of a handful of daughters and a heartless husband in search of a son. When his wife became pregnant again, the husband clearly announced his preference that she give birth to the devil before another girl. That bitter proclamation sealed the child's fate.

Just as the causes of the catastrophe varied, so did descriptions of the resulting imp. Though most described a simple horned baby, the more animated narrators added a tail or hooves. Many told of how the child had been born blaspheming and cursing its parents with unimaginable language. In other accounts, the child was fond of smoking cigars and laughing incessantly at its poor parents. Finally, after struggling to control the damned thing, the father hopelessly took it to the heroine of Hull House, Jane Addams herself. Allegedly, Hull House workers had the baby taken to a local church for baptism, but it struggled out of the priest's grasp and began to dance along the back pews. Unable to pacify the evil infant, Addams kept it locked under supervision in an upstairs room at Hull House, where, according to most later versions of the story, it eventually died.

After the first group of women pushed through the front door demanding a look at the child, the parade of the curious appeared

Left: Jane Addams, one of the first social workers, is renowned today for her progressive reform, but Hull House, the settlement house she founded on Chicago's Near West Side, is known as the city's most haunted house—and was known to be haunted even when Addams moved in well over a century ago. *Library of Congress; photograph by Underwood and Underwood.*

Below: Hull House became a point of pilgrimage for Chicagoans, who flocked here to see the "Devil Baby." *John B. Stephens.*

unstoppable. Each day for six weeks, women of every class and culture streamed into the settlement house hoping to return home with a tale of the alleged incarnation. Each day, Addams turned them away with growing annoyance at what she saw as a pathetic oppression of immigrant women by their old-world superstitions, and "the 'contagion of emotion' added to that 'aesthetic sociability' which impels any one of us to drag the entire household to the window when a procession comes into the street or a rainbow appears in the sky."

Bewildered by the story's hold on the public imagination, yet unable to persuade the curious of the tale's falsehood, Addams resorted to private interviews with each of the older visitors. In the course of these sessions, she discovered a common quality of desperation among them. Listening with interest to their versions of the stories and the circumstances of their own lives, Addams became aware that the tale was serving a serious need—that of exhausted, ignored and forgotten women to be heard. By hastening to Hull House in search of this monstrous infant, they were rushing for a chance to win the respect of their husbands, children and neighbors, to seize the spotlight for a moment before slipping back into a painful obscurity. As Jane Addams herself wrote, "Because the Devil Baby embodied an underserved wrong to a poor mother, whose tender child had been claimed by the forces of evil, his merely reputed presence had power to attract to Hull-House hundreds of women who had been humbled and disgraced by their children."[53]

Intriguingly, one obscure version of the Devil Baby story ties it to the urban legend known as the "Devil in the Dancehall," one incidence of which was alleged to have occurred in Chicago's Bridgeport neighborhood, a short distance from Hull House. Some curiosity apparently arose as to whether a hooved stranger who appeared in the crowd at that dancehall may have impregnated one of the young women at the dance, perhaps a Hull House resident out for an evening of merriment, a welcome reprieve from the trials of everyday life.

Though most accounts of the Devil Baby story begin and end at Hull House, others have speculated that the baby was taken out of the house and sent by the humanitarian Addams to a more isolated home, perhaps even the Waukegan retreat house she founded on the North Shore.

Today, among believers in the existence of a so-called Devil Baby of Hull House, there continues a debate between those who believe that the baby was just that—an earthly manifestation of diabolical origin—and those convinced that the child was, sadly but simply, a deformed infant brought to Hull House by a destitute mother. Believers in the second likelihood also assume that the child either died at Hull House or was sent from public scrutiny to a quieter shelter outside the city.

Whether or not a baby, deformed or demonic, was ever brought to Hull House, belief in the fact has remained fierce. The widespread popularity of the Hollywood film *Rosemary's Baby*, which legend holds was inspired by the Hull House story, has proven that the appeal of the tale is hardly provincial, though local accounts persist of an evil little mug that glares out of the upstairs window, as do reports of foggy upper windows and feelings of unease.

Adding to the building's mystery have been the paranormal reports of so many visitors over the years, who claim that not only is the house haunted but also the garden between the original house and the dining hall built by Addams after she moved in. Mediums and clairvoyants claim there is a "portal" or interdimensional doorway in this area, possibly opened by Native Americans when white encroachment forced them from early Chicago.

Others have spoken about an "abortion graveyard" here in the garden, as Addams was an early advocate of birth control and abortion, which she and other progressives held to be tools of empowerment for women. Whether abortions were done at Hull House we do not know, but it is certainly possible given the radically progressive nature of Addams and many of her staff.

During her lifetime, Addams did what she could to prevent this "haunting" of Hull House. Soon after the phenomenon, she seized the opportunity to proselytize on the wretched state of women's lives, sharing her visitors' stories with the readership of the *Atlantic Monthly* in October 1916 and emphasizing her belief that the old women who came to visit the Devil Baby believed that the story "would secure them a hearing at home…and as they prepared themselves with every detail of it, their old faces shone with a timid satisfaction."

These days, as busloads of ghost hunters eyeball Hull House hoping for a glimpse of a gruesome little face, a misty window or a filmy form on the staircase, Jane Addams must turn in her grave, disgusted by what she felt was a foul and fantastic fairy tale. Yet even the realistic progressivist was not altogether grounded in "modern" convictions. During her own administration of Hull House, Addams engaged in at least one superstition of her own: placing pails of water at the threshold of her bedroom…to keep the ghosts away.

THE HAUNTING
OF BACHELORS GROVE

Bachelors Grove was a tiny but important settlement that had grown up around a timber stand in present-day Oak Forest. Stephen Rexford, the area's first settler, had come from New England to the future site of Chicago with a wave of English bachelors in the early 1830s and was part of the first land sales in that era. Other bachelors followed and, later, German farm families who improved the area with farms and homesteads. But the coming of the railroads and the burgeoning of cities emptied out the area by the turn of the twentieth century, with many going on to Iowa, Nebraska or California—or back to Chicago with the growth of opportunities there. The little cemetery, however, remained. When the Forest Preserve District of Cook County forced out the few remaining families in the 1920s, the farms were forested, and the cemetery became shrouded by trees—and mystery. The twentieth century would see Bachelors Grove Cemetery gain notoriety as one of the most haunted cemeteries in the world; that haunting was directly tied to the World's Fair of 1893.

At the Columbian Exposition, Americans first encountered many cultural curiosities. The game of golf was one of them. Enraptured, businessmen—and well-heeled women—established a quick and impressive following for this "new" pastime. In 1889, Harlow Niles Higinbotham—the president of the World's Columbian Exposition, director of the Northern Trust Bank and partner at Marshall Field & Company—proposed the creation of a golf club to be built outside of Chicago. A landscape architect was chosen, and a site was earmarked, near present-day 147th Street and Cicero Avenue, less than a mile from Bachelors Grove Cemetery.

Some histories suggest that the site of the Midlothian Country Club was specifically chosen for its remoteness, as the directors did not want the usual country club set to know about the development. But the club quickly became a sensation, not only in Chicago but also around the world. Immediately, however, the problem of actually getting to the club became a big one. Before the building of the Midlothian/Blue Island spur line (MBI Railroad) to bring country club guests to the grounds, visitors had to take the train to Rexford's Crossing and travel the last leg over dirt roads. Those coming from Blue Island took the Midlothian Turnpike, an ancient Indian road called the "Old Blue Island Road" on the first maps of Cook County. This road led from Blue Island, diagonally southwest through Bachelors Grove (and past the cemetery). Many made use of the club's famed "Tally Ho Wagon," a rather ramshackle-looking vehicle that required as many as six horses to pull it through the often muddy trail. After the building of the rail extension to the country club, the turnpike was used less and less and almost exclusively by travelers on foot going to Blue Island to catch the train to Chicago to work or shop. In 1927, 147th Street was paved, creating the first paved street in the area and making both the spur line and the old roads obsolete. This same year saw the closing of most of the sales of private land to the Forest Preserve District of Cook County and the final vacating of most of the area homesteads.

It wasn't until 1941, however, that the FPD revealed plans for the future of the district; maps from that year clearly show the turnpike road "to be abandoned." But some evidence suggests that, by that time, there may have already been trouble—and ghost stories—brewing on this once busy highway.

According to an *Examiner* article published in October 2012, a man named Huburt Geist claimed to have started the haunting tales of Bachelors Grove as far back as the 1930s.[54] According to the author of the article, Geist had written a pamphlet in that era and distributed it to area libraries. In his pamphlet, Geist said that he'd come to the area in the 1870s and opened a blacksmith shop, tending to horses traveling the old turnpike road between Blue Island and the pioneer settlements. With the coming of the country club and the motor age, he opened a filling station and continued his roadside service. However, when the road fell into disuse after the building of the rail line, he found that, often, the only travelers on the road were young people, high on bootleg gin, most of them the kids of the country club set, who would drive to Bachelors Grove Cemetery from 147th Street and park, engaging in all sorts of untoward behaviors, most of which Geist claimed he could overhear. He decided to take matters into his own hands.

One night, Geist crept through the woods with a lantern, making "hooing and booing" sounds, thoroughly scaring off a young couple in the throes of mischief. Greatly satisfied, Geist made this a nightly ritual—until it backfired on him. To his chagrin, young people began coming to the area purposely to "look for spooks," and the more he tried to scare them off, the more they came. Moreover, the new crowd didn't seem to be afraid of spooks at all—the first wave of Bachelors Grove's ghost hunters, it seems.

Backing up these stories, researcher Wendy Moxley Roe interviewed one elderly gentleman in recent years who shared that, by the late 1930s or early 1940s, it was common practice to meet young women at the Bachelors Grove tavern and picnic area—where Carlson Springs Preserve is today—and then walk the girls to the cemetery to scare them. The popular spot (which featured barbeques, "beer by the pitcher" and Hawaiian and country-and-western musical acts) was at the edge of the forest preserve land, and these young people would have walked along the old turnpike road and over the creek bridge to reach the cemetery. In light of these circumstances, it now seems likely that by the time the Midlothian Turnpike was scheduled for closure, there had already been revelers and even ghost hunters coming to the cemetery at night for a number of years, using the turnpike road and the bridge over the creek.

However and whenever the ghost stories began at the enigmatic Grove, their staying power has been something to behold. Hundreds of encounters have been reported by visitors, some looking for them, some not. A woman in white, phantom dogs and houses, strange lights, sounds and sensations and even reports of time loops and other anomalies—they all not only survive but also thrive at the tiny pioneer burial ground called Bachelors Grove.

THE LAKE MONSTER

In the early 1890s, Captain Brinkerhoff was one of the most respected officers at Fort Sheridan on Chicago's North Shore, living in one of the most beautiful officers' houses overlooking the vastness of Lake Michigan. One afternoon in the spring of 1893, Brinkerhoff was sitting near a window on the second floor of his home, occasionally looking up from his reading to gaze out on the water. During one such reverie, a black form caught his eye. The object was moving toward the shoreline in the area of his house, and as it came nearer, the captain was shocked to see it dive below the waves and appear again a minute later. As it continued on this way, he saw that the object was immense in size and that it was—unbelievably—alive.[55]

Brinkerhoff grabbed a telescope and raced out to the bluff below. When he gazed through it out to the lake, shock washed over him, and he called to Lieutenant Biauvelt, who lived in the house next door, to come quickly and bring his telescope as well. Biauvelt joined him a minute later, quizzically. Brinkerhoff pointed out toward the creature, and his colleague had a look. What Biauvelt saw was the most astonishing thing he had ever seen in his years of adventuresome military life. There, in the waters of Lake Michigan, swimming toward shore, was what could only be described as a sea monster.

Its head was enormous and dark, resembling the pointed head of an alligator. The monster appeared to be hurt in some way, ceasing its swimming after several minutes and drifting toward an ice floe. The creature became surrounded by ice and fought to free itself, swimming again toward the spot where the men had first observed it. The body of the monster, the men said, made a perfect letter *S* as it swam away from shore and then turned back again, eventually disappearing under the waves near Waukegan.

Recently, a sea lion had escaped from Lincoln Park Zoo, and someone suggested that this was the "sea monster" that had been seen by the officers, but they quickly dismissed the idea—reiterating that the creature was of a totally different description.

During the weeks that followed the Fort Sheridan sighting, a flurry of reports descended on local newspaper offices from witnesses claiming to have seen the mysterious and terrifying creature, but after a brief bout of celebrity, the fervor died down.

As for Fort Sheridan, though no more was seen of the "lake monster," something interesting continued there after that strange afternoon and inspired by the sighting. Distressed by the fantastical tale, and subtly suggesting the witnesses were inebriated, the chaplain of Fort Sheridan persuaded two hundred enlisted men to sign a vow to give up the drink.

THE LOSS OF THE *CHICORA*

O ne of the most compelling aspects of Chicago's supernatural life is the belief that Lake Michigan boasts a supernatural "triangle." This triangle seems to share many qualities with the famed Bermuda Triangle, that enigmatic portion of sea that has—reportedly since the voyages of Columbus—claimed strange effects on navigational instruments, wild jags in time perception by travelers and frequent disappearances of ships and planes. Even more haunting than these anomalies, however, are the legends of the ghost ships of our own beloved waters: misty masts and lost crewmen forever searching for ports and homes long gone.

During my research these past years into the hauntings of Gary, Indiana, I encountered stories of Lake Michigan ghost ships I hadn't heard before. One fascinating story features the phantom of *Flying Cloud*, a filmy form glimpsed off the coast of Miller Beach where the schooner capsized in November 1857, taking the lives of seven. Nearby sails the ghost of the vanquished *John Marshall*, which is said to affect the instruments of those who pass through its ill-fated course today.

As a Chicago ghostlorist, I've long been familiar with many of the phantom remains of this city's maritime past. There are the sorrowful souls yet seen and heard in the waters off the Wacker Drive dock, where the 844 victims of the *Eastland* disaster met their fate on the Chicago River on a summer morning in 1915. At times, too, passersby still feel compelled to leap into the river, possibly influenced by the panic of observers who made the plunge that day to save their loved ones.

There are those ghosts of the *Lady Elgin*, which we've met, that steamer having sunk during a violent storm in 1860. Over a century later, victims are still seen walking out of the Lake Michigan waters, clothed in period dress, both on the shore at Northwestern University and at Whihala Beach in Whiting, Indiana, where many bodies washed up days later.

Late in each year, ghost hunters in Chicago search for signs of the *Rouse Simmons*, the so-called Christmas Tree Ship, which vanished from Lake Michigan in November 1912 while ferrying pine trees to the city to be used as holiday decorations. No trace of the vessel or the crew—save for the captain's wallet—was found for years, until a diver, searching for another wreck, discovered *Rouse Simmons*'s remains with the Christmas trees still on board. During all those lost years, visitors to the site of the grave of the captain's widow—in Acacia Park Cemetery—reported the strong scent of pine needles. After the discovery of the vessel, pine trees were planted near the grave in honor of the lost crew and captain. Pedestrians traversing the riverside dock area near the Clark Street bridge, where the ship was scheduled to arrive, report the strong scent of Christmas trees there too.

While these ghost ships have all found a welcome home in Chicago ghostlore, a fascinating figure I'd never encountered until now is Louis Groh, captain of the tug *O.B. Green*, who was apparently a well-known Spiritualist who frequently consulted the spirits for advice as he navigated the Great Lakes waters. Like so many Americans of the time, Groh accepted spirit communication—and aid—as part of normal life, a progressive advance that was as much a part of scientific growth as a thousand other advances of the nineteenth century.

In a *Chicago Tribune* article titled "Captain of O.B. Green Aided by Spirits," the captain confided that he and his wife maintained contact through a sort of turn-of-the-nineteenth-century Skype/GPS tracking service, thanks to the spirits:

Why my wife puts them to frequent use. When she mislays anything and cannot find it she asks the spirits. They write in words of fire just where it is, and sure enough there we find it. We put them to daily use thus in countless ways.... Often my wife feels worried about me and wants to know just where I am and what I am doing. She calls upon her guiding spirit and asks the question. The spirit goes out and sees me and comes back and tells her, all in the twinkling of an eye. Sometimes even she wants to send to me and has no way to do so. She merely calls in spirit, asks to have me told, and knows it is done. The spirit appears to me here and writes the message for me. Sometimes I can see just the hand, tracing the burning letters. I am used to these things and they do not seem at all strange to me though they might to another.[56]

Groh was known for the numerous spirits that populated his vessel, causing a variety of paranormal phenomena on board, and, in talking about his long career, related numerous stories of mysterious ghost ships that were frequently sighted by crews sailing the Great Lakes and beyond:

> [W]*hen the* Maine *was blown up it was said by New England fishermen that the specter of the destroyed vessel manned by a spirit crew was often seen cruising up and down the coast. It used to come along in a fog, and when it was abreast of a vessel the breeze would die out. A chill would come over the water and the vessel passed would seem to shiver as its sails hung idle. The specter crew stood at the guns and the foghorn was moaning. From the masthead flew the signal, "Cannot rest until avenged."*
>
> *The* Thomas Hume *sailed out of port one evening, and since then, not a vestige of it has been found. Annually, however, on the date of its disappearance, a specter schooner glides from under the lee of the northeast breakwater and moves off down the lake, regardless of wind. Once, a tug captain followed it to find where it was going, but when it was off Grosse Point and about ten miles from shore, the masts and sails tottered and fell and the hull lurched and disappeared into the sea, while a wail from the crew came across the water.*

The captain was very public about his practice of "trumpeting" séances. A spirit or séance trumpet is made of tin or aluminum and is traditionally used in physical mediumship as a means of allowing spirits to communicate with the living. It was during his talk of trumpeting that the captain's attention turned to the vanquished *Chicora*, a beautiful vessel regarded as the gem of the Great Lakes when, on January 21, 1895, it disappeared during a voyage from Milwaukee to St. Joseph, Michigan. January 1895 had brought unusually thick ice to the waters of the Great Lakes, and experts theorize that the ice tore holes in the hull as the *Chicora* battled a ruthless gale on its return trip. The vessel was lost, seeming to vanish into thin air.

The disappearance of the *Chicora* was a popular sensation, as many Wisconsin and Michigan residents had traveled on this state-of-the-art vessel to the World's Fair of 1893. Days after the vanishing, barrels of flour began

The *Chicora* was a well-known vessel on the Great Lakes. When it was lost, Captain Groh of the tug *O.B. Green*, a Spiritualist, attempted to locate the *Chicora* with the help of his spirit friends. *Port of Luddington Historical Society.*

washing up near South Haven, Michigan, forcing loved ones to accept that their hopes should be laid to rest.

After the disappearance, Groh claimed he had been contacted during a trumpet séance by the spirit of a man named John Ericson. Ericson had been a fireman on another vessel, *T.T. Morford*, which had exploded, leading to Ericson's death. After the *Chicora*'s disappearance, Captain Groh claimed that the spirit of Ericson had promised to help him locate the wreckage of the elegant ship with the aid of ghostly knowledge. Through mediumship, Ericson had vowed: "I'm coming back to see you again and locate it on paper. But if you pass over the spot before that I'll strike you with a chill and throw you to the floor of the pilot-house so you'll know it's the place."

Sadly, and despite the unswerving faith of Groh in his spirit friends, the information never came through. To this day, the *Chicora* remains lost under the icy waters of the Great Lakes, though its phantom counterpart still sails. One can only believe that Captain Groh, too, still pilots the ghost tug *O.B. Green*, sailing the routes of time past, out on the Lake Michigan waves.

THE MYSTIFYING SILENCE
AND THE GHOSTS OF GRACELAND

When real estate investor Thomas B. Bryan founded Graceland Cemetery in 1860—just three blocks from Wrigley Field today—the now bustling neighborhood was practically wilderness. Over the years, a number of architects and designers worked to civilize this 120-acre enclosure in typical Chicago fashion. Bryan's nephew, Bryan Lathrop, served as president of the cemetery for a number of years and was enchanted by naturalism. As a result, architects William Le Baron Jenney and Ossian Cole Simonds were hired to enhance the grounds. Simonds was so taken with the project that he ended up turning his professional attention fully toward landscape design. Through the work he did at Graceland and afterward, Simonds foreshadowed the gracious natural appreciation of the Prairie School artists.

Names found in many of the stories in this book can be found on the stones and monuments here: Chicago's much-maligned "first settler," John Kinzie; railroad magnate George Pullman; merchant king Marshall Field; the great detective Allan Pinkerton, whose men subdued the chaos in the days after the Great Fire; Fazlur Kahn, structural engineer of the cursed Hancock building; Mayor Carter Harrison, who was shot at the end of October 1893, bringing the triumphant World's Fair to a grim close; and Sherlock Holmes scholar Vincent Starrett. And so many others.

Ghosts roam here—though in recent years, many have sought to debunk the thrilling stories I and others have passed on from the folklore that flourished during our childhoods in the area. Thankfully, the stories remain, despite the attempts.

The tomb of Ludwig Wolff, which stands right over the Montrose Avenue fence, has been carved from a built-up mound, with stairs leading down to the entrance. A vent at the top feeds the legend that Wolff was terrified of being buried alive and included a ventilation system—and literal bells and whistles—to guard against the chance of it. Residents of the apartment buildings that tower over Montrose Avenue say that, on nights when the full moon illuminates the cemetery grounds, one may see the phantom figure of Wolff's faithful wolf hound pacing in front of the tomb's entrance, its fur shining and its eyes glowing a fluorescent green. Some have dismissed these tales, as coyotes do live here… "Just the light reflecting off their eyes," they say.

Perhaps.

Strollers through the cemetery have told of seeing a somber figure standing on the veranda that tops the tomb of the Goodman family, gazing across the beautiful man-made Lake Willowmere, a placid retreat surrounded by willow trees and the graves of Chicago's great architects and artists and "Mr. Cub," Ernie Banks.

A wondrous surprise at this lake is a recently refurbished footbridge that leads to the island burials of World's Fair architect Daniel Burnham and family. Burnham's ghost was reported frequently after his death, but few knew who the ghost was until the publication of *The Devil in the White City*. They see him, hands in pockets, standing on the banks of his island here, walking the fairgrounds in Jackson Park and even in his old offices at the Rookery Building on LaSalle Street, where he designed the World's Fair. In fact, some have wondered if it is his ghost, and not defense attorney Clarence

World's Fair architect Daniel Burnham and his family are interred on a small island in Lake Willowmere, Graceland Cemetery. His ghost has been seen here and, I believe, at the old fairgrounds in Jackson Park. *Photograph by Eva Cowan.*

Lorado Taft's looming memorial, *The Eternal Silence* (or "Statue of Death"), stands watch over the grave of hotel keeper Dexter Graves at Graceland Cemetery. The statue has been said to have a supernatural power since its erection. *Photograph by Eva Cowan.*

Darrow's, that has been seen so often on the steps of the old Palace of Fine Arts of Burnham's design.

The haunting tales of Lorado Taft's foreboding monument, *The Eternal Silence*, have now passed completely into legend. That eerie creation, a larger-than-life tower of oxidized bronze depicting a looming, hooded figure, was said to be unphotographable when it was erected over the grave of Ohio-born hotel owner Dexter Graves. As it is one of the most fascinating, and hence, most photographed, monuments in Chicago cemetery art, that tale is obviously untrue. Yet some still insist that a look into the deep-set eyes of the so-called Statue of Death will give the beholder a glimpse of his own death to come.

A friend of mine, Robert Murch, is the world's greatest historian of Ouija boards, or talking boards, as they are more generically called. During a visit to Chicago to speak at a paranormal conference I was hosting, Murch made a visit to Graceland Cemetery hoping to find the grave of J.M. Simmons, who was one of the largest producers of Ouija boards in the world in the early twentieth century—so many that he was called the "Ouija King of Chicago." Along with Simmons were other Chicago-based talking board companies that sprang up in the 1940s. As Murch says, Ouija boards and Chicago were "like peas and carrots."

Murch was extremely disappointed when the management of the cemetery told him Simmons wasn't there, but he and his friend toured the cemetery anyway, as he had heard about its stunning beauty and history. Rounding a curve, he came upon the towering Statue of Death and stopped dead in his tracks. He couldn't believe what he was seeing.

The figure, Murch said, was a dead ringer for the one that donned the boxes of William Fuld's and later Parker Brothers' Ouija and Mystifying Oracles from 1941 to 1972. "Could it really be that I just came face to face with the inspiration of what Hubert Fuld called affectionately the Blue Ghost?"[57]

When I saw him later that day, Murch had a huge smile on his face. He came and knelt down next to the chair where I was sitting and said, "I want to show you something." He said, "My friend took me to Graceland Cemetery" and took out his phone and showed me a montage he had quickly made, the side-by-side photographs of the Blue Ghost and the Statue of Death.

I started to cry and laugh at the same time. Not knowing about Chicago's connection to the marketing of the Ouija board, I had never realized the similarity. It truly was an amazing one.

Murch knew he would probably never know if Lorado Taft's stunning statue was really the inspiration for the likeness of the "mystifying oracle"

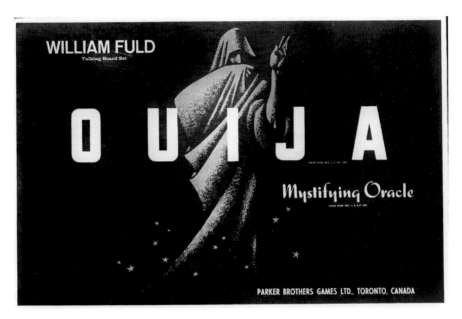

Ouija board historian Robert Murch discovered the eerie similarity between the "Statue of Death" and the signature "Blue Ghost" seen on the cover of the Ouija board game. Chicago was a center of Ouija board manufacturing in the early days of the game's popularity. *Robert Murch, the Museum of Talking Boards.*

that appeared on countless Ouija board boxes produced in Chicago, but we both like to think it was. As Murch says, rather than seeing a premonition of his death when he looked into the eyes of *The Eternal Silence*, he "simply saw a ghost with a story to tell."

One of Graceland's ghost stories has been ruthlessly and regularly dismembered for two decades by a long line of historians and journalists: the story of the little ghost girl known as Inez Clarke.

When I first started lecturing on Chicago's ghosts, a well-known cemetery historian showed up at one of my lectures, waited until I asked for questions and then started scolding me about "spreading falsehoods about cemetery history" regarding Inez Clarke. It was one of countless times I would have to explain to "experts" the difference between history and folklore.

Struck down in her girlhood by either tuberculosis or a lightning bolt (the versions of the tale often differ), the story goes that Inez was buried in Graceland by her devastated parents, who proceeded to commission a statue of their lost angel for her gravesite. That monument, perhaps the most affecting of any Chicago child's, depicts the little lady in her favorite dress, perched on a *faux bois* chair and holding a dainty parasol. Her gleaming eyes hover above a whisper of a smile. Surrounding the masterpiece is a box made of glass, securely cemented to the monument's base.

Years ago, reports began to circulate that the statue had come up missing one night, only to be found in place the next morning. Apparently, this happened on several occasions until, according to the story, the glass case was placed over the monument to prevent further theft. When a security guard making his rounds discovered the empty case one night, despite it being securely anchored to the base, he fled the cemetery at once, leaving the grounds unattended and the gates standing open.

Accounts differ as to whether Inez's statue began disappearing before or after her monument was encased in glass. Those who attest to her death by lightning say that she only disappears during violent storms, perhaps seeking shelter from the frightening weather, while those who credit her death to tuberculosis say that she runs off at random. Occasionally, a visitor will claim to have seen a child who wanders and disappears among the graves near the Clarke monument, and stories tell of children visiting the cemetery with their families and wandering off, only to be found near the statue, uttering claims that they were "playing with Inez."

Cemetery records do indicate that a child was buried in that spot in August 1880 but that the child's name was Amos Briggs. No "Inez Clarke" exists in Graceland's records at all.

In 2009, Chicago historian John Binder got to the bottom of the confusing mystery behind Graceland's most famous ghost. The Inez who was buried here was Inez Briggs, who died of diphtheria at the age of six, in August 1880. Her death certificate specifies Graceland as the intended burial site. Binder theorized that the names "Inez" and "Amos" had been mixed up in the cemetery record. He found that at the time of her death,

Memorial monument to the mysterious Inez Clarke, one of Chicago's most enduring ghost stories, despite much controversy over her existence. *Graveyards of Chicago, Matt Hucke.*

Inez was living with her mother, Mary McClure, and her grandparents David and Jane Rothrock in what is now the 800 block of West Armitage Avenue. By 1872, Inez's father, Walter Briggs, was gone, and Mary wed John Clarke. Though Inez was not his daughter, the family had her new stepfather's surname carved on her tombstone, leading to almost a century and a half of mystery.[58]

Though the puzzle of Inez's name has been solved, her ghost has not been laid to rest. She still wanders on stormy nights here, defying all who call her a fairy tale.

PHILOMENA AND
THE MERCHANT KINGS

Behind a fortress-like facade at 5800 North Ravenswood Avenue lie the 350 acres of Rosehill Cemetery. Here you'll find 16 Civil War generals, 14 Chicago mayors, scores of rags-to-riches millionaires, hundreds of local heroes and pioneers, about 200,000 other assorted personalities of varying note and notoriety—and at least 5 ghosts.

Adorning the place is the world's largest collection of secular Tiffany glass housed in the world's first communal mausoleum, a memorial chapel once named the most beautiful building in Chicago by the American Institute of Architects and more than five thousand pieces of funerary art, among them the exquisite Pearce monument hailed by *Chicago Magazine* as the city's best.

The city's oldest and largest cemetery lured cemetery historian David Wendell here in 1993. When Wendell first came to Rosehill, he brought with him a list of some 1,500 notable but deceased Chicagoans, confident that a good number of those were buried at Rosehill. He was surprised to discover that no census had ever been taken to verify the particular prestige of the Rosehill population. Thus, the position of Rosehill Cemetery historian was simultaneously created and filled.

As he searched the cemetery records and their accompanying stones, Wendell found that, indeed, hundreds of notable Chicagoans had been resting largely unnoticed at Rosehill. Although Rosehill's "no ghost" policy prohibits the staff from alluding to the cemetery's more "active" residents, nosy ghost hunters can seek out some particularly spirited sites.

The main entrance to Rosehill is itself haunted—reportedly by the granddaughter of its architect, H.H. Boyington. According to legend,

Rosehill Cemetery train depot, where spur lines ran from the city center to bring mourners to the cemetery grounds. *Source unknown. Photograph courtesy of Chicago and Cook County Cemeteries.*

Philomena Boyington loved coming to work with her grandad and playing at the construction site. Before the gate was finished, however, the little girl tragically died. Today, she can still be seen playing near the gate or looking out of one of the gate windows.[59]

Among the more famous of those sites is the Hopkinson Mausoleum. Charles Hopkinson was a real estate investor who made his fortune around the time of the Civil War. In his will, Hopkinson provided for the erection of a mausoleum to serve as a temple and burial space for his family. When Hopkinson died in 1885, architect James Eagan designed a miniature Gothic cathedral to satisfy the wishes of the deceased. The property owners behind the Hopkinson lots, however, took both Hopkinson's family and the cemetery to court, charging that the finished mausoleum would disrespectfully obstruct their site. The family pushed the case through to the Illinois Supreme Court, which ruled that the prosecuting families should have foreseen the possibility of such a project. Construction resumed.

Notwithstanding the fact that the Hopkinsons' initial turmoil met with a happy ending, it is said that on the anniversary of Hopkinson's death, a faint but ghastly moaning rises from the crypt inside the mausoleum, accompanied by the unmistakable rattle of chains. Charles Hopkinson, it seems, continues to carry a grudge against the property owners who attempted to destroy his vision.

Backing up the eyewitness accounts of Rosehill employees, another source has testified to the genuine nature of the Hopkinson haunting. The *National Enquirer* printed a photograph of the Hopkinson Mausoleum in 1992 with an account of the site's alleged phenomena. Typical of a newspaper that routinely undermines its own already infamous credibility, the paper falsely stated that the mausoleum is situated in Chicago's Graceland Cemetery, several miles away.

Across the road from the Hopkinson family is the grave of Frances Willard, founder of the Woman's Christian Temperance Union. In testament to Willard's charisma and organizational talent, she persuaded three million people worldwide to sign a document swearing never to drink a drop of alcohol.

Although the progressive leader's willful personality might certainly have lived on after her death, there have been no reports of a phantom Frances. Her movement, however, seems to have received an inadvertent boost from her sister's ghost. For when Frances's closest friend and associate, Belle Milner, contracted a mild but persistent case of tuberculosis, doctors urged her to move from her North Shore home to a more hospitable climate. According to Frances, as her associate languished in her room one muggy afternoon, Frances's late sister, Mary, appeared to the sickly girl and pleaded with her to take the advice of friends and doctors and move west in the interest of her survival. As the apparition reasoned, Frances would not want her friend to die a martyr with so much work left to be done for the cause. And so Belle went west to Arizona, where she survived for two more years, establishing successful chapters of the WCTU in the challenging surroundings of the Wild West.

For her part, Frances insisted that upon her death she be buried in the casket of her mother, also named Mary. To this day, they rest together at Rosehill in a single grave, according to Frances's wishes.

Specifications for burial are not always spoken before death. Sometimes the deceased seem disappointed in postmortem arrangements. In October 1995, one of the groundskeepers at Rosehill came rushing into the administrative offices at around eight o'clock in the evening. He spoke excitedly about having seen a woman out on the grounds, standing next to a tree off the access road, near the Peterson Avenue wall. He went on to explain that after seeing this woman, he left his car to confront her and find out her business. As he attempted to approach the figure, however, what he saw froze him in his tracks. The apparition, dressed in a long garment, seemed to be floating above the ground. Gradually, the vision dissolved into a mist, and the groundskeeper, freed from his paralysis, hurried to report the incident.

According to rumor, the next day an excited Des Plaines woman phoned Rosehill's office: "You're not going to believe this, but…" She went on to relate that her aunt had come to her as a spirit the preceding night, expressing her concern that after her death she had not been properly remembered. The woman, giving the surname of Kalbas, requested that a marker be ordered for her aunt Karrie's previously unmarked grave, which was part of an old family plot. When the staff went out to the site to verify the lot and the type of stone that should be ordered, it was discovered that the grave with no stone was the same site where the apparition had been seen the night before.

With the stone ordered, Karrie Kalbas was never seen again, either by her niece or by anyone at Rosehill.

One of Rosehill's most interesting sites has no known haunting legends associated with it—yet, it is connected to one of the most intriguing and enduring of all Chicago mysteries. When the old City Cemetery was disbanded by the city council in 1837, it was foreseen that all of the interred bodies would be moved to other sites. One of those bodies belonged to Ira Couch. Couch died young in 1856, but not before he had established himself as a successful haberdasher and one of Chicago's business pioneers. In tribute to his achievements, the Couch family built a mausoleum sixteen feet wide by thirty feet long by eleven feet high, using stone imported all the way from New York. In 1863, when the city council ordered all remaining bodies removed from the cemetery, the Couch family fought for the mausoleum to stay where it was. The Couch family won that battle, and to this day, the obstinate Couch Mausoleum holds its ground as a rather conspicuous oddity behind the Chicago Historical Society at the south end of Lincoln Park.

Ironically, the cemetery records maintain that Ira Couch rests in his family's plot at Rosehill Cemetery. However, because the tomb in Lincoln Park has been sealed, it would take an order by the Chicago City Council to have the mausoleum opened for investigation. Until then, though, one of Chicago's favorite questions remains: Who is buried in Couch's tomb?

There is another artifact from the old City Cemetery with a curious story. Nearly lost among the thousands of beautiful sculptures at Rosehill, the marble images of Frances Pearce and her infant daughter command the attention of all who behold the monument's famed beauty.

When Horatio Stone married Frances Pearce in the mid-nineteenth century, he looked forward to a bright future with his young bride. Tragedy struck early, however—not once, but twice. In 1854, Frances was dead at the age of twenty; four months later, their infant daughter followed her.

In commemoration of his beloved ones, Stone commissioned Chauncey Ives to create a memorial statue for placement at the Lincoln Park graves of his wife and child. Later, the graves and the memorial were moved to Rosehill, and a glass casing was added to protect the figures from the elements. According to legend, on the anniversaries of their deaths a white haze fills the glass encasement, and as visitors approach, mother and child rise to greet their guests. Believers say that Frances and her daughter, having died so young, return to bid farewell to the life and loved ones they never knew.

Such gravesite funerary art at Rosehill is arguably without peer in Chicago, but it is joined by another exceptional art collection of a different kind. It is the largest collection of secular glass ever created by Louis Comfort Tiffany, and it is housed in Rosehill's Community Mausoleum, where it is spread among the family rooms of some of Chicago's wealthiest and most influential personalities.

The Rosehill Cemetery Company proposed the erection of a community mausoleum around 1912, foreseeing the need for aboveground crypts that would serve Chicagoans longer. In their attempts to raise subscriptions for this project, the cemetery appealed to the city's elite businessmen, impressing upon them its revolutionary nature and comparing the concept to the burial customs of the Greco-Roman Empire. Their idea sold, and by 1914, Rosehill had raised enough money to begin construction of the massive project.

One of the subscribers to the mausoleum was John G. Shedd, president of Marshall Field and Company from 1909 to 1926, who contributed $3 million toward the establishment of Chicagoans' much-beloved Shedd Aquarium. Shedd's family room was to become the centerpiece of the structure, and indeed, this portion of the mausoleum testifies to Shedd's profound love of aquatic life. The chapel outside that room forms the apex of the building, and chairs in the chapel feature intricately crafted backs depicting seahorses

This monument to Frances Pearce and her infant daughter is known not only as one of the most beautiful funerary monuments in Chicago but also as one of the most haunted. *Photograph by Eva Cowan.*

The Community Mausoleum at Rosehill, modeled after the Parthenon in Athens, was the first such structure to be erected, funded by some of Chicago's wealthiest citizens, including John G. Shedd and Richard Warren Sears, whose family room has its own entrance, to the left of the dramatic front columns. Sears is sometimes seen standing outside his family room, dressed in top hat and tails, or strolling through the corridors of the massive crypt. *Photograph by Eva Cowan.*

and shells; urns of flowers crafted of shells adorn the crypt. For the family room itself, Shedd commissioned Tiffany to create a unique window for his family alone—one that, at sunset, would bathe the room in a blue haze to mimic the underwater atmosphere to which Shedd was so drawn in life. Shedd had Tiffany sign a contract specifying that no other such window could ever be created by Tiffany again. Shedd's insistence on the provision becomes understandable when one stands in this room at dusk. At every sunset since his death, Shedd's coveted blue haze has blessed his family's sleep.

Though no hauntings are associated with John Shedd, the same cannot be said of the mausoleum's two most famous residents, mail-order pioneer Aaron Montgomery Ward and Richard Warren Sears, the watch salesman from Minnesota who went on to found one of the world's greatest retail businesses, Sears, Roebuck and Company. Ward's death in 1913 was quickly followed by that of Sears, in 1914. Since they were bitter rivals in life, it is not surprising that the sole specter said to haunt Rosehill's Community Mausoleum should be one of these two competitors. Long after the dreamy haze has fled from the Shedd chamber and the last footfalls have retreated from the clammy corridors of this massive tomb, the towering figure of Sears, in top hat and tails, has been seen through the private doors of his family room, leaving that chamber to walk the halls of the mausoleum, between his own crypt and that of Ward's. Perhaps Sears tries in vain to provoke Ward into late-night argumentation; perhaps he wants merely to discuss business or days gone by; perhaps he only wishes, after all, to make amends. But Ward has refused to stir. We know that Sears, restless in life, feared an eternity of compulsory rest. In fact, his family room is the only such room in the whole mausoleum that was designed with an outside entrance.

Joining Miss Boyington in Rosehill's shadows is Elizabeth Archer, who committed suicide in aching response to the accidental death of her high school sweetheart, Arnold Fischel. Students at North Side Senn High School, their pairing was evidently approved by Archer's father, who erected to their memory the so-called Archer-Fischel Monument, where Elizabeth is sometimes spotted at chilly November dusks.

The teenage Archer may find solace in the friendship of another set of lovers here who have been sighted between the commemorative Smith column in section 11 and the Smith memorial bench near the intersection of sections 11 and 18. They appear distraught and, when approached about their well-being, calmly explain that they cannot leave, as they are buried nearby. At this, both vanish. Some believe that these unfortunate wanderers were star-crossed lovers who died as a result of their suicide pact: a drug overdose meant to keep them together despite their parents' disfavor. Whoever they are, a number of witnesses attest to their ongoing angst, including a Roman Catholic priest and a funeral director.

Freemasons and their fans will want to join ghost hunters at a rather lively memorial at Rosehill erected by the Lincoln Park Masonic Lodge, which had its charter revoked by the Grand Lodge of Joliet when the Lincoln Parkers were accused of dealings in the black arts. The defunct lodge's monument features a large sphere affixed to its pinnacle. Weighing in at several tons, the sphere has reportedly fallen off about once every ten years, affirming, some say, the divine disfavor of the underlying members.

Joining the banished brothers here is Gerhardt Foreman, a pal of Englishman Aleister Crowley, the so-called wickedest man in the world, with whom Foreman studied for a number of years. Returning to the United States, Foreman founded the AMORC, the Golden Dawn and other Masonic orders while dabbling in any number of esoteric pastimes. Buried here at Rosehill, Foreman's family mausoleum is said to have been chained shut to keep Gerhardt from wandering.

Keeping watch on Foreman and others is the phantom of Stephen Hansson, a caretaker and grave digger who was murdered in his then rural Lake View home and buried at Rosehill. Visitors infrequently catch a twilight glimpse of Hansson in his old coveralls, leaning on a spade in the driveway of the retaining vaults behind the May Chapel.

Darius Miller died too soon to be buried by Hansson, but no matter. Miller was buried in an Egyptian-inspired crypt that stands on the lakeshore near the May Chapel at Rosehill. According to legend, Miller was a victim of the curse of King Tut and was the curator of Egyptology at Chicago's Field

Museum of Natural History at the time of the discovery of Tutankhamen's tomb. There when the ancient sepulcher was unsealed, he was thus among those marked for death by the famous curse. History reveals that all members of the archaeological team were dead within a year of the tomb's opening. Adding to Darius Miller's mysterious demise is the rumor of a blue light seen seeping from his tomb in the early morning hours of each May 1. Alas, none of the stories of Darius Miller is true. Miller was a railroad executive with a distinguished career and merely interested in Egyptian themes. He died almost a decade before the opening of the tomb of King Tut—of appendicitis while hiking in Glacier Park, Montana.

Despite their dubious origins, such stories abound at Rosehill. Many visitors to the grave of Lulu Fellows are treated to the scent of fresh flowers as they leave coins, toys and other tokens at Lulu's monument, an uncanny likeness encased in glass and labeled with the tragic epitaph: Many Hopes Lie Buried Here.

And legend has long held that visitors at the gravestone of Mary Shedden, allegedly poisoned by her own husband in 1931, will see one of two startling visions: a glimpse of Mary's warm, inviting face or the leering skull of her hapless corpse. Skeptics brush off this tale, claiming that the stone's material (mica, a shimmering, gold-like substance) is responsible for these tricks of the eye.

Yet, those close to Rosehill's heart believe, just as they believe in the uncanny mobility of the Frank M. Baker monument, the statue of a graceful deer that has been seen on many occasions far from its home over the Baker lot. In fact, while hurrying to his duties during an evening storm, former caretaker James Hutchenson caught a glimpse of this unmistakable animal "grazing" near the Ravenswood Avenue gates, only to find it back in place the next morning—lodged, as ever, in concrete.

THE PETRIFIED NUNS AND THE
GHOST OF MOTHER GALWAY

On the night of September 18, 1908, in the heart of Chicago's west side ghetto, a reported five thousand spectators gathered at the site of the former Sacred Heart Convent and Seminary girls' school at Taylor and Lytle Streets. The throng had begun to gather when an elderly couple, the caretakers of the building, rushed into the streets, the man crying, "It is a spirit! I saw it with my eyes!"[60]

Those drawn to the scene were entranced by the claims of the old man, who swore to have seen the shadowy figure of a woman in black gliding down the dark halls of the building bearing a lantern in her diaphanous hand.

The account soon gathered other testimonies to back it up. Spectators said they saw "a pale, ghostly light" flit from window to window through the old convent, the vision convincing many present that a phantom was afoot.

It wasn't long before the spectral sightings were tied to the ghost of the long-dead Mother General of the convent, the revered Mother Galway, who had passed away some twenty years before. Those gathered believed the nun had returned, in agony that her beloved convent had been recently closed and her body disinterred from the convent grounds for removal to another resting place.

The suggestion of it caused an immediate sensation and spread like fire through the streets. It was reported that, within an hour, from seven to eight o'clock in the evening, a crowd of five thousand had filled the streets surrounding the old fortress:

With every hour the excitement grew. The crowd became so great that traffic in the street was blocked and two riot calls were sent into Maxwell Street Police Station. A detail of a dozen policemen was rushed to the scene to preserve order.

A little after eight, a "thin, white glow" had reportedly been seen in an upper window by a number of the crowd, and in response (as was customary at the time), spectators responded to the ghost sighting by physically attacking it, throwing objects from the street at the window where the apparition had appeared, shattering the glass. Patrolman Frank Fournier, who had been detailed to the scene, ran up into the building to investigate the vision but, to the disappointment of the crowd, emerged with the news that he had seen nothing.

The crowd had grown so great by that time that the streetcars were stopped from passing, and backup officers were brought in to disperse the crowd. By morning, the thrilling hours of the night before were only a memory.

Like most things Catholic on Chicago's South Side, Mother Galway's ventures were connected to Father Arnold Damen and the parish of the Holy Family. Father Damen was one of a dozen Belgian Jesuits who had been sent to America to take on various missions. The group first regrouped in St. Louis before spreading out across the developing nation to follow their instructions. Father Damen was to establish a Roman Catholic church and parish in Chicago where he was to minister to the poor and convert citizens to the Catholic faith. Damen, in 1858, had barely secured authority to purchase the land for his future church before he received instructions from the bishop of Chicago to ensure that the Sisters of the Sacred Heart would be called upon to establish a girls' school in the city.

The sisters had already been living in Chicago. Their first school was a rented brick house on Wabash, but the school quickly outgrew its accommodations as news of the quality of the school's education spread. The sisters moved the school to a large frame house at Rush and Illinois Streets, but again the growth of the school led to the enrollment soon bursting the seams. The sisters bought a large parcel of land in the parish of the Holy Family, Damen's own. The order was one of the wealthiest on earth, having enjoyed the generosity of the wealthy who praised the nuns' teaching of their children going back to the order's inception in France. Mother Galway and the order decided to build a new seminary on the Near West Side, within Father Damen's parish of the Holy Family. The new school was designed by the same architect who had been contracted to design the inside of the parish church, and by the summer of 1860, the spire of Holy Family and the sisters' nearby convent and girls' seminary school could be seen rising from the landscape along present-day Roosevelt Road. The old frame school at Rush and Illinois Streets was floated down the river to serve as a free school for the poor, according to a long-standing tradition of the order: where there was a private, tuition-based school, there must also be a free one. One reporter observed the exodus from the old quarters the day of the move:

> *Yesterday the Seminary of the Sacred Heart was removed from its late quarters in the North Division, on the corner of Rush and Illinois street to its new edifice on West Twelfth street. This removal of ordinary household goods, chattels and fixtures was made quite imposing by a procession of forty drays and thirty-five express wagons, in all seventy-five loaded vehicles, looking, especially the last in the line, like the evacuation of the North Side.*[61]

Many prominent Chicagoans (both Catholic and non) sent their daughters to the school, as the parish it was affiliated with grew to a reported five thousand students, which was the largest in the world, according to a written account in a 1953 dissertation about Chicago parochial schools by Sister Mary Innocenta Montay. But another immigration influx in Chicago and the Midwest in the 1890s led to the movement of well-to-do locals, with the immigrants who moved in sending their children to the free school run by the order. As a result, only twenty-two students remained at Sacred Heart when the order moved its school to Lake Forest in 1904. There they experienced another increase of students to one hundred before long. There, in the new well-to-do digs, enrollment increased again. The school, too, was beginning to offer junior college courses, leading to the growth of Barat College in 1918. Sacred Heart graduated its last high school student in 1961 and was renamed Woodlands Academy of the Sacred Heart, which still operates today. Barat College was closed in recent years.

When she died, the body of Mother Galway was laid to rest on the grounds of the Sacred Heart Convent and Seminary at Taylor and Lytle Streets in Chicago, one of the last private burial sites in the city.

At the time the woman in black began to haunt the building, the convent was undergoing a major transition. Two months before the sightings, the building had been sold for $150,000 to a local Jewish society that planned to use it as an orphanage. As part of the conversion, the graves of Mother Galway and her colleagues had been dug up for reinterment in the Roman Catholic Calvary Cemetery at the Chicago-Evanston border on the lakefront.

When the bodies of the nuns were disinterred, Mother Galway and her successor, Mother Gauthreaux, were found to have been "turned to stone" or petrified, their bodies described as "pillars of ivory" by astonished viewers who saw that, upon exhumation, their cloth habits and even the wooden crosses on their chests had crumbled away, but their bodies remained untouched by decomposition.[62]

The story was a national one, reported in many local papers, including Colorado's *Ordway New Era*:

[W]*hen the men sought to raise the coffins the task was one which taxed their strength to the utmost. Neither casket had survived the test of time perfectly, and that in which Mother Gauthreaux was buried was badly crushed. Because of the tremendous weight the caskets were opened and a startling state of affairs discovered. There was the body of each woman almost exactly as it had appeared the day the casket had been closed and lowered into the earth beside the seminary. When a member of the ladies of the Sacred Heart is buried she is clothed in the same black habit she wore during life. Instead of the silver cross on her breast a small wooden one is placed there and nothing metallic is allowed to remain. Then the folds of the black veil are carefully drawn across the face of the dead nun. When the wondering nuns looked upon the bodies of Mother Galway and Mother Gauthreaux the little wooden cross was gone with the passing of the years, and the features looked upon for the last time when the veil was placed over the face were no longer visible. But the outline of the figures was there as perfect as ever. Every line of the body that had been visible 20 years ago was still there, and the color of the black habit gave the somber hue to the solid figure weighing more than 1,000 pounds, where both of the women had been but slight in stature during life and weighing hardly more than 100 pounds. For a moment the nuns of the institution were allowed to contemplate the wonders nature had wrought with the bodies of their predecessors. They saw where the familiar white cap had crumbled away, as had the texture of the habits, leaving only a solid figure as if hewn out of ivory. Then the bodies of the dead nuns were incased in new caskets and they were borne to Calvary to the little plot where the sisters of the institution now bury their dead.*

Many believed the sisters had been preserved by the metallic caskets in which they'd been interred or that water had seeped into the caskets, changing the structure of the cells of their bodies. Certainly, many others, including numerous of the thousands who gathered on that thrilling night later that fall, just wondered.

MULDOON

When Rocco Facchini was given his first assignment as a young priest in Chicago in the 1950s, he was full of fervor to go save souls and minister to the people of the church, wherever he was sent. He couldn't have asked for a worse place to be. Facchini, who had grown up in Chicago with Italian immigrant parents, was one of only about two dozen Italian American seminarians in the Chicago Archdiocese at the time. Most seminarians were expected to be Irish, German or Polish, and the rest were considered kind of the "bottom of the barrel." Undeterred, Rocco had gone through Quigley Seminary, the Gothic gray fortress near the Water Tower, and after twelve years he was ready for duty.[63]

Rocco longed for an assignment to an Italian American parish, preferably one on the Near West Side of Chicago, where he had grown up with most of the other Italian families in Chicago. What happened, instead, proved to be extremely fateful for his vocation—and not in a good way.

Facchini got his assignment—but it wasn't quite what he had in mind. He was sent to serve at St. Charles Borromeo near Western Avenue and Roosevelt Road—a once thriving Catholic church that was by then almost empty of parishioners; the neighborhood had greatly transitioned since the church's nineteenth-century erection, becoming predominantly African American and decidedly not Roman Catholic. The pastor of the church—Charles Kane—had fallen out of his faith. Agnostic, his only concern was the weekly public bingo game hosted by the parish, which brought in money for the coffers. But Rocco was undaunted. He was full of verve and vigor and ready to convert the surrounding neighbors to members of the Catholic flock, dreaming of filling the church again as it had once hummed with life.

From day one, life at the church was—well—hell. Father Kane was even worse than Facchini expected. He served meals, giving a small portion to Rocco and the rest to his dog; spoke boldly about his disbelief in the Gospel; padlocked the refrigerator; and openly reveled in a relationship with the rectory housekeeper. Rocco found no support from the pastor when he voiced his hopes to proactively convert the non-Catholic people of the area. All Kane cared about was the bingo money being counted.

In addition to his issues with the current pastor, Facchini had another priest to deal with in the rectory of St. Charles: one who had been dead since 1927.

By the time of his assignment, the rectory of St. Charles Borromeo was already known to be "haunted," and tales of its resident ghost had been eagerly traded at seminary by Rocco's classmates and teachers. Rocco knew well that former pastor Peter Muldoon, who had gone on to become one of the most influential bishops in Chicago, still walked the halls of the old rectory, as he had lovingly built the church himself so many years before. In fact, Muldoon had planned to be interred at St. Charles upon his death and chose a spot behind the altar for his tomb.

Bishop Muldoon had been a crucial figure in the cohesion of the Irish American faithful in Chicago. A deep division existed between the foreign-born Irish and the American born, the former jealously guarding the administrative positions in the church. Muldoon, though American by birth, knew how to smooth over relations and proved himself quickly as a gifted leader. By 1901, Archbishop Feehan had named Muldoon auxiliary bishop, bringing him to live in the archbishop's mansion in Lincoln Park.

Less than a decade later, Muldoon was sent to Rockford, Illinois, to found the Rockford Archdiocese, after his image was smeared by a jealous foreign-born Irish priest who concocted atrocious lies about Muldoon, even publishing a book about them. Though Feehan had every faith in Muldoon's innocence, he felt forced to send him away to preserve the integrity of the Chicago Church.

Muldoon went to Rockford and served well. There, in 1927, he died. Though he had longed to be buried behind the altar at St. Charles in Chicago, he was laid to rest in Rockford, among his adopted flock. A final wish of Muldoon's was that his episcopal ring be sent to St. Charles Borromeo, but before it arrived, it disappeared.

The parish church of St. Charles Borromeo became the subject of a book by a former Chicago priest who wrote of the haunting of the rectory by the church's founder, Bishop Peter Muldoon. The rectory may be seen to the right of the church in this image. *Author's photograph.*

It was not long after Facchini's arrival at the parish before he made the personal acquaintance of the ghost of Bishop Muldoon, who made himself well known by slamming doors, walking heavily up and down the halls at night, moving furniture and turning on radios in empty rooms. Sometimes, the heady scent of lilacs would waft by, filling the room or hall with an overpowering scent, and the pastor's dog would bark and wail at unseen somethings. Returning home from outings, Rocco would often find his locked door standing open. Rocco began to speak to his invisible colleague: "I'm your friend, Peter," he would whisper. "Talk to me."

One day, a visiting friend entered the rectory and noticed an older priest writing in his office. When Facchini later pointed out a large framed portrait of Muldoon hanging in the hall and told him the ghost stories, the young priest went pale, saying, "That's the priest I saw writing in the office when I came in."

But while Facchini felt no fear from Muldoon, Father Kane lived in terror of the bishop's ghost. When the large framed portrait of Muldoon, bolted to the wall, was found on the floor one day, Kane exclaimed, "It's Muldoon! He's out to get me!" The pastor would lock himself in his room at night, convinced that Muldoon walked the halls seeking his doom, and his dog stood guard at the door.

After fifteen years, Rocco Facchini left the priesthood and married, going on to raise two sons. In 1967, St. Charles Borromeo's church, rectory and school were razed. Today, the area, which was largely burned down over time during its impoverished era, is home to the FBI's Chicago field office, hospitals and research facilities and the Cook County Juvenile Courts, which stand on the site where the steeple of St. Charles once towered. Next door to the courts, where the rectory once stood, is the court parking garage.

Bishop Muldoon's ring has never been found.

THE NORTH SHORE ROAD

Sheridan Road starts in Chicago's north side Lakeview neighborhood and travels almost directly along the lakeshore up through Uptown, Edgewater and Rogers Park to reach the north end of the city. There it zigzags quickly to run right along the rocky lakeshore and into the posh North Shore suburbs, and those towns are filled with ghost stories that seep from the area's dark ravines, winding roads and towering, forested mansions.

Indeed, from the moment one crosses the Chicago-Evanston border, haunting tales ride along. Just at the border is famed Calvary Cemetery, a nineteenth-century Irish Catholic burial ground hosting one of Chicago's most famous ghosts. The Aviator—or "Seaweed Charlie" as he is sometimes called—has been seen dragging himself up from the lake and over the rocks, dressed in World War II pilot gear, dripping wet and dazed, since his plane went down over the lake during training exercises long ago. He makes his weary way across treacherous Sheridan Road, oblivious to cars, and disappears through the cemetery gates.

A bit farther along Sheridan Road looms Northwestern University, the halls of its nineteenth-century buildings haunted by the spirits of devastated scholars and professors, and beaches haunted by the vanquished passengers of the *Lady Elgin*, most notably a Woman in Black seen wandering among the abandoned graves of unknown passengers near the Village of Highwood.

Farther north along the North Shore Road one travels past the sites of suicides and murders, including the site where a girl named Annie Russell, victim of unrequited love, jumped into the lake from the bluffs.

Among the lavishly forested lairs of the Lake Forest rich stands the peerless Schweppe Mansion. Despite its twenty bedrooms and eighteen bathrooms, not a living soul inhabited this elaborate structure for nearly fifty years after its owner, Charles Schweppe, killed himself with a bullet to the head in 1941. Charles moved into the Tudor and Gothic masterpiece on Mayflower Place upon his marriage to Laura Shedd. Her father, aquarium namesake John G. Shedd, had built the house for Laura as a wedding gift.

When Laura died in 1937, Charles lived a lonely life of apparent emotional torment, roaming the house's staggering thirty-three thousand square feet. His suicide note explained little of his ghastly experiences in the echoing house, though he tried to express the relentless turmoil he'd endured. In two lines, he tallied his awesome misery:

"I've been awake all night. It is terrible."

Thereafter, as the house stood empty for forty-seven years, rumors spread that Charles remained in torment, haunting the mansion's master bedroom. Of particular interest to psi-searchers is a window overlooking the driveway. According to ongoing testimony, this lone pane has never needed cleaning, even when the house has been otherwise covered in grime. Over the years, these eerie tales only added to the house's grim atmosphere, keeping many vandals and potential buyers at bay. Then, Donna Denten Desplenter bought the house and immediately started its renovation. When she began her overhaul, Desplenter discovered a curious reality: the mansion has what its caretaker has called a "doorway to hell." Apparently, this entryway in the basement leads only to narrow, black corridors, turning into other snaking passageways, dead ends and desolate rooms. Such a wonderland, especially nestled in a reputedly haunted house, necessarily drew the braver partygoers of the area's teenagers. The purchase of the home by Desplenter has once again put the Schweppe Mansion on the path to livability, driving out the potential vandals and relieving the neighbors. Still, while local interest in the haunting of this haven has certainly dissipated, it is uncertain whether Charles's spirit has done the same.

In the last week of May 1881, a North Shore resident and his twelve-year-old son were out looking for birds' nests in Hubbard's Woods, between the train tracks and Lake Michigan's Winnetka shoreline. At the base of an ash tree, hidden in a clump of currant bushes, the boy found the body of a man. His clothing and shoes appeared to have been slashed with a knife or other sharp object. His pockets had been pulled inside out. The flesh was badly decomposed. The corpse had no head.[64]

It was soon discovered that, about a month and a half prior, a young man had been strolling on the beach near the woods and had come upon a decomposed human head. As the area of the coast of the shore there was known as an exceedingly dangerous—and deadly—one for ships, the man assumed the head belonged to a long-dead shipwreck victim whose head had been severed by lake ice after his death. He left the head where it was and thought no more of it. It washed out with the waves but then washed up on the beach again some days later, where some boys saw it and ran to town with their report. By the time the police reached the shore, however, the head was gone again, swept out to the lake, and was never seen again.

After the discovery of the body, it was buried where it was found, as the identity of the corpse could not be determined. When the rest of Chicago found out about the ghastly discoveries, it was revealed that another head had been found on the beach near the site some two months earlier and had also been left where it was discovered, eventually washing up on a beach farther north in the Lake View area.

The press was disgusted with the people of the North Shore, finding them wanting in basic human instinct:

> *Two months ago the head of a man was discovered in the water along the lake shore within a short distance of the spot where this body was discovered Friday. No one thought enough of the matter to get the head or hold a coroner's inquest or decently bury it, and from that time it has been floating in the Lake and only a few days ago was sighted in the vicinity of Lake View. But barbarity did not stop there, for this body which is found cannot even have a place in a potter's field. Within ten feet of where it lay, a hole was dug two feet deep and the putrid corpse pushed into it with a pole, without even a decent box to cover it, and to-day cows feed in the same field and tread down the grave…a subject to disgust a cannibal.*[65]

The identity of the headless body was never found—or reunited with its lost head, which is still believed to be lost on Lake Michigan. But each night on the anniversary of the corpse's death, a headless form is said to walk through the trees of Winnetka, in search of its missing portion.

THE BOY WHO DRANK
HOLY WATER

In the summer of 1896, Chicago was chilled by reports that the largely Polish Catholic parish of St. Hedwig was harboring a child who had been possessed by the devil. Ignatius Kojiolek was just eleven years old and an ordinary child, popular among his peers, when the bizarre goings-on began in his family home.[66]

Ignatius's family related to reporters the first sign of something deeply wrong: Ignatius had walked up to a hot stove and laid a hand on it, leaving it there for many seconds. A visitor to the house who observed this cried out, "Haven't you burned yourself?"

Ignatius responded, in what would become known as his devil voice, that the stove felt as cold as an icicle.

Soon, another visitor—a neighbor—reported that the child had blown from his mouth a "sulphorous blast" that drove her out of the house in terror.

On numerous subsequent occasions, other neighbors, friends and relatives were horrified to be confronted with Ignatius's recitations of their deepest, darkest secrets. Surely, they believed, there was no rational explanation for this supernatural knowledge.

Many wondered, naturally, how Ignatius had come to be possessed. The explanation was given that he had, some months earlier, fallen down and injured one of his knees. Although his knee healed, the pain migrated to his side and, later, to his shoulder and his eyes. Numerous doctors were consulted but could not discern the cause. After much frustration by the family, a faith healer was sent for. After some time attending to the child, however, the latest visitor had some bad news.

The healer said he had tried his tried-and-true remedies on Ignatius, with no success. The prayers and incantations that never failed him refused to affect the child. When the boy's parents asked the healer why, he told them Ignatius was possessed by the devil.

A hypnotist was then consulted who attempted to cure Ignatius with his own, more modern methods. In response to his attempts, however, the boy just lay there as still as if dead. Ignatius's father then placed a crucifix on the boy's lips; his son responded with guttural noises and spitting and refused to bend his arms when his father tried to help the child make the sign of the cross on his forehead.

Things soon became even worse, as Ignatius began to speak to his terrified siblings in a guttural voice and to mock his parents, who had become sick with concern for their son. The faith healer returned to the house, this time bearing a bottle of some mysterious liquid, sold for three dollars a bottle, which he claimed could cure the possession. Since his first visit, it had been determined—though it is unclear by whom—that Ignatius was now possessed by the spirit of a vicious dog and its equally unpleasant owner. It is unknown whether the three-dollar serum had any effect.

Then, in November 1897, almost a year after the initial news story of the possession broke, the jig was up. Following eighteen attempted exorcisms, during which numerous priests had—among other tests—asked Ignatius to give information unknown to him about the exorcists and to speak in Latin and Greek, also unknown to him except for texts used as Mass, one pastor was resolved to end the saga. Ignatius had failed all of these standard tests for possession, and during a last attempt, Casimir Stuczko, a priest at Holy Family Parish, reminded Ignatius that if he were the devil he would feel no pain. Then, Father Stuczko bent the boy's fingers back to the point where they were almost broken.

A full confession was immediately forthcoming.

Ignatius admitted to the priest that he had started his sham "for fun." It had been a lark, he said, to watch his parents and siblings cower in fear of him, as he impersonated the voice of the devil. It had been amusing, he admitted, to see doctors and healers of the highest rank stymied by his condition, unable to fix it.

Despite his confession, many were unconvinced that Ignatius had made it all up. After all, he had known of so many skeletons in the closets of the family's relatives and friends. Ignatius confided in return that he had simply listened in on many adult conversations and that these adults didn't give children enough credit to hear, let alone remember, what the grownups said.

As a final proof that Ignatius was truly not possessed by the devil, Father Stuczko presented the boy with a half pint of holy water and told Ignatius to drink it—though his parents had previously said the boy had recoiled from a cup of water with just one drop of dried, blessed water at the bottom.

Ignatius passed with flying colors, downing the lot of it in one gulp.

After a full confession by the boy, Father Stuczko recommended a full absolution and said he felt Ignatius to be exceedingly bright, with a promising future.[67]

THE FIRE DOORS

C hicago is a dear friend to disaster. From the 1812 massacre on the Lake Michigan dunes to the 1915 capsizing of the *Eastland* steamer on the Chicago River, to the crash of Flight 191 in the spring of 1979, the city has exchanged lives for infamy time and time again, establishing Chicago as an unlucky town. In particular, fire has battled the town's heart an astonishing number of times, marking the passage of decades with blazing reminders of the fallibility of our grandest plans. From pre-founding infernos that reduced whole blocks to cinders, to the infamous fire of 1871, to the unthinkable fire that, in 1958, ended the lives of ninety-two children at Our Lady of the Angels School, fire has been to Chicago an enemy, always waiting around the next corner, eager for heartache and headlines.

Despite the reaping of lives, many of them young, and the destruction of incalculable property, fire has not only destroyed but also created. Perhaps the most famous example of this idea is the plan of Chicago itself, the way to which was opened by the wholesale destruction of the city by the Great Fire. In fact, a number of years ago, the City of Chicago formally thanked Catherine O'Leary for keeping the cow that started it all. It was because of that fire, they said, that Chicago, with its grid system and great vistas, is as beautiful and sensible as it is today. More soberly, the Our Lady of the Angels fire inspired fast and sweeping changes in fire safety codes around the country, as did another early Chicago inferno: the devastating 1903 fire at the old Iroquois Theatre.[68]

December 30, 1903, found thousands of Chicago children in the throes of leisure. Christmas had come and gone, but this was only Wednesday, and five days remained before the start of school. Ahead lay the New Year's festivities and, for many, days on the town with siblings, cousins and friends, the groups of cheerful youngsters snaking through the Loop, headed up by weary mothers and aunts.

Turn-of-the-century Chicago was nothing to sniff at; the sights and sounds of its bustling downtown district were enough to hold the most insatiable adolescent in awe of its sheer variety. The usual fare consisted of enormous department store windows, packed with untold goods, street vendors hawking their own wares, a never-ending throng of people clad in all manner of dress and rushing to a thousand appointments, a crush of horses and wagons and, above it all, the thundering elevated train, carrying carloads of passengers over the crush of life below.

But today was even better. For a Christmas holiday treat, nearly two thousand schoolchildren and their chaperones were due at a special matinee performance of *Mr. Blue Beard*, starring popular comedian Eddie Foy. The venue was the new Iroquois Theatre, a peach of a theater that had opened only five weeks earlier on Randolph Street. Built like a rock with the latest in safety equipment, the palace-like lobby elicited many an *ooh* and *aah* from the people who piled in that December afternoon. They would be the last accolades that the Iroquois would hear.

The first act of the upbeat musical passed without incident, the audience delighting in the antics of the cast, the luxury of the surroundings and the impressive orchestra and lighting effects. Then, as the second act forged ahead, disaster crept in.

Unnoticed by the audience, a light to the left of the stage area flashed, setting a painted drape on fire. It swiftly carried the flame into the space above the performers, igniting the top of the fabric backdrops. Without warning, the blazing drapery crashed down, setting on fire the costume of at least one performer, who rushed offstage in a panic. As the stunned audience blindly rushed out, Eddie Foy attempted to stop the disorderly retreat. With mild success, Foy urged the crowd to remain calm. But when the actors opened a stage door to escape, the draft sent the existing fire blazing, and panic flared, too.

An asbestos curtain had been installed in the "fireproof" theater, but when crew members tried to lower it against the fire, it jammed several feet from the stage floor. Not long after the snafu, part of the stage collapsed. Then, to the horror of all present, the lights went out.

Twenty-seven exits had been designed for the Iroquois, but many had been locked against nonpaying guests. Others were hidden by curtains so as not to spoil the elegance. The stampede of people, the horror of the pitch-blackness and the lack of available exits combined to create one of the grisliest scenes ever encountered by firefighters anywhere.

By the time they fought their way inside, past a main exit sealed shut by a seven-foot-high wall of corpses, not a living soul remained. Hundreds, most of them women and children, lay, trampled and asphyxiated, behind the main theater doors, doors that opened inward.

The Iroquois itself was a shambles of ashes and charred marble, the critically acclaimed "temple of beauty" turned chamber of horrors in a matter of minutes. Over the weeks that followed, more than two dozen with fire-related injuries would join the departed audience members, and hundreds would nurse injuries, some for a lifetime. The indictments that ensued against managers and officials who, in the rush to complete the theater, glossed over inspections and unfinished safety features offered little consolation to the thousands who lost loved ones in the unspeakable tragedy.

Those who lived tried as best they could to blend back into the lives they had known. Scars physical, mental and emotional made the attempt

IN THE THEATER, DOORS LOCKED, PANIC, FIRE, AND DEATH.

A stampede erupted at Chicago's Iroquois Theatre after fire broke out on the afternoon of December 30, 1903. The horrific scene led to massive changes in fire safety law around the world—and enduring ghost stories at the theater site today. *Wikimedia Commons.*

a brutal struggle. One North Center woman, an Iroquois organist, came away from the disaster alive, but with a face so badly marred that she wore a veil ever after along with the turn-of-the-century costumes she had worn before the fire. Known only as Mrs. Meyers, neighbors would see her well into the 1940s, keeping far from others, outfitted in her somber Gibson Girl attire. On rare daylight outings, she would pause frequently to touch up heavy makeup. In the evenings, neighborhood children followed her stealthily as she made her way, in the safe darkness, to window shop at Broadway and Lawrence and recall the days when the bustle of the Loop was open to her.

Mrs. Meyers died in 1970, sixty-seven years after the tragedy. With her went one of the last living witnesses to that devastating day on Randolph Street. Theater life there, however, would go on. Sometime after the demolition of the Iroquois, the Oriental Theatre was erected on the same land. Decades passed, and after waning attendance at Loop theaters, the Oriental, too, was shuttered. A massive rehabilitation effort, inspired by Mayor Richard M. Daley's push for the renaissance of the old Randolph Street downtown theater district, threw open the doors on the old Oriental, sparkling again and renamed the Ford Center for the Performing Arts. Yet while the doors all open outward and state-of-the-art sprinkler systems stand at the ready, prepared to saturate the tiniest of sparks, something here remains unconvinced of the preparedness of this place.

The alley behind the Ford Center is the same alley that ran behind the ill-fated Iroquois in the waning days of 1903. Though rescuers found at the theater's front the unopened doors barricaded with bodies, the horror out back was, if possible, even worse:

> *The rear alley was a smoking, flaming hell....Firefighters heard the pounding behind iron-shuttered doors and windows and tried to wrench them open with axes and claw bars. Above them, the unfinished fire escape door suddenly flew open. People, many on fire, were pushed onto the platform that led nowhere but down. Body after body thudded onto the cobblestones.*
>
> *Another fire escape door was pried open and people were running down it when the door directly underneath was blown open by pent-up heat and gasses. Fire spewing from the door spiraled upward and engulfed people coming down the escape. Firefighters spread black nets, but few of the trapped saw them through the smoke. More jumped and survived only because their bodies were cushioned by those who had leaped before them.*[69]

Left: A memorial bas-relief plaque, created by sculptor Lorado Taft, was placed in the Iroquois Emergency Hospital to commemorate the dead of the fire.

Below: The alley behind the Iroquois, known today as Couch Place, is known as one of the most haunted sites in Chicago, with myriad phenomena experienced by pedestrians as well as cast and crew of the current theater that was built on the site after the fire. *John B. Stephens.*

Adding to the death toll in the alleyway were others, mostly women and children, who had attempted to crawl across a makeshift bridge extended by students and workers from the Northwestern University building located across the way, many tumbling to the pile of corpses below. When the mania was over, 125 bodies lay in the space that Chicagoans would forever call "Death Alley."

Bishop Samuel Fallows of St. Paul's Reformed Episcopal Church was among the volunteers at the theater. "I saw great battlefields of the Civil War, but they were as nothing to this," he said.

Today, the alley behind the fully restored Oriental Theatre/Ford Center for the Performing Arts is usually empty, its narrow passage maneuvered only by the occasional delivery truck, stagehand or performer, or by a pedestrian grabbing a shortcut to a late appointment.

The void, however, may be deceiving.

Those who do find themselves in Death Alley never feel quite alone here, and never quite comfortable. When I first began investigating Chicago's hauntings, there were no stories at all about the Iroquois fire. I was sure, however, that this site absolutely must exhibit phenomena to betray the then largely forgotten disaster that had happened here. And so I began to visit the site regularly in an attempt to collect evidence of this. I was amazed by what I found.

I soon began to meet stagehands, actors and property managers who attested to the paranormality of the "new" theater space that had been built here and even—or more so—that of the alley that ran behind it. They told me of hearing children playing in the alley during performances—sometimes laughing so loudly that a stagehand would be sent out to quiet them…only to find no one there but the laughter still echoing away. They told of actors and staff coming into work through the alley who would feel little hands try to take theirs, as if a child were trying to walk with them. Others talked about coming out of the stage door and smelling an overpowering smell of smoke as of a house fire—there one minute and utterly gone the next.

When the Broadway smash *Wicked* enjoyed its run here of many years, we began to be flooded with stories from the cast and crew. The property manager told us that, each night before turning the lights out after the show, one could hear children's laughter in the women's bathroom and a toilet flushing. When entering the bathroom, however, no one could be found. The toilet, however (which was not a sensory toilet but manually flushed), could be heard with its old tank filling up after a recent flush. He said it was as if little girls were playing at flushing the toilet for fun. Chorus members told of the apparition of a teenage girl they would see padding up and down the backstage stairs in her bare feet, wearing a sequined leotard—perhaps the phantom of one of the only cast members who died that day in 1903: Nellie Reed, a young aerialist who was part of the tightrope troupe.

The property manager also told us that he had come out to the alley to smoke one night after finally getting a particularly rough show beginning off to a start. He was sitting on the little curb that runs along the theater building and looking down at the cobblestoned alleyway. A woman's voice said to him, "The smoke will kill you." He laughed and looked up, saying, "I know, I know."

There before him was a woman dressed in period clothing, her full skirts falling to the ground and high, feathered hat framing an ivory face. An instant after he saw her, she vanished.

The theater and alley are not the only places that still ring with residue of the terrible fire. As the tragedy unfolded, the eighth floor of the Marshall Field & Company Department Store was converted into a hospital where fire victims were bandaged and bound with dish and bath towels from the housewares department. Those who died during treatment were wrapped in sheets and blankets from the bedding department to await the coroner's wagons. The day after the disaster, the *Chicago Tribune* reported that

> *the west room and employees' sitting room on the eighth floor were filled within thirty minutes after the work of rescue began. Anxious men seeking relatives and friends pushed their way through the crowd. One had heard that his wife and boy had been taken to the store. He found his son safe, but the search for the woman failed.*[70]

One woman, whose two children had not been heard from, went into convulsions, and another half dragged and half carried in her two children, whose clothing had been almost all torn off of them.

Throughout the years, rumors arose of various employee suicides said to have occurred from the eighth level of the open-air atrium in Marshall Field & Company; coworkers were said to claim that the victims had all spoken of a "heaviness" or depression while working on that floor. Could the use of the floor as a hospital—and morgue—for the Iroquois fire victims have left some kind of deadly impression on the building itself? No one can know for sure, but there seemed to be no stopping the macabre events.

As recently as the summer of 2007, a man entered Macy's just before closing time and—according to employees—purchased a white suit, white hat, white shoes and gloves. He donned his purchases in the men's room, rode the elevator to the eighth floor and leaped to his death from the atrium rail, ending up splayed across the Coach handbag display. This action led to the installation of thick plexiglass walls above the original railing walls around each atrium floor.

A hospital was founded to memorialize the victims of the Iroquois fire. In the lobby was installed a bas-relief bronze plaque designed by Lorado Taft, portraying the figure of Sympathy leading a procession of humanity. When the Iroquois Emergency Hospital closed, the plaque disappeared. It was found in a basement storage area at city hall and installed in the lobby of the

Cook County building in the Loop. There, in October 2003, one hundred years after the Iroquois disaster, a fire broke out, killing six people. It was discovered that stairwell doors had been locked, trapping victims inside.

Though the Iroquois Theatre fire is only one of hundreds of ghost stories I have researched and shared over these many years, and though I have visited the site with ghost tour guests literally thousands of times, the site of the tragedy and telling of the story never fail to cause me to choke up with emotion. So much so that, many years ago, I stopped taking people there on my tours.

Sometime after, I was invited to speak at a paranormal conference in Sault Ste. Marie, in the Upper Peninsula of Michigan. I am relatively unknown by paranormal enthusiasts outside of Chicago, and few people at the event knew of my work in Chicago, but the organizers thought my lecture—about children and the paranormal—would go over well. I was billed as an "expert" on children and the paranormal, not on Chicago ghosts. Again, few knew me. There was a woman there who was giving readings. She was an empath—someone who picks up on energies surrounding people. I had never met her or even heard her name before, and the conference hadn't started yet. An empath can tap into your own emotions and the emotions of any spirits that may be surrounding you.

I decided to have a reading with her, and she said, "There are many people around you. They live in what looks like an alley, a long dark stretch in a city. They died together in a fire. They want to know why you don't come to see them anymore."

THE AFTER-DEATH EXPERIMENTS

In late Victorian Chicago, Cottage Grove Avenue ran through one of the most fashionable districts in the city. Among the local businesses serving the posh residents of the area was the funeral parlor run by the Boydston Brothers, one of the most respected and busy funeral homes on the South Side.

Funeral homes had enjoyed a booming business since the Civil War, when families looked for a way to preserve their dead sons long enough to be shipped home and "waked" before burial. For grieving military families whose hopes for reunion were so quickly and heartbreakingly lost, a final view of an intact loved one was a small but necessary comfort. Later, in 1865, when Chicagoans and other mourners along the route of President Lincoln's famed funeral train paid their respects to the assassinated leader, the body had been "touched up" many times along the route, as the embalming lost its hold, but it was enough to convince millions that preservation after death was desirable.

The Boydston Brothers enjoyed their popularity with the Victorians in large part because of their cutting-edge practices. Along with providing the very latest in caskets and burial arrangements, they also conducted their own experiments in embalming, right in the basement of their Cottage Avenue funeral chapel. In December 1898, a reporter paid them a visit and discovered that the brothers had been keeping two bodies in the building that had been deceased for some four to five months. The corpses were the subject of experiments to find a method of "petrifaction"—a way to actually turn human bodies to "stone."[71]

According to the reporter, the woman in the basement had been brought in for preparation in July but then remained unclaimed by family or friends. The brothers took the opportunity to experiment on the corpse, injecting a "peculiar fluid" at intervals as the weeks passed. Though the death had occurred in the hot summer months, no decomposition or even darkening of the skin was observed. As the months passed, the brothers noted a "hardness of the body…and none of the usual falling of the features, which are as full and round as they were during life."

The second body in question was that of a sixteen-year-old girl. The girl had perished in August, some four months before, appearing as fresh and alive as the day of her death. According to the brothers, relatives of the girl continued to visit the body and bring flowers and trinkets to place in the casket.

As it turns out, the Boydstons had been experimenting for quite some time. Earlier that same year, they had made the headlines when it was discovered that a woman who had died in 1896 and was allegedly buried at the Dunning cemeteries had actually been lying in the Boydstons' embalming chamber for two years. The burial record of one Julia A. Clerc was declared a fraud, and it was expected that the coroner's office would give order to disinter the body in the Dunning grave.

The Boydstons explained that the woman had been sent to their parlor when she died after surgery for peritonitis. The Boydstons had prepared the body with a new embalming method they were working on and waited for someone to claim her—but no one did. They decided to keep the body, rather than selling it to a medical school, in order to observe the effects, which were apparently astounding.

Amazingly, it was the pastor of a south side Spiritualist church, Georgia Gladys Cooley, who identified the body as Clerc's, claiming she had received the woman's name via "spiritualistic communication" when she and several other south side pastors proposed to pay for a funeral for the unclaimed woman. Soon after, Cooley was arrested for shoplifting when she was charged with stealing a bolt of lace veiling, which she claimed she was going to use for the dead woman's funeral.

At the opening of Cooley's shoplifting trial, just as attorney William P. Black arose to make his opening argument in defense of Cooley, nearly one hundred square feet of plaster fell from the ceiling upon the court, including Cooley, whose forehead was badly scratched. Several women fainted and had to be carried out. Cooley was eventually acquitted, after ten weeks of hearings.

Despite all the unrest, the body from the Boydstons' was eventually interred at Oakwoods Cemetery. It is unknown whether the mysterious grave at Dunning was ever opened.

Nothing more is known about how the Boydstons' embalming experiments proceeded, though apparently they did not pan out. A few later appearances in the local papers don't speak about their methods. In 1903, they prepared the bodies of five victims of the devastating Iroquois Theatre fire. In 1904, a man walked in their chapel to make funeral arrangements for a "friend" who had committed suicide and, moments later, shot himself in the funeral parlor bathroom. And in 1908, the Health Department asked the county to suspend the brothers' license for cremating a body without a permit at Graceland Cemetery.

One wonders what plans the Boydston Brothers had for the method if it succeeded. Perhaps they imagined a futuristic cemetery, with preserved corpses in glass cases; perhaps an addition to the funeral home where bodies could be displayed in a sort of "museum of the dead." Perhaps they hoped to offer families the option of installing their loved ones back in the family home, delaying burial indefinitely.

In any case, the Boydstons' strange moment in Chicago history still lives on, a testament to the excitement and innovation of the nineteenth-century funeral industry.

THE POOR FARM

In my more than thirty years of career ghost hunting, more than two decades of research and writing and a lifetime of interest in Chicago's paranormal history, no person, no event, no legend or lore has inspired the question of haunting more than the name of Dunning. Yet, through all those years, not a shred of a story had ever surfaced to suggest that any of the site's dreadful history still lives. But that changed a few years ago.

I first saw the Dunning property when I was in the last years of elementary school, when my girlfriends and I would take the Irving Park bus no. 80 west from the Northcenter neighborhood where we lived to shop at the Harlem and Irving Plaza, affectionately known as "The HIP." By then, the Dunning buildings were long gone, having been replaced by the Chicago-Read Mental Health Center, and the Read Center had replaced the dreadful Dunning name for younger Chicagoans like me, who often heard of crazy people being locked up there for the rest of their lives.

The complex first opened as a poorhouse in 1851, where indigent individuals and families lived and worked an adjoining farm. It was during this early time that the Dunning name became affixed to the place, hailing from a local man's name on the nearby rail stop. The Dunning poor farm sprawled over more than 150 acres that had been purchased from Peter Ludby, a farmer who had held the land via squatter's rights since 1839. Seven years after the poor farm opened, the Cook County Insane Asylum was completed on the acreage, directed by a Dr. D.B. Fonda. From the beginning, underfinancing and overcrowding were problems.

Despite the inadequate resources, the need for a larger facility became increasingly apparent, and in 1871, the year of the Great Fire, a new structure was completed. It was serving around six hundred patients by 1885. Two fires, in 1912 and 1923, destroyed great portions of the asylum structures and sent the city into a panic when, each time, a number of inmates escaped from the grounds. In 1912, a *Nashua Reporter* headline proclaimed the day after the fire: "Steward of Institution Struggles for Life with Crazy Man 75 Feet in Air—Police Stops Scores from Suicide."[72]

In reality, a hospital employee who was trying to lead patients to safety from a burning building had to restrain one man who tried to run back inside. The two ended up in a skirmish near a bridge railing over a deep ditch. The "suicides" that were stopped were patients trying to escape upper rooms that were hopelessly aflame. In 1923, a second fire broke out; according to the *Mansfield (OH) News*, "[It] took a toll of at least 17 lives and loosed a score of dangerously insane patients as a menace to the city."[73]

New construction soon began to replace the destroyed infirmary buildings, and in the summer of 1912, Cook County transferred the property and institution to the State of Illinois. The fearful name was officially changed to Chicago State Hospital, though for Chicagoans, the Dunning moniker would always remain.

Richard Vachula lived much of his life in the Dunning area and wrote a great deal about the experience for internet researchers. Some of his work may still be found at AbandonedAsylum.com, where I found his work with the help of Daniel Pogorzelski of the Jefferson Park Historical Society. Vachula writes about the welcome change that came in the 1950s, when electroshock therapy (ECT) was largely replaced by chemotherapy at Dunning:

> *When ECT was administered to the patients, neighbors along Narragansett [Avenue] could hear loud screams and pleas for mercy. I can recall as a youngster while riding my bicycle along Narragansett and hearing these cacophonous sounds. It was enough to unnerve anybody.*

Life in the Dunning neighborhood meant days and nights perpetually undermined by a constant, though largely unfounded fear of patient escape. As Vachula recalls:

> *Besides the unrelenting screams, there always existed a fear among the neighborhood surrounding CSH (Chicago State Hospital) that an inmate would escape at night, break into one's home, and strangle someone in their*

*bed. People living around CSH locked their doors, slept with a pipe or
baseball bat by their beds or even kept a gun or knife in reaching distance.
Their irrational fear caused strange behavior.*

There was the occasional patient who did manage to escape, sometimes
regularly, like the so-called Wolfman, who would flee to nearby Mount
Olive Cemetery during full moons and howl until retrieved by security and
police. Others' attempts were not so easily rectified, like that of a woman
who became impaled on the eight-foot hospital fence during a 1951 bid at
freedom.

In the late 1980s, Pontarelli, a prolific Chicago real estate developer,
purchased the land with the intention of building a residential community
on the old Dunning grounds. When digging began, workers shocked the boss
with the news that skeletal remains were being uncovered, and in astonishing
numbers. According to the *Chicago Tribune* of July 9, 1990:

*Among them was the mummified torso of a man so well preserved that he
showed the handlebar mustache and mutton-chop sideburns of the 1890s.
There were other remains: several baskets of bones, perhaps representing the
bodies of several dozen people.*

Archaeologists at Loyola University were hired to excavate, and many
university students volunteered to assist in the painstaking process. It was
revealed that three separate cemeteries had occupied the land, containing
unclaimed victims from the Great Fire, orphaned children, penniless veterans
of the Civil War, the dead of the poor farm and Dunning inmates who had
perished as patients. Also presumably among them were the bodies from
the potter's field at the original City Cemetery in Lincoln Park, which were
reportedly moved to the poor farm after the cemetery was closed and are
likely included among the "Itinerant Poor" memorialized at the new Read-
Dunning Memorial Park. The park was built on a three-acre tract of land
set aside for reinterment of the remains found at the Dunning site, and today
the site is complete, its final design a snaking pathway connected by seven
concrete circles. At its dedication on December 18, 2001, the remains of the
182 disturbed graves were reburied in an official memorial service to dedicate
the park. There was much talk that day of the unfortunate of Dunning finally
being at peace. But perhaps not all have found the rest they deserve.

I finally heard of the haunting of the Dunning property several years ago,
at a meeting of the Jefferson Park Historical Society. I had been invited to

speak there by Daniel Pogorzelski, vice president of the society, and during the question-and-answer session, someone asked if I knew of any hauntings at the nearby Dunning site. I admitted that I had searched in vain for years for stories of phenomena there, and I jokingly pleaded for someone to come forward with even a ghostly rumor of the place.

After the presentation, I was approached by a half-dozen members who, in fact, had some amazing stories to tell of the old asylum grounds. I went into the night blissful, entranced and more than a little unnerved.

As part of the development of the Dunning property, Wright Community College, previously housed in an early twentieth-century building, designed a new, relatively sprawling modern campus, centered on a pyramidal structure housing faculty offices, the campus library and computer labs. Tales of the paranormal are rife among the Mexican and Polish American cleaning persons on staff at the college, who have witnessed everything from lights turning on and off to full-scale apparitions of figures in nineteenth-century clothing.

Pogorzelski told me of a woman he knows, an immigrant from Ireland, who refuses to shop at the Jewel food store in Dunning Square Mall because it was built on the asylum property and is rumored to be haunted. She deliberately shops across the street, at the Polish market, Wally's, though she is one of the only non-Poles who patronizes the place.

Most unsettling are the encounters that reportedly continue at the local ward office on Irving Park Road, where employees have seen a gray-haired elderly woman in a hospital gown.

One Chicago-area investigator held a "ghost box" session at the Read-Dunning Memorial Park, attempting to communicate in real time with the ghosts of the vanquished asylum. A ghost box is a popular tool used by increasing numbers of researchers to collect what many believe to be spirit voices. A ghost box is simply a radio that has been built—or adjusted—to consistently and quickly scan through the AM or FM band. Box enthusiasts believe that the resulting indecipherable sounds provide spirits with vocal bytes from which they can create words to answer our questions. At Dunning, this particular researcher picked up some astounding samples (later posted on YouTube), including "All of us are dead," "I'm backwards," "Children bike on our heads" and "You're sitting on our carcasses."

THE STAND AND THE JAIL

One of Chicago's most recognized locations is the intersection of Twenty-Sixth Street and California Avenue—a.k.a. "26th and Cal" or simply "26th Street"—home of the Cook County Criminal Courthouse and its adjoining jail. A major player in Chicago's dramatic history, the jail has held some of the nation's most notorious inmates, from gangland kingpins Al Capone, Tony Accardo and Frank Nitti to modern-day monsters like Richard Speck and John Wayne Gacy.

Cook County, the Illinois county that includes Chicago and many of its surrounding suburbs, was founded in the early 1830s with unincorporated Chicago as its county seat. Chicago's first jailhouse was not erected until 1835, some two years after the city's incorporation, but by mid-century, the tiny stockade that had served until then could no longer accommodate the escalating crime rates of the burgeoning county seat.

A larger jail was then created near the Chicago River at present-day Hubbard Street, behind the old courthouse, and inmates from the old prison were brought over to the new in the midst of the dedication ceremonies. The *Chicago Tribune* wrote of one Joseph Gilholley's move to the new jail

during the noon recess. As the guard escorted him across the court, he heard the sounds of the banqueters who were dedicating the new building, and he tried to wrest himself away from the bailiff. Finally he was placed again in his cell and the guard went to get him his luncheon and returned with a tin vessel containing hot soup. When it was handed to him he hurled the contents of the bowl in the guard's face and then belabored him over the head with the empty dish. He was placed in the dungeon.[74]

Despite the "bright cells and fresh, clean beds" and "an up-to-date fumigation" described by the *Chicago Tribune*, the new jail had room for only the city's most dangerous criminals, whose trials were staged at the courthouse next door. Much like today, the guilty were sent away to live out their sentences at state penitentiaries. Those who had been arrested for less serious crimes were thrown in Chicago's bridewell, the city's common lockup in the heart of the vice district, near Polk and Wells Streets.

By 1871, the bridewell had been given new digs at Twenty-Sixth Street and California Avenue and a new name: the Chicago House of Corrections. In that devastating year of the Great Fire, inmate populations swelled at both the new House of Corrections and the Hubbard Street jail. When the riverside jail could no longer accommodate the rising crowds, a new county jail was built next to the city lockup at Twenty-Sixth and Cal.

The "new" courthouse there is filled with dreadful memories—the stuff, literally, of Chicago's nightmares. There is the room where, on September 4, 1946, William Heirens—the "Lipstick Killer"—pleaded guilty to three murders, including the dismemberment of six-year-old Suzanne Degnan, and attempted to hang himself in the adjoining jail the same night. There is the courtroom where, in 1966, Richard Speck calmly sat through testimony condemning him and his eight abominable slayings. There is the hall of sorrow where John Wayne Gacy was tried, the trial spanning those heartbreaking five weeks in 1980. Mike, a longtime sheriff's deputy with the courthouse, reports, "They claim the room is haunted by the kids. They hear giggling, running around, shuffling around the benches, as if [they] were fidgeting in court."

Gacy, like most maximum-security risks, would have been held in the spare, foreboding chamber known as "The Max," a steel-walled cell with gates at either end. Today, after years of harboring the penned-in anxiety of killers—and worse—the Max has its own memories. Stories abound of disembodied voices, singing and crying. Dark figures glide effortlessly through its walls. Lights fail.

Legends run rampant through the unfathomable history—and elusive physical makeup—of the criminal courts. As Mike says, "Twenty-Sixth Street is weird. They don't take anything out. They just put stuff in." Anything no longer in service, they say, is simply locked up or closed off, but remains.

The most notorious of these spaces was Division One. Mike has never seen it himself, but the "electricians talk about it. When they talk about

The old Cook County Courthouse still stands today as a mixed-use building. The gallows occupied a place in the courtyard behind the building, where an alley runs today. Reports of strange phenomena are still told by firefighters staffing a firehouse to the immediate north of the site. *Library of Congress.*

seclusion it was literally dog cages in Division One. I've heard this through stories only. They called it 'The Hole.' You literally couldn't move."

Particularly puzzling is the courthouse's eighth floor, completely closed off for years from public and staff access. According to oral accounts that still pass among the staff, the eighth floor served as a morgue until fifty years ago. Backing up the rumors are reports of paranormal activity: sounds of commotion from behind the locked doors.

One of the Cook County Courthouse's many secrets was brought to light in 2006 when the jail's storied gallows were put up for auction with a starting bid of $5,000. The world-famous Cook County gallows were originally built to execute the anarchists associated with the 1886 Haymarket Riot. Between those first executions and the last, in 1927, the gallows ushered in the deaths of more than eighty men.

After the last hanging, the county disallowed death by hanging in favor of the electric chair; however, a curious circumstance kept the structure on site—in the jailhouse basement, to be exact—for fifty more years. In 1921, "Terrible" Tommy O'Connor escaped from the Cook County Jail just days before his anticipated execution. (The story of Tommy O'Connor was first made famous by Chicago journalist Ben Hecht in *The Front Page*, which was adapted for the screen in *His Girl Friday*.) As his sentence specified death by hanging, the county kept the gallows at Twenty-Sixth Street just in case O'Connor was ever caught. Finally, in 1977, a judge deemed that the capture of O'Connor would likely never be realized. He ordered the gallows to be sold.

The gallows went—then, without a ripple—to Mike Donley, who operated Wild West Town in the village of Union, Illinois, about an hour northwest of Chicago. When, in 2006, Donley pronounced the attraction too macabre for the youthful patrons of his Union museum, he put the gallows back on the auction block.

Unlike the first sale, the gallows had many offers the second time around, including that of Libby Mahoney, chief curator of the Chicago History Museum, who wanted to make the structure part of a permanent Haymarket Riot exhibit, and longtime American exploiter of the strange, Ripley's Believe It or Not! In the end, the gallows sold to Ripley's for nearly $70,000, disappointing the many historical associations, labor unions and opponents of capital punishment who'd hoped for a more educational installation of the gruesome artifact.

In Chicago, the passageway that once led to the courtyard of the old Hubbard Street courthouse—and its sinister gallows—still exists today, between the old courthouse building (now a mixed-use building called Courthouse Square) and a modern firehouse across the alleyway. Tales have been told by the firefighters of phantom visitors in their bunkroom and bay in the wee hours who appear and vanish without warning, and passersby, too, share stories of chilling encounters in the alleyway: touches on the arm or face, shoves and slaps and other gentle or violent gestures by invisible hands.

THE SAUSAGE MAKER

When, in 1897, Chicago sausage mogul Adolph Luetgert was convicted of murdering his wife, Louisa, and sentenced to life imprisonment at Joliet State Penitentiary, the word on the streets was that Louisa's scheming husband had, according to an evil children's rhyme, "made sausage out of his wife."

Adolph's methods weren't quite as extreme, however, as the city's nose-diving sausage sales suggested. Louisa did enter her husband's sausage factory in one piece on the night of May 1, 1897, never to be seen whole again. But the job Adolph did on his bride was a private affair, discovered by determined detectives—not unsuspecting diners.

That spring before Louisa's disappearance, heated arguments had cut through the neighborhood surrounding the Luetgert house, near Hermitage and Diversey Avenues. Brash and unembarrassed, the words between the Luetgerts made clear the couple's trouble: Louisa's niece, Mary Siemering, had come to work for the Luetgerts as a housekeeper. Demure and darling, she had captured the fancy of the man of the house, and Louisa was on to their trysts. Friends and relatives of Louisa were alarmed when one morning Louisa was simply gone. She had, without notice, decided to take a trip to visit an aunt in Kenosha. Or so Adolph explained.

Wasting little time, friends of the absentee housewife besieged police, laying their unease on the table, backing up their fear with frank tales of the Luetgerts' marriage woes. Well aware of the couple's instability, the law latched on.

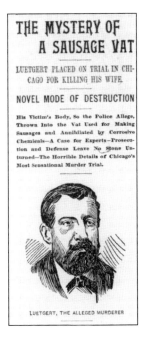

THE MYSTERY OF A SAUSAGE VAT

LUETGERT PLACED ON TRIAL IN CHICAGO FOR KILLING HIS WIFE.

NOVEL MODE OF DESTRUCTION

His Victim's Body, So the Police Allege, Thrown Into the Vat Used for Making Sausages and Annihilated by Corrosive Chemicals—A Case for Experts—Prosecution and Defense Leave No Stone Unturned—The Horrible Details of Chicago's Most Sensational Murder Trial.

LUETGERT, THE ALLEGED MURDERER

Adolph Luetgert became known as the "Sausage Vat Murderer" for gruesome reasons. His factory is today condominiums on Diversey Avenue. *From the* Chicago Tribune.

Gaining access to Adolph's sausage works, detectives soon discovered two gold rings in a twelve-foot-long potash vat, one of them inscribed with the initials L.L. Fragments of a human skull were tediously removed from the smokestack, from which an anonymous witness had seen smoke pouring on the night of Louisa's disappearance, even though the factory had been closed for some two months due to reorganization. Circumstantial evidence piled high enough to suffocate Adolph Luetgert, who was arrested within the week and taken to a holding cell in the east Chicago Avenue police station to await trial.

No witnesses testified to Luetgert's guilt; still, the rings, the unidentified but obvious remains and the ready tools of death in the shape of meat saws, furnaces and boiling vats convinced all but one jury member of Adolph's evil deed. The jury was dismissed, and Luetgert was retried a second time. The has-been meat maker was convicted of murder and sentenced to life imprisonment, despite the fact that Louisa's body had never been found.

Adolph Luetgert spent a scant two years in prison, but what years they were. From his cell far south of his old factory, he wailed through the days and nights, crying for release, claiming his innocence. Inmates believed in Luetgert's guilt, convinced that Louisa's spirit was incarcerated with him—taunting him, terrorizing him. Relatives and other visitors who witnessed Luetgert's scenes became convinced of the truth of this tale—but not Adolph's defense attorney, Lawrence Harmon. Harmon was determined to prove that Luetgert was innocent of his wife's murder; to this end, he spent thousands of dollars of his own savings in his personal hunt for the "lost" Louisa. Ultimately, he entered an insane asylum. Luetgert himself died at the turn of the century, haunted to death, they say, by his vengeful wife.

After Adolph's passing, rumors arose that Louisa's ghost had returned to the couple's home adjoining the sausage factory on Chicago's North Side. There, the new owner would catch frequent glimpses of her standing by the mantel in the parlor. Legend says that he was so annoyed with this pesky boarder that he actually had the house removed from the site, relocating it to a lot on Marshfield Avenue. After the house was gone, Louisa began appearing to security guards in the old sausage factory next door, where she would wander between the basement incinerator and the vat where her rings had been found by police.

When fire severely damaged the factory, Louisa actually moved again—this time back to her old house, now on Marshfield. Frustrated by the phantom's return, the owner sought to placate Louisa by moving the building a second time, back near its original spot at Diversey and Hermitage, in order to give the ghost some peace and, hopefully, get rid of her for good.

No one knows if he was successful or if the ghost of Louisa Luetgert continues her quest for justice along the streets of Chicago's North Side.

As for the old sausage factory, I visited it several years ago with a local news network affiliate. The superintendent of the building—now a condominium complex—let us into the basement, where the furnace used to be. Neither he nor any residents we met from the condominiums that were made from the structure had any ghost stories to tell of the site where Louisa met her death.

As with so many of these things, the spirit world is—as Adoloph Luetgert was—here, holding its secrets close.

MEDIUMS AT LARGE

On the night of March 31, 1848, a deeply spiritual Poughkeepsie, New York man named Andrew Jackson Davis sat straight up in bed, awakened by a voice that told him that the "work" had begun. This cryptic "work" was to be realized as nothing less than the marvelous project of establishing communication with the dead.

For it was on this same night that Katherine Fox, a young girl whose family had long been disturbed by strange noises in their Hydesville, New York home, had snapped her fingers at an invisible guest and commanded, "Here, old Splitfoot, do as I do!" When a responding rap came from the air, the Spiritualist movement was born.

Kate Fox's "spirit rapping" began the so-called modern communication with spirits through a structured technological system of Morse-like code. This type of spiritual telegraphing was only the first example of the trendiness of the nineteenth-century spirits, who used advances in technology—like automatic writing with graphite pencils—to prove their existence.

Spiritualism also wove seamlessly into the existing fad of Mesmerism, a type of mental healing, whose patients sometimes claimed visitations with the dead, clairvoyance and precognition when "magnetized." Andrew Jackson Davis was a Mesmerist, familiar enough with that hypnotically induced step-off into the other sphere. Known locally as the "Poughkeepsie Seer," Davis claimed that when hypnotized or magnetized he could communicate with those of other realms, who suggested to him ways for improving the human condition.

Confronted with the paradox of Spiritualism in an age of mechanical positivism, historians long assumed the nineteenth-century Spiritualist movement to be just one more part of that era's revolt against rampant society—a physical and ideological neighbor of New York State's Utopian communities. Remembered, when at all, as a quirk in the works of the century's larger-than-lifers (William Lloyd Garrison, Joshua Giddings, Harriet Beecher Stowe, Horace Greeley, William Cullen Bryant, James Fenimore Cooper, Elizabeth Cady Stanton and others), the movement was much more to many others.

In 1865, Theodore Parker observed that Spiritualism as a religion was more likely "to become the religion of America than in 156 A.D. that Christianity would be the religion of the Roman Empire." And although that prophecy seems a bit off the mark in retrospect, the true principles of the phenomenon did become enmeshed in American thought and culture.

It was puzzlement, though, rather than rapping spirits that haunted the movement's skeptics, like George Templeton Strong, disturbed by Spiritualism's popularity in "that enlightened nineteenth century." Still, although fraud would make the gullible easy prey for the movement, the promise of evidence of immortality inspired the rational minds of the age's most respected thinkers and kept that "enlightened nineteenth century" utterly enchanted.

In fact, it was the nineteenth-century fanaticism with empirical science that made Spiritualism seem so promising. Ironically materialistic, its increasing reliance on materialization of spirits prompted disgust in metaphysicians like Ralph Waldo Emerson.

Spiritualists rejected supernaturalism, trumpeted the inviolability of natural law, demanded external facts rather than intuition and threw their faith behind the progressive development of natural knowledge.

The weird marriage of the mechanical and the spiritual was an easy one for many Americans, who in the years before Spiritualism's rage had marveled at inventions of innovators like Benjamin Franklin. As historian Werner Sollors recognized, Spiritualism was actually a sacralization of empiricism, an attempt to "find transcendental meaning in graphite pencils and gaslight...batteries, locomotives, and the telegraph itself."[75]

The telegraph. It was this single invention that opened wide the doors to Spiritualist possibility. For if real-time communication could be accomplished across thousands of miles of space, why not communication to other realms, where the dearly beloved reportedly reside? Benjamin Franklin, discover of electricity and magnetism, made frequent appearances at the séances of earlier times, thrilling mediums and sitters in his role of "heavenly inventor" of the "spiritual telegraph" of modern spirit communication.

With spiritual advocates like Franklin, earthbound proselytizers like Davis and the support of a generous portion of the literary and philosophical giants of the age, Spiritualism won over a conservatively estimated 1.5 million Americans who had rejected orthodox Christianity in the belief that life had only so many questions, all of which humanity—innovative, rational and clever—was quite capable of answering. Taking their regular places in séance parlors and Spiritualist churches, they sought evidence of the unknown in the form of ectoplasmic hands and trivial information from the great beyond.

It was both fraud and a failure to evolve that halted the thrust of the Spiritualist movement. As "flimflammers" were jailed by the dozens, men of science thrust mediums under controlled conditions, where most floundered. Those who remained sought refuge in Spiritualist churches and camps, the latter as havens where mediums and believers might come together to live in community with the otherworldlies who were summoned nightly at camp séances, where nineteenth-century culture was preserved in its earnestness or—as others called it—naivete.

In February 1901, a respected businessman told a fascinating tale to a reporter at Chicago's *Inter Ocean*. He related how, for months, he had been frequenting the home of a Mr. and Mrs. Arnold on South Prairie Avenue. Arnold, he said, was a candy manufacturer who had enjoyed great business success, and the couple's elegant home was a pleasure to visit. After the first few dinners there, however, their new friend was in for a shock.

After the meal, the man was urged to take a seat in the parlor, around a card table. Mrs. Arnold returned his questioning gaze with a wondrous explanation: the couple's apartment was haunted! Over the next hour, their visitor was stunned by voices, touches and other proof of his hosts' claim. Over several more visits, he became a firm believer in the mediumship of Mrs. Arnold and the reality of Spiritualism.[76]

Little did this poor fellow know that he had fallen into the hands of Oscar and Dessie Arnold (a.k.a. John and Mary Orloff), two of the most relentless flimflamming "mediums" of the era. His hosts would, in the years to come, be revealed to be at the top of the game of defrauding and fleecing anyone with a dollar in his pocket. In Chicago, the Arnolds gained the confidence of many powerful citizens, including "Bathhouse" John Coughlin, the uber-crooked and influential alderman.

Dessie Arnold was convicted of grand larceny in 1910 after her husband's own conviction and sent to San Quentin prison for, among other things, convincing Spiritualist clients to invest in a fake toothbrush company, on the advice of the spirits she summoned.[77]

It was hardly the first time Chicagoans had been exposed as frauds in the Spiritualist world. In 1888, two sisters, Mary (known as "May") and Elizabeth "Lizzie" Bangs—whose mother was a medium—were arrested by detectives during a séance after a series of run-ins with the police. Having moved to Chicago with their family from Atchison, Kansas, in 1868, by the early 1870s the children were performing for visitors as part of séances advertised as "An Evening with the Bangs Children," during which messages from the spirit world appeared on slates and furniture migrated around the parlor. As part of the display, the sisters would be tied up and locked in a cabinet. When they emerged later, the girls would be holding a cat, said to be a "spirit kitten" form the Other Side.

A grand jury failed to bring charges against the sisters in 1890, but the next spring, a bill was passed by the Illinois Senate "prohibiting anyone from impersonating the spirits of the dead, commonly known as spirit-medium séances, on penalty of fine and imprisonment."

The Bangs ladies, however, were undaunted. At some point, May convinced chemical manufacturer Henry Graham that his dead wife wanted him to marry her. Not long after the marriage, they divorced. May took everything.

The sisters also dazzled one of the main investors in the new invention of the typewriter with their "spirit typewriter," which delivered messages from dead celebrities as old as, literally, Moses.

By the mid-1890s, the Bangs sisters were advertising their ability to paint "spirit portraits" of the dead, which sold for between $50 and $150. They had many takers. In fact, Dr. Isaac Funk (of Funk and Wagnall's) became a sort of patron to the pair, paying $1,500 for a single one of their paintings. When the press accused the sisters of having tunnels, trapdoors and other secret fixtures at their Chicago home to bring their "spirit" painters inside unnoticed, the sisters scoffed that Funk had "crawled on his hands and knees all over the premises to learn if any secreted second-rate artist was hidden somewhere."[78]

The celebrity of the sisters boomed with their portrait industry, and at the height of their art career, the sisters went to Massachusetts to perform a wedding ceremony between a woman and her fiancé, the latter of whom had died.

In 1901, Stanley LeFevre Krebs, a psychologist who had taken an interest in the Bangses' claims, attended one of their séances with a mirror hidden in his clothes. With it, Krebs discovered the sisters writing "letters from spirit" themselves where the clients could not see them. A long line of debunkers followed, all of whom attended the sisters' sittings undercover, emerging with further proof of their fraud. Others, however, examining the portraits, were puzzled by the lifelike quality of them—and the absence of any apparent brushstrokes.

In 1907, Mary married again—this time, the dead mother of leather manufacturer Jacob Lesher brought the order for her son to marry. Bangs divorced him and cleaned him out before two years had passed.

The Bangs sisters retreated from the growing scrutiny to Camp Chesterfield, a Spiritualist camp in Indiana that still operates today. There they hosted many pilgrims to their parlor, all asking for their famed spirit portraits or messages from their "spirit typewriter." One visitor brought his own canvas, sealed in a wooden crate that was nailed shut. After a long while—during which the visitor almost despaired—the sisters told him to open the box.

> *We accordingly opened the box and to my great surprise and joy beheld a complete life-sized picture of my wife and child in the spirit world. The picture is so natural and life-like hat many of my neighbors and friends fully recognize it although they have been in the spirit life for 33 years.*[79]

In 1913, David P. Abbott, an amateur magician and sort of pre-Houdini debunker of the paranormal, published a pamphlet explaining the Bangs sisters' methods of producing their paintings, titled *The Spirit Portrait Mystery: Its Final Solution.*

Meanwhile, Vice Admiral W. Usborne Moore, a retired British naval officer, had visited the sisters under a different name and, on his first visit, was presented with more than nine pages of slate writing referring to events that had happened some forty years earlier, allegedly written by a friend who had died long before. Moore continued to test the two women, each time receiving pages and pages of messages from friends who had passed, usually after marking them so the pages could not be substituted. At one point, Moore's friend, the psychical researcher Sir William Crookes, added lithium to the ink Moore had brought to use in a test. Upon Crookes's later examination, he found lithium in the ink from the resulting messages—proving to him that the sisters had not written them before the sitting.

May and Lizzie Bangs died in 1917 and 1920, respectively, after myriad sensational legal cases erupted from their marriages and financial intrigue. They are both interred in Forest Home Cemetery outside Chicago, under their married names. It is uncertain whether they have been in contact with the physical world since their deaths.

In the midst of the Bangs sisters controversy, another larger debate was raging in Chicago: the arguments that swirled around the question of "spirit photography." The sensation of spirit photography had begun with William H. Mumler, a former Boston jewelry engraver who accidentally took a photo of himself in which his dead cousin seemed to have appeared. He left his job to pursue this new "art" full time, gaining fame with his most famous photo: that of Mary Todd Lincoln with the ghost of her husband, the dead president.

Mumler was eventually tried for fraud and larceny after years of notoriety. P.T. Barnum, who had long felt Mumler was capitalizing on the grief of mourners, testified against him. The photographer was acquitted by a judge and died penniless, but not before his techniques were discerned and improved on by many. Chicago would be among many other cities to produce photographers who seemed to also be mediums—who could coax out of their darkrooms the wondrous kinds of images that Mumler had pioneered.

Around 1905, Chicago's Dr. George Warne had gone undercover to the Wells Street studio of S.W. Fallis, a well-known spirit photographer in the city. Warne told Fallis he was greatly suffering after being left alone following the deaths of so many of his loved ones. He gave Fallis photographs of some "dead" relatives and friends, and in short order, Fallis produced a photograph of Warne surrounded by the spirits of the man's dearly departed. Unfortunately for Fallis, two of the people in the photographs he'd brought along weren't dead yet. Further evidence of the fraud was, for Warne, the addition of the faces of several "old Puritans and an Indian."[80]

Number 704 Fulton Street was likewise a place of controversy in turn-of-the-century Chicago, when in the late 1890s, a Mr. and Mrs. Foster hung out a shingle advertising themselves as "Occult Photographers." Avid Spiritualists, the Fosters had been counseled by another like-minded local to supplement their meager income with spirit photography. When Foster said he didn't know how to do it, the friend scoffed: "If you can take a picture of the living, you can take one of the dead."[81]

S.W. Fallis took many "spirit photographs" in his Chicago studio, such as this one in 1901. He was virulently protested as a fraud by numerous attackers. *Library of Congress, S.W. Fallis.*

As they tried to make a living from photographing the dead, the Fosters were relentlessly attacked, in particular by John C. Bundy, editor of the *Religio-Philosophical Journal*, who breathlessly pointed out some countenances of Indians in the Fosters' photographs that had previously appeared in *Harper's Weekly*, each line of the images an obvious duplication.

Undaunted, Mr. Foster rebuffed Bundy's charges: "My Indians are Mr. Bundy's Indians." Yet, "If the Indians in *Harper's*…want to be photographed, how do you suppose we could keep them away??"

AT LEAST ONE OF Chicago's mediums seemed to have motives that were unquestionably "pure": a man named Abraham James, who in the early 1860s made geological drawings—often in the dark or blindfolded—that he said were directed by the spirit world.

A lawyer named George Shufeldt Jr. took an interest in James after the medium claimed that not only petroleum but also a spring of exquisite, health-giving water could be found by digging on a certain piece of Chicago land. With Shufeldt heading a team of investors, the ground was broken there, in 1864, at the northwestern corner of Chicago and Western Avenues, and a brilliant spring burst forth. The well and an icehouse operated there for a year with great success; however, the petroleum was a no-show.

The "spirit well" that had been located in Chicago by otherworldlies—and Abraham James—was a sensation, drawing as many as a thousand people a day to view the miracle. Alas, it wasn't long before other companies arrived, drilling even deeper for water near the original site and eventually destroying the pressure and bringing an end to the heyday of Chicago's "spirit well."

Today, the only reminder of the spring is one of Chicago's many mysterious street names: that of Artesian Street, a lingering souvenir of that century when the materialistic and spiritualistic enjoyed a matchless moment—especially in Chicago.

NOTES

Introduction

1. "Seeks a Haunted House," *Inter Ocean* (Chicago, IL), January 22, 1901, 7.
2. "Haunted Houses in Demand," *Inter Ocean* (Chicago, IL), January 30, 1901, 6.
3. "Ghosts Dwell in Chicago," *Chicago Tribune*, January 27, 1901, 45.
4. "It's a Sprightly Spook," *Chicago Tribune*, February 15, 1891, 5.
5. "Ghosts Dwell in Chicago."
6. Paulette D. Kilmer, "Haunted Times? Ghosts in Crime Stories Printed by the New York Times 1851–1901," in Lisica and Sachsman, *After the War: The Press in a Changing America*.

The Massacre Tree

7. Algren, *Chicago*.

An Occurrence at Sag Bridge

8. "Spooks at Sag Bridge," *Chicago Tribune*, September 20, 1897, 5.
9. Heise, *Resurrection Mary*.
10. "Will Examine the Skeletons," *Chicago Tribune*, November 30, 1897.

The Indian Cemetery

11. Verlyn Spreeman, "History of the Robinson Family," unpublished pamphlet, Schiller Park Historical Society, Schiller Park, Illinois.

The Watchman

12. Jason Berry, "The Spirit of Black Hawk," *Chicago Reader*, June 30, 1994.

The Water Stop

13. "Awful Tragedy," *Chicago Tribune*, August 18, 1873, 8.
14. This and subsequent quotes from *The Conductor and Brakeman*, vol. 13 (1896): 595.

The Beach People

15. This and the following quote from "Ghosts of the Lady Elgin Dead Desecrated," *Chicago Tribune*, March 26, 1899, 29.
16. Don Terras, maritime historian and director of the Grosse Point Lighthouse National Landmark, related to me that the only lighthouses standing in the area of and at the time of the *Lady Elgin* disaster would have been those built in 1855 in Port Clinton (Highland Park) and Taylorsport (Glencoe), both of which went out of service in 1859. The lighthouse mentioned in the *Tribune* article was most certainly that at Port Clinton.

The Missionaries and the Acolytes

17. "Beginnings of Holy Family Parish, Chicago," in *Illinois Catholic Historical Review*, vol. 1, 441 (Illinois Catholic Historical Society, 1918).

The Hanging Man

18. Everett Chamberlain, "Five Months After," *The Lakeside Monthly*, vol. 7 (April 1872): 314.
19. Excerpts in this section are from the Chicago Historical Society's *The Great Chicago Fire*.
20. "Self-Destruction," *Chicago Tribune*, October 22, 1875, 8.
21. "A Sensational Suicide," *Wayne County Herald*, June 23, 1881, 2.

The Custom House

22. "Custom House Believed to Be Haunted," *Chicago Tribune*, December 21, 1871, 3.

The Soldiers' Lot

23. "Coolbaugh: Startling Suicide of the Well-Known Chicago Banker," *Chicago Tribune*, November 15, 1877, 5.
24. "A Pitiful Tale," *Buffalo (NY) Weekly Courier*, July 9, 1879, 3.

The Omen

25. "Bird of Evil Omen," *Inter Ocean* (Chicago, IL), March 8, 1896, 1.
26. "A Lake Loon and the Storms," *Chicago Tribune*, April 25, 1892, 6.

The Vampire Hunters

27. "The Lake View Vampire," *Chicago Tribune*, September 30, 1888, 7.
28. "Vampire of Lake View," *Chicago Tribune*, November 4, 1888, 25.
29. "100 Children Hunt Cemetery 'Vampire,'" *Boston Globe*, September 25, 1954, 1.

The Fort

30. "Haunts His Enemies," *Chicago Tribune*, December 27, 1893, 1.

Ghosts of Englewood and the Curse of H.H. Holmes

31. "Suburban Gossip: Englewood," *Inter Ocean* (Chicago, IL), March 27, 1878, 8.
32. The "Englewood Spook" was chronicled in various news agencies and articles, including "Ghost Seen, but Escapes," *Chicago Tribune*, October 22, 1906, 2.
33. "The Haunted Police Stations of Chicago," *Chicago Tribune*, May 5, 1907, 48.
34. There are no better resources for the study of the life and killings of H.H. Holmes beyond Erik Larson's *The Devil in the White City* and Jeff Mudgett's *Bloodstains*.

The Haunted Palace

35. Quotes in this section are from Goebeler and Vanzo, *Steel Boat, Iron Hearts*.

Wild Nights

36. "The Monkey Sees Ghosts," *Chicago Tribune*, August 28, 1887, 5.

The Wood Walkers

37. Serhii Chrucky, "Wood Block Alleys," ForgottenChicago.com.
38. Sean Buino, "Gold Coast Ghost Story," *The Handy Dad*, ChicagoNow.com.

The Bridge of Sighs

39. Reports of death in Lincoln Park between 1893 and 1920 are too numerous to reference in a volume such as this. I have included references

for only direct quotes used in this section. For each incident included I have tried to indicate the month and year for the reader's further research. All incidents were reported by either the *Inter Ocean* or the *Chicago Tribune*.

40. "People Struck by Lightning in Lincoln Park," *Chicago Tribune*, June 17, 1892, 1.
41. "May Take Action on Suicides," *Chicago Tribune*, December 10, 1897, 10.
42. "His Theme the Fatal Bridge," *Chicago Tribune*, December 13, 1897.
43. "Visited by Ghosts," *Chicago Tribune*, February 13, 1898, 25.
44. *Chicago Tribune*, July 22, 1898.
45. Article proposing ban on suicide coverage in papers 1901.
46. "Suicide Bridge Falters Toward Ghosts Its Made," *Times Recorder* (Zanesville, OH), October 7, 1919, 3.
47. "Worker on Suicide Bridge Swept into Lagoon; Saved," *Chicago Tribune*, November 16, 1919, 15.

The Head of Belle Gunness

48. Griffin, *Extreme Paranormal Investigations*.

The Great Ghost Panic of 1908

49. "Police Charge Mob; H'ant Stalks About," *Inter Ocean* (Chicago, IL), July 31, 1908, 5.
50. "5,000 Fight to See Ghosts," *Chicago Tribune*, July 31, 1908, 3.

The Demon of Lemont

51. "Queer Antics of a Ghost that Annoys Lemont People," *Inter Ocean* (Chicago, IL), November 1901, 41.

Mrs. Jekyll and Hyde

52. "Blames Ghost for Romadka Thefts," *Inter Ocean* (Chicago, IL), October 21, 1907, 3.

The Devil Baby

53. Addams, "Devil-Baby at Hill House."

The Haunting of Bachelors Grove

54. Richard Davis, "The Bachelors Grove Cemetery Report, circa 1933," *Life Is a TV Dinner*, ChicagoNow.com.

The Lake Monster

55. "Saw a Sea Serpent," *Chicago Tribune*, March 25, 1893, 1.

The Loss of Chicora

56. "Spirits in a Pilot House," *Courier* (Waterloo, IA), October 8, 1900, 6.

The Mystifying Silence and the Ghosts of Graceland

57. "The Ouija Files: Murch Meets the Blue Ghost in Chicago," ParanormalPopCulture.com.
58. Mark Konkol, "Ghost Story Back from the Dead," *Chicago Sun-Times*, October 30, 2009.

Philomena and the Merchant Kings

59. I spoke with the archivist Nancy Webster at the Highland Park Historical Society, who sadly was unable to find any evidence of a Boyingdon granddaughter named Philomena or of a death of any of his grandchildren at all.

The Petrified Nuns and the Ghost of Mother Galway

60. "5,000 in Mob Surge about Old Convent," *Inter Ocean* (Chicago, IL), September 19, 1908, 2.
61. "The City," *Chicago Tribune*, August 23, 1860, 1.
62. "Bodies of Nuns Turned to Stone," *San Francisco Chronicle*, October 13, 1907, 51.

Muldoon

63. Facchini and Facchini, *Muldoon.*

The North Shore Road

64. "A Ghastly Find," *Inter Ocean* (Chicago, IL), May 30, 1881, 8.
65. Ibid.

The Boy Who Drank Holy Water

66. "Ruled by a Dog Spook," *Chicago Tribune*, May 30, 1896, 1.
67. "Acted the Evil One," *Chicago Tribune*, November 15, 1896, 25.

The Fire Doors

68. An excellent account of the Iroquois Theatre fire many be found in David Cowan's *Great Chicago Fires* as well as the book *Tinder Box* by Anthony P. Hatch. The website IroquoisTheater.com is invaluable for researchers of the fire and anyone interested in Chicago or fire history.
69. Bielski, *Chicago Haunts.*
70. "Dead and Dying Heaped in Café," *Chicago Tribune*, December 30, 1903, 4.

The After-Death Experiments

71. "Will Investigate a Mystery," *Chicago Tribune*, March 20, 1898, 7.

The Poor Farm

72. "Maniacs Battle Rescuers in Fire," *Marshfield (WI) News* and *Wisconsin Hub*, January 25, 1912, 2.
73. "Eighteen Dead in Chicago Insane Asylum Fire," *News-Journal* (Mansfield, OH), December 27, 1923, 1.

The Stand and the Jail

74. "New Jail Thrown Open," *Chicago Tribune*, July 11, 1897, 15.

Mediums at Large

75. Sollors, "Dr. Benjamin Franklin's Celestial Telegraph."
76. "Odd Ways of Ghosts," *Inter Ocean* (Chicago, IL), February 24, 1901, 42.
77. "Medium Collapses When Sentenced," *San Francisco Examiner*, December 4, 1910, 25.
78. "Spiritualists Open War against Fakes," *Inter Ocean* (Chicago, IL), February 28, 1905, 3.
79. Heagerty, *Portraits from Beyond.*
80. "Spiritualists Open War."
81. "Spirits in Photographs," *Chicago Tribune*, February 14, 1889, 1.

Selected Bibliography

Addams, Jane. "The Devil-Baby at Hill House." *Atlantic Monthly* (October 1916): 441–50.

Algren, Nelson. *Chicago: City on the Make.* Sausalito, CA: Contact Editions, 1961.

Andreas, A.T. *History of Chicago: From the Earliest Period to the Present Time.* Salem, MA: Higginson Book Company, 1997.

———. *History of Cook County, Illinois.* Evansville, IN: Unigraphic Inc., 1976.

Berry, Jason. *The Spirit of Black Hawk: A Mystery of Africans and Indians.* Jackson: University Press of Mississippi, 1995.

Bielski, Ursula. *Chicago Haunts: Ghostlore of the Windy City.* Holt, MI: Thunder Bay Press, 2009.

———. *Chicago Haunts 3: Locked Up Stories from an October City.* Holt, MI: Thunder Bay Press, 2009.

———. *Haunted Bachelors Grove.* Charleston, SC: The History Press, 2016.

———. *More Chicago Haunts: Scenes from Myth and Memory.* Holt, MI: Thunder Bay Press, 2008.

Chicago Historical Society and R.R. Donnelley and Sons Company. *The Great Chicago Fire.* Chicago: Chicago Historical Society, 1971.

Cowan, David. *Great Chicago Fires: Historic Blazes that Shaped a City.* Chicago: Lake Claremont Press, 2001.

Eckert, Allan W. *Gateway to Empire.* Ashland, KY: Jesse Stuart Foundation, 2004.

Facchini, Rocco A., and Daniel J. Facchini. *Muldoon, a True Chicago Ghost Story: Tales of a Forgotten Rectory.* Chicago: Lake Claremont Press, 2003.

Goebeler, Hans Jacob, and John P. Vanzo. *Steel Boat, Iron Hearts*. London: Chatham, 2005.

Griffin, Marcus F. *Extreme Paranormal Investigations: The Blood Farm Hooror, the Legend of Primrose Road, and Other Disturbing Hauntings*. Woodbury, MN: Llewelyn, 2011

Grossman, James R., Ann Durkin Keating and Janice L. Reiff. *The Encyclopedia of Chicago*. Chicago: University of Chicago Press, 2004.

Hatch, Anthony P. *Tinder Box: The Iroquois Theatre Disaster, 1903*. Chicago: Academy Chicago Publishers, 2010.

Heagerty, N. Riley. *Portraits from Beyond: The Mediumship of the Bangs Sisters*. Surrey, UK: White Crow Books, 2016.

Heise, Kenan. *Resurrection Mary: A Ghost Story*. Chicago: Chicago Historical Bookwooks, 1990.

Hucke, Matt, and Ursula Bielski. *Graveyards of Chicago: The People, History, Art and Lore of Cook County Cemeteries*. Chicago: Lake Claremont Press, 2013.

Jackson, Herbert G. *The Spirit Rappers*. Garden City, NY: Doubleday, 1972.

Kaplan, Louis. *The Strange Case of William Mumler, Spirit Photographer*. Minneapolis: University of Minnesota Press, 2008.

Larson, Erik. *The Devil in the White City: Murder, Magic and Madness at the Fair that Changed America*. New York: Crown Publishers, 2003.

Lisica, Dea, and David B. Sachsman. *After the War: The Press in a Changing America, 1865–1900*. New York: Transaction Publishers, 2017.

Miller, Donald. *City of the Century: The Epic of Chicago and the Making of America*. New York: RosettaBooks, 2014.

Moore, R. Laurence. *In Search of White Crows: Spiritualism, Parapsychology, and American Culture*. New York: Oxford University Press, 1977.

Mudgett, Jeff. 2011. *Bloodstains: [based on a true story]*. Los Gatos, CA: Smashwords, 2011.

Schapper, Ferdinand. *Southern Cook County and History of Blue Island before the Civil War*. N.d.

Sollors, Werner. "Dr. Benjamin Franklin's Celestial Telegraph, or Indian Blessings to Gas-Lit American Drawing Rooms." *American Quarterly* 35, no 5 (Winter 1983): 459–80.

ABOUT THE AUTHOR

U rsula Bielski is a Chicago historian and folklorist specializing in cemetery history and the folklore of the preternatural. A respected paranormal researcher, this is her tenth book on Chicago ghostlore.

Visit us at
www.historypress.com